THE
TEMPLE

THE
TEMPLE

Its Symbolism and Meaning
Then and Now

Joshua Berman

JASON ARONSON INC.
Northvale, New Jersey
London

This book was set in 11 pt. Goudy Oldstyle by Alpha Graphics of Pittsfield, N.H.

Copyright © 1995 Joshua Berman

10 9 8 7 6 5 4 3 2 1

Library of Congress Cataloging-in-Publication Data

Berman, Joshua.
    The Temple : its symbolism and meaning then and now / by Joshua
Berman.
        p.   cm.
    Includes bibliographical references and index.
    ISBN 1-56821-415-4
    1. Temple of Jerusalem (Jerusalem)   2. Judaism—History—To 70
A.D.   I. Title.
    BM655.B47   1995
    296.4—dc20   95-5211

Manufactured in the United States of America. Jason Aronson Inc. offers books and cassettes. For information and catalog write to Jason Aronson Inc., 230 Livingston Street, Northvale, New Jersey 07647.

In loving dedication to my parents

George and Rochel Berman

Contents

Acknowledgments

The formative years of my *yeshivah* development were spent at a seat by the window in the great *beit midrash* of Yeshivat Har Etzion, perched high in the Judean Hills with a commanding view that stretches from the Mediterranean to the Jordan Valley. At times my seat would allow for an inspiring glance at terraced hills; at others, I would be motioned to open the window slightly more, or shut it, depending on the winds and the season.

With the appearance of this book, I find myself once again at my seat alongside the window of the Har Etzion *beit midrash*. It is with reverence and gratitude that I open the *yeshivah*'s window and share with a wider audience the inspiration and enlightenment that I received there. My illustrious *rashei yeshivah*, Rabbi Yehudah Amital, *shlita*, and Rabbi Aharon Lichtenstein, *shlita*, have created a spiritual cradle that has nurtured thousands of young men with a vision of an increasingly complex world through a wonderfully sensitive and rooted interpretation of the rabbinic tradition. It was a privilege to be one of these young men. The tone and tenor of this book reflect their deep influence on my thinking and feeling as a human being, as a Jew, and as a *ben Torah*.

Like all classical *yeshivot*, Yeshivat Har Etzion places its main emphasis on study and mastery of the Talmud. Yet, it is a *yeshivah* uniquely sensitive to the relevance and significance of the study of the Bible in an age of national rebirth. Led by the pioneering spirit of Rabbi Yoel Bin-Nun, Bible study at the Herzog Teachers College at Yeshivat Har Etzion is approached with rigor and dedication. The following pages are deeply infused with the approach to Bible study that is practiced there. The fourth chapter of this book is based on lectures by Rabbi Bin-Nun of incredible scope and creativity.

Many friends at Yeshivat Har-Etzion reviewed various parts of the manuscript, and I was privileged to receive their collective insight. These include David Jackson, Rabbi Yair Kahn, Jeffrey Kobrin, and Ronnie Ziegler.

This book would not have come to be without the guidance of Menachem Leibtag, director of the Overseas Program at Yeshivat Har Etzion. Menachem possesses a deep love and mastery of the Bible and has brought the richness of the prophetic word to hundreds of young men around the world. It was Menachem who convinced me that a full-length book could be written on this topic, it was Menachem who suggested an outline and hammered out many ideas with me, and it was Menachem who critically reviewed each chapter, offering insight to replace ignorance in numerous sections of the manuscript. To open the window of our *beit midrash* and share the wisdom of all these men with a wider audience is a great privilege. It is also an awesome responsibility. Credit for the wisdom in these pages is due to all of them. Final decisions, however, have been entirely my own and errors in fact or in interpretation are solely my responsibility.

I wish to thank Arthur Kurzweil of Jason Aronson Inc. for lending his confidence to an unpublished author, and to his staff for their assistance in editing and producing this volume. Artwork has been reproduced with the gracious permission of Rabbi Leibel Reznick from his authoritative book *The Holy Temple Revisited* (Jason Aronson, 1990).

The Talmud (*Kiddushin* 30b) says that there are three partners in the creation of a man; his Maker, his mother, and his father. There are many with greater wisdom and knowledge than I who have not been afforded the opportunity to publish. I am grateful to the Almighty for having orchestrated events in my life in such a way that I had the rare opportunity at a young age to invest in this work. The greatest of His gifts in this regard has been my dear wife, Michal, who for several years shouldered more than her portion of our shared responsibilities. Finally I am eternally indebted to my parents for having instilled within me a strong sense of Jewish values and a love for the written word. It is to them that these firstfruits are dedicated.

The Talmud (*Baba Batra* 60b) reports a custom of leaving a small section of one's wall unfinished in commemoration of the destruction of the Temple, for completion in any realm is unattainable when the Temple lies in ruins. This book contains unfinished sections, sections that will not benefit from the tremendous erudition of Baruch Berman, *z"l*, who perished in an automobile accident at the age of thirty-four as composition of this book was beginning in February of 1992. Prior to his *aliyah* to Alon Shevut in 1988, Baruch had been one of the paramount figures of Jewish learning in Moscow, a man whose courage faced down the Soviet establishment as dozens crammed into his tiny apartment to be inspired by his presentations. Baruch was a savant, fully conversant in history, philosophy, literature, Bible, midrash, and fluent in several languages. While studying and teaching at Yeshivat Har Etzion, Baruch once challenged a student who was about to embark on his undergraduate education. "Do you know how modern Jerusalem was built?" he quizzed. "First they built the outlying suburbs and then they built inward, gradually connecting the disparate parts into a single city. This is how you should pursue your education. Study disciplines that have nothing to do with one another and then build bridges between them yourself." The void that he left has been a *churban* for all who knew him.

Introduction

When a man rises to pray, if he is situated outside the land of Israel he should face toward Israel and direct his thoughts toward Jerusalem, the Temple and the Holy of Holies. If he is situated in the land of Israel, he should face toward Jerusalem and fix his thoughts toward the Temple and the Holy of Holies. If he is situated in Jerusalem, he should face toward the Temple, and direct his thoughts toward the Holy of Holies.[1]

At the entrance to the plaza of the Western Wall, the cry of "*Hinachta tefillin?*—Have you donned phylacteries today?" draws one's focus toward a stall to the left. A young man in bermuda shorts and sunglasses stiffly twists the shiny black leather straps around his left forearm, his eyes intently meeting those of his instructor as he responsively enunciates the guttural intonations of the Hebrew blessing.

A few paces further into the plaza, another cry catches the ear: "*Minchah! Minchah!*" Waving his arm, a man in a business suit, playing the role of ritual traffic cop, steers the incoming flow of men toward a velvet-covered lectern, where, in the tones and accents of Eastern Europe and of Yemen, of Brooklyn and of Birmingham, they will collectively recite the afternoon service. On the other side of the *mechitzah*—the partition dividing the men's section from the women's—the activity is quieter and more private. In a long dress and black stockings, her hair tucked under a simple kerchief, a woman sits swaying slowly over a large-print edition of the Psalms, her whispers broken only by the cries emanating from the baby carriage she gently rocks.

An older woman limps her way from person to person with both hands out; in the one, she bears a worn, laminated, Hebrew certificate from the chief rabbinate attesting to her destitution, and in the other, coins jangle against one another, vocalizing her silent appeal.

Back on the men's side of the *mechitzah*, a tourist adjusts his public-issue, gray, cardboard skullcap and approaches the Wall. Taking up an open spot next to a soldier in olive drabs, he raises his finger and traces the contours of the massive, dressed stones. As the tourist carefully eyes a crevice stuffed with small notes of paper, an exuberant Jew in black garb rushes up; his lips and swaying ear locks brush the Wall simultaneously, and the gush of memorized prayers begins to flow from his lips.

Just as stones and shells of many shapes and colors from a vast sea are drawn inexorably to a common shoreline, the tide of history and culture draws Jews of all backgrounds to stand together before the Western Wall. They see in it an enduring symbolic strength, which derives from its identity as the last remnant of the second Temple complex, destroyed in 70 C.E.

The liturgy and the Bible—the classical sources that are accessible to every Jew—point to the centrality of the Temple in Jewish thought. The traditional prayers recited three times a day include petitions that the Temple service be restored. When a Jew recites the Grace after Meals, which is ostensibly a litany of thanks, he offers a digressive and lengthy appeal for the reconstruction of the Temple. Over one-third

of the verses of the Torah and over half of the 613 biblical commandments relate directly to the Temple and the activities within it. From
the conquest of Joshua until the return of Ezra, the Temple—in its
road to construction, destruction, and reconstruction—emerges as a
central theme of the entire Bible.

However, for all its centrality in classical sources and within the
hearts of Jews everywhere, the Temple suffers in contemporary circles
from a "bad" reputation. Critics from the more liberal branches of
Judaism label it and its rites the vestiges of paganism. The concept of
a "house" for an omnipresent and incorporeal creator is said to be
theologically inconsistent with enlightened man's view of God.

The image of the Temple is problematic, not only for liberal Jews,
but oftentimes for Orthodox Jews as well. Many traditionally minded
Jews have little to say about the Temple other than that it is the place
where God's presence dwells, and even less to say about its relevance
to the present age. When the traditional Jew is summoned to think
about the Temple, he is forced to abandon his own frame of experi-
ential reference, for he lives in a Temple-less age. Often he will con-
jure two complementary images. In the one, he feels nostalgia for the
days—which, in fact, were few in number—when valorous kings ruled
the land, prophets spoke the word of God in absolute authority,
miracles documented His existence and power, and sacrifices were offered in the Temple. In the other image he sighs in anticipation of a
rarefied age in which the dead will be resurrected, all exiles will be
gathered into the holy land, and the messiah will cause lion and lamb
to dwell in harmony. It is within this apocalyptic frame that the Jew
envisions the rebuilding of the Temple.

This sense of distance from the reality of the Temple is heightened
in the language of halakhic discourse as well. The labels a person
applies to great periods of time are a telling indicator of his prime
values. In the life of a nation, time may be oriented around independence—its citizens will speak of the age of statehood and the era of
preindependence that preceded it. Alternatively, a culture that has

endured armed conflict will speak of the prewar and postwar periods in its history. In the life of an individual, a chronological orientation often made is that between bachelorhood and married life.

How is history oriented for the individual whose worldview stems from halakhic writings? A primary distinction made by medieval rabbinic scholars was between commandments that are applicable *bizman ha-zeh* (the present age) and those that can only be fulfilled *bizman ha-bayit* (in an age when the Temple stands). For those whose convictions stem from talmudic writings, the distinction between the *zeman ha-zeh* and the *zeman ha-bayit* is a pillar of chronological orientation. There are no similar terms to describe the distinction between a period when the majority of the Jewish people observe the *Halakhah* and a period when they do not.[2] The most significant qualitative distinction that this Jew makes with regard to history is between an age when the Temple stands and an age when it does not. This phenomenon has a subliminal effect on the time-consciousness of the halakhically sensitive Jew. Because he is infused with a consciousness of the radical distinction between the two, even the most devout cannot help but feel a sense of distance from the Temple and its significance, as he lives in what has been a very protracted *zeman ha-zeh*—a present age in which the Temple plays no role in the life of the people.

Nowadays, when prophets no longer speak and the messiah is yet to come, the Temple is anticipated but rarely discussed or understood. Although the Temple takes a central place in our supplications, many would be hard-pressed to explain why. It lies dormant as a vestigial organ within the body of modern Jewish thought.

While the Temple is assailed by some on theological grounds, it suffers attacks from another realm as well. The Six-Day War in 1967 saw the recapture of Jerusalem and of the Temple Mount. Possession of, and access to, the Temple Mount and the very concept of a third Temple have emerged as politically explosive issues. Since the site is holy to both Judaism and Islam, it is the focal point for much religious and political tension. Occasionally these tensions spill over, as they did in October 1990, resulting in rioting and bloodshed on and around the Temple Mount.

It is generally extreme religious right-wing political groups that raise the banner of the third Temple. Because the very concept of Temple has been commandeered by the religious political right, it has become tainted in the eyes of many with more moderate views. Associations are quickly made. It is not only that the concrete desire to rebuild the Temple has become taboo, but any positive value attached to the concept of Temple is seen as equally suspect. To be "pro-Temple" in any sense of the term is to be antipeace. To be pro-Temple is to be religiously intolerant, for the Temple could only be rebuilt if the Dome of the Rock were destroyed. To be pro-Temple is to be branded a fundamentalist in an age when fundamentalism is the anathema of the Western world.

It is the desire of the author to rebuild the Temple's image. One is hard-pressed to find a written overview in either English or Hebrew devoted to the theology of the Temple from a classical Jewish perspective. The talmudic passage cited at the outset calls upon us to concentrate on Israel, more narrowly on Jerusalem, and most fixedly on the Temple. The centrality of the Temple in the Bible, the liturgy, and the Talmud mandates a study that restores the Temple's meaning and significance to a modern, Temple-less world. The geopolitical climate likewise focuses our attention, and the world's, on Israel, more narrowly on Jerusalem, and most fixedly on the Temple Mount. If we are to make absolutist claims to Jerusalem and to the Western Wall, it behooves us to have an understanding of the role of the Temple within our tradition.

Sources relating to the Temple can be found in every genre of Jewish literature—biblical, talmudic, kabbalistic, and poetic. The present study incorporates sources from the entire spectrum of the rabbinic tradition. However, it is the Bible that gives the earliest and most comprehensive overview of the meaning of the Temple and its role in society. This work hopes to give insight into the Temple through an exploration of its biblical roots.

THE TEMPLE AS SYMBOL

Contrary to the popular misconception that the Temple is solely a sacrificial center, the Temple needs to be construed as part of an organic whole and cannot be studied in isolation. As the center of Israel's national and spiritual life, it relates integrally to many of the institutional pillars of the Jewish faith—the Sabbath, the land of Israel, kingship, and justice, to mention just a few.

In this study we will address the symbolism and iconography of the Temple. Symbols are a cornerstone of the collective consciousness of a culture, and it behooves us to mention a few notes about symbolism as a backdrop for this study. Many voices within the rabbinic tradition maintain that belief in God is meant to be practiced and manifested amid the symbolic actions embodied in the *mitzvot*.[3] But why are all these actions necessary? Why is faith alone insufficient? It is through concrete acts of religious observance that religious conviction emerges on the human plane. Symbols provide us a vocabulary with which to perceive metaphysical and divine reality.

Seen in this perspective, the need to understand the symbolism of the Temple is particularly acute. The Temple represents the presence of the infinite, omnipresent, and incorporeal—what the kabbalists called the *ein sof*—in a limited, physical space: "Make for Me a sanctuary and I shall dwell in their midst" (Exodus 25:8). Man lacks the conceptual framework with which to comprehend God's true essence, let alone its limitation, in some way, to a house of stone. It is when man's analytic capacities fail him that symbols allow him to relate to such phenomena and integrate them into his weltanschauung.[4] Our conception of God and relationship to Him stand to be sharpened through understanding the form and structure of the Temple and its rituals.

Beyond their significance as the embodiment of concepts, symbols also play an important role in the cohesion of a society. Individuals are bonded due to the influence of the symbols upheld by society. This was the opinion of Emile Durkheim, the father of modern sociology, in his 1912 *The Elementary Forms of the Religious Life*. If every symbol contributes to the collective identity of a culture, then within Judaism the symbolic social function of the Temple is of paramount importance, for the Temple is the symbol that lies at the very heart of the biblical conception of society. In an age of national renewal, an understanding of this symbolic focal point can only help inform our reemerging national identity.

A study of the symbolism of the Temple can shed light, not only on our conception of God and on our collective identity, but on other symbols as well. The structuralist school of sociology emphasizes the interconnection of symbols as threads of a tapestry. The synagogue and its appurtenances, such as the Ark, the city of Jerusalem, and the institution of collective prayer, are only a few of the symbols and rituals directly related to the Temple. To understand the Temple is to shed new light on them all.

It is worth noting at the outset, for the sake of precision, that when speaking of the Temple, we need to distinguish between three related, yet distinct, terms. *Tabernacle* will refer to the transient structure that was erected by the Israelites in the wilderness and remained their central site of worship upon entry into the land of Israel. *Temple* will refer to the structure erected in Jerusalem by Solomon, and later again by the returnees from Babylon. *Sanctuary* will be used as a generic term that refers to both, with reference to the elements that are constant between them.

HERMENEUTICS: A MODERN APPROACH
TO TRADITIONAL EXEGESIS

This book is an exploration of the concept of Temple in Jewish thought, through its biblical roots. The Bible, however, is read in very different ways by different readers. It is necessary, therefore, at the outset, to delineate the approach to the biblical text that will be employed in this study.

My analysis will address the masoretic text from a conceptual framework that is in consonance with the rabbinic tradition. This book employs an exegetical strategy that has gained far wider exposure to a

Hebrew readership than it has in the pages of English Judaica. This
strategy combines elements of medieval exegesis, on the one hand,
and midrashic scope, on the other. The medieval exegetes, by and
large, engaged in close readings of the biblical text. Their primary
concern was to elucidate the local meaning of a word or verse. With
the notable exception of R. Moses Nachmanides (1194–1270), the
commentaries of these exegetes rarely demonstrate a concern for the
evolution of broad themes, or motifs, across entire books. The genre
of midrash, on the other hand, is often telescopic in its view, weaving
together disparate figures and passages in sweeping thematic and conceptual statements. These *midrashim*, however, often seem to use the
biblical verse as a springboard for broader discussions, rather than as
a text to be closely read within its own context. In this book, I attempt to combine these two genres. On the one hand, we will read
the biblical text with the precision and commitment to the meaning
of the text itself of the medieval exegetes. At the same time, however, we will attempt to draw broad parallels between sections and
develop themes and leitmotifs across passages, across entire books,
and, indeed, across the entire Bible.

For those approaching the work from outside a traditional Jewish
framework, this work is one of Orthodox biblical theology and does
not relate to the historical development of the concept of Temple in
ancient Israel. The exegetical approach is literary, and it has been inspired by the writings of the likes of Benno Jacob, Robert Alter, James
Kugel, and Gustav Fokkelman. Through close readings, it offers a
distinct emphasis on compositional structure, leitmotif, and language.

When a Jew prays, he is called upon to direct his thoughts toward
the Temple and toward the Holy of Holies. It is my hope that this
book will enable the reader to attain a deeper understanding of the
Temple, and consequently, a greater place for it in his heart.

Joshua Berman
Alon Shevut

1

What Is *Kedushah*?

In Hebrew, the term *beit ha-mikdash*, conventionally rendered as temple, literally means a house of *kedushah*—of holiness. At the outset, then, it is appropriate to ask, what is *kedushah*?

NOT "HOLY," NOT "SACRED"

It is of little help to simply translate the term *kedushah* into English. Something *kadosh* is interchangeably said to be either sacred, or holy, or endowed with sanctity. However, because our culture is one in which religion plays only a peripheral role, our sensitivity to the distinctions of religious language has eroded. Seen in their original contexts, these three words are hardly synonymous. *Holy* comes from the German *heilig*, meaning "complete or whole."[1] *Sanctity* stems from the Latin *sanctum*, meaning "walled off." *Sacred*, also Latin in origin, comes from the word *sacrum*, which means "dedicated to the gods."[2] In a predominantly secular society, the words *sanctity* and *sacred* are often

1

used in a sense denuded of religious connotation and are taken to
mean "inviolate." This is a usage that relates neither to their etymo-
logical origins, nor to their later religious connotations. It is in this
vein that we speak of the *sanctity* of marriage. Likewise, when we refuse
to deviate from a small detail of etiquette or object to the deletion of
an item in an annual budget, we often do so on the grounds that each
is *sacred*. The many translations of *kedushah*, therefore, allow only a
distorted glimpse of the original meaning of the term.

MANY JEWISH MEANINGS

The temptation, then, is to try to define *kedushah* from within—to
examine Jewish sources alone and deduce an understanding of
kedushah that is independent of the terminology of other cultures.
However, when the Jew examines the spectrum of his tradition, he
can only conclude that *kedushah* has meant different things in different contexts throughout the ages. For the Italian poet and ethicist
R. Moshe Chaim Luzzatto (1707–1746), in the last chapter of his
Mesilat Yesharim, and for the late-sixteenth-century kabbalist R. Chaim
Vital, in his *Sha'ar Kedushah*, *kedushah* referred to a person's character and his traits. Within this conception, a person achieves a state of
kedushah when he reaches a degree of moral and spiritual perfection.
Nachmanides, in his commentary to Leviticus 19:2, understood that
the call to *kedushah* was a call to asceticism, to limit one's engagement
with earthly pleasures, even when these are permitted within the literal
letter of the *Halakhah*. For the kabbalists and their philosophical descendants, *kedushah* was a metaphysical property whose theurgic significance is discerned in the heavenly realms. For R. Joseph Soloveitchik,
kedushah referred to the experience man feels as he encounters God
through the *Halakhah*. Thus, even when examining Jewish sources
alone, a single definition of the term *kedushah* seems unavailable.[3] In
this chapter we will examine the context in which the term *kedushah*
originates—the biblical context.

A BIBLICAL DEFINITION

The list of entities described as *kadosh* in the Bible is lengthy and varied. On the one hand, *kedushah* describes God's essence. "Who is like You, majestic in holiness" (Exodus 15:11), declared the Children of Israel at the crossing of the Red Sea. "My Lord God swears by His holiness" (Amos 4:2), proclaims the prophet Amos.[4]

However, the term *kedushah* has broad application with regard to mundane entities as well. It can describe groups of people, such as the priests and the nation of Israel; periods of time, such as the Sabbath and festivals; objects, such as first fruits, tithes, and sacrificial animals; places, like Jerusalem and the Temple—all are described as being *kadosh.*

For one familiar with the Bible, or with halakhic practice, the notion that God is *kadosh*, or that the Sabbath, the priests, the Temple, et. al. are *kadosh*, is commonplace, even if it is somewhat unclear exactly what is meant when it is said that these entities are *kadosh.*

However, the precise meaning of the term *kedushah* becomes elusive indeed when we note two ways in which it is strikingly absent from the biblical record. The first concerns the use of the term *kedushah* with reference to individuals. In our culture, we are apt to call a righteous person, one who is saintly and pious, a "holy" person. The Bible is replete with characters who would seem apt for the appellation *kadosh*. However, when we examine the nomenclature that the Bible uses to describe its heroes, we arrive at a surprising conclusion. Noah is termed *ish tzadik*—a righteous man (Genesis 6:9). Moses is called *ish Elokim*—a man of God (Deuteronomy 33:1). Caleb is described by God as *avdi*—My servant (Numbers 14:24). Samuel is described as *ne'eman*—faithful or loyal to God (1 Samuel 3:20). None, however, are called *kadosh*. The Book of Psalms may be seen as a record of the righteous individual's relationship with God. Its protagonists are called by many names—*tzadik* (righteous), *chasid* (pious), *yashar* (straight in the path of God), *ohev Torah* (a lover of the Torah)—to mention several, but none are called *kadosh*. It would seem, then, that the term *kadosh* cannot be used to describe an individual's character, no matter how "holy" he may be.[5] In fact, throughout the entire Bible there is but a single occasion where an individual is described as *kadosh*. The wealthy woman of Shunem says, in reference to the prophet Elisha, "I am sure that it is a holy man of God (*ish Elokim kadosh*) who comes this way regularly" (2 Kings 4:9). The fact that this term is used neither by God, nor by a prophet, nor even by the biblical narrator, but merely by a minor character within the story, serves only to highlight the exceptional nature of this usage. The general rule remains: the Bible does not characterize a righteous individual as *kadosh*.

A second peculiar aspect of the biblical use of the term *kedushah* concerns its absence from the patriarchal record of Genesis. In light of our discussion concerning the use of the term *kadosh* to describe righteous individuals, it is no surprise that none of the patriarchs is called *kadosh*. If, as a rule, throughout the Bible, individuals are not described as *kadosh*, there is no reason why the heroes of Genesis should serve as an exception. What is astonishing, however, is that not a single entity is described as *kadosh* in the entire narrative covering the careers of the patriarchs. By contrast, when God appeared to Moses at the burning bush (Exodus 3:5), Moses was told to hold his distance because he was treading on *admat kodesh*—holy ground. In like fashion, we find that as Joshua prepared for the capture of Jericho, the angel of God appeared to him and commanded him to bare his feet, "for the place where you stand is holy" (Joshua 5:15). If sites of revelation become holy, why are none of the sites of revelation in the Book of Genesis likewise declared holy? In light of the experiences of Moses and of Joshua, we might have expected the banks of the Jabbok River (Genesis 32:24) to become *kadosh* once the angel revealed himself to Jacob. The same could be said for Beth-El, where God appeared to Jacob in a dream, and which Jacob concluded was the very house of God and portal to the heavens (Genesis 28:17). Nowhere is this question more pertinent, however, than with regard to the site of the binding of Isaac. Mount Moriah emerges later in the Bible as the site of the Temple itself (2 Chronicles 3:1)—the apex of *kedushah* in the spacial realm. Nonetheless, Abraham is not told that the spot is one of *kedushah!* Why did sites of revelation assume *kedushah* when God spoke to Moses and Joshua but not when He communicated with the patriarchs?

The omission of the term *kedushah* from the patriarchal annals becomes even more striking when we examine the promises to the patriarchs concerning the future of the Jewish people. The patriarchs were told that their descendants would become a great nation (Genesis 12:2)—a blessed people (Genesis 22:18)—that kings would emerge from their midst (Genesis 17:6, 35:11), and that they would enter a special relationship with God as His people (Genesis 17:8). Never were they told, however, that their descendants would become an *am kadosh*—a *holy* people. The Jewish people are called an *am kadosh* dozens of times throughout the Bible. Why, then, were the patriarchs unapprised of this destiny?

A review of the entire Book of Genesis reveals that *kedushah* is mentioned precisely once: "And God blessed the seventh day and declared it holy, because on it God ceased from all the work of creation which He had done" (2:3). The Sabbath seems never to have been revealed to the patriarchs, and is only related to the Children of Israel following the splitting of the Red Sea (Exodus 16:23). What, then, does it mean when the Bible labels something *kadosh*? Why is the term nearly absent from the Book of Genesis, and why are righteous individuals never termed *kadosh*?

Our understanding of *kedushah* in the sense that we call *holiness* can be sharpened by examining how the root *k.d.sh.* is biblically applied in nonsacral contexts. A prostitute is sometimes referred to as a *kedeshah* (Genesis 38:21–22; Deuteronomy 23:18). When God threatens the king of Judah for fraudulent behavior, He says, "I will make *kadosh* (*ve-kidashti*) destroyers against you" (Jeremiah 22:7). Certainly, there is nothing holy about a prostitute or the destroyers of Judea! On the basis of these occurrences, which have absolutely no sacral overtones, many have noted that the root *k.d.sh.* means "set aside" or "dedicated."[6] A prostitute is a *kedeshah* because she dedicates herself not to one man but to the act of harlotry. The adversaries of the king of Judah are made *kadosh* in the sense that they are *set aside* for that purpose.

The meaning of the root *k.d.sh.* as "set aside" or "differentiated" is the key to understanding *kedushah* in its sacral sense as well. When the prophets declare God to be *kadosh*, it is a declaration that He is, in the most profound sense, *set apart* from this world. The statement that God is *kadosh* is a statement of His awe and transcendence above this world.

An examination of the mundane entities termed *kadosh* in the Bible also reveals that they are set aside, or designated, as well. They are all *set apart for the service of God by formal, legal restrictions and limitations.* The *kedushah* of periods of *time* such as the Sabbath and the festivals, is marked by limits on man's activities of work and construction. Tithes and sacrificial animals—*objects* endowed with *kedushah*—are proscribed from use in mundane purposes. The sets of *people* endowed with *kedushah*, such as the Priests, may not come into contact with a corpse and are restricted in their choice of spouse. *Kedushah,* then, implies separation and differentiation. When referring to God, it is a reference to his ultimate transcendency. When mundane entities are termed *kadosh*, it implies that they are separated for the service of God by formal legal restrictions and regulations.

The understanding of *kedushah* as set apart for the service of God through regulation is particularly salient for understanding the notion of *am kadosh*—a holy people. The Torah refers to the Jewish people as *kadosh* over a dozen times throughout the Torah alone.[7] In every instance, it is in conjunction with a call for Israel to observe the commandments. Leviticus, chapter 19, is a telling example of the significance of the juxtaposition of the terms *kedushah* and *commandment.* Verse 2 proclaims that we must be *kadosh* because God is *kadosh*. The chapter then lists some two dozen commandments that stem from the status of being an *am kadosh*. As some have noted, these commandments are almost entirely prohibitions that limit the activity of the *am kadosh.*[8] Oftentimes, the appellation *am kadosh* introduces or concludes a set of commandments that distinguish the Jewish people from other nations, such as the section of the dietary laws (Leviticus 11:45, Deuteronomy 14:21) and the section outlining illicit relationships (Leviticus 20:26).[9]

As we noted before, the term *kedushah* is strangely absent from the patriarchal record of Genesis. However, this phenomenon is understandable when the term *kedushah* is seen in relationship to another term—*covenant.*

KEDUSHAH AND COVENANT

The first time that Israel is called an *am kadosh* is at the moment of the consecration of the covenant itself—the revelation at Sinai. In Exodus, chapter 19, the prelude to the giving of the Torah, the Torah says (Exodus 19:5–6): "Now then, if you will obey Me faithfully and keep My *covenant,* you shall be My treasured possession among all the peoples. Indeed all the earth is mine, but you shall be to Me a kingdom of priests and a *holy* nation."[10] The implication of the passage is that the *kedushah* of Israel stems from the fact that it has entered into a collective national *covenant* with the Almighty. Why couldn't the Jewish people have been declared an *am kadosh* prior to the covenant of Sinai?

The patriarchs—even as forefathers of the Jewish people—stood in relationship with the Almighty only as *individuals.* Their affiliation and affinity with God constituted the basis of the election of Israel. However, the bond between God and the Jewish people reaches its pinnacle when the *nation* of Israel accedes to the norms of the Torah, thereby entering into a *collective* covenantal bond with God. This is the key to understanding the term *am kadosh*—a nation endowed with *kedushah.* When something is endowed with *kedushah,* it is segregated for the service of God through regulation and restriction. The Children of Israel become an *am kadosh*—a nation segregated for the service of God through regulation by virtue of entering into a covenantal pact with God at Sinai. *Kedushah*, in all realms—time, space, and objects—is a function of the emergence of the *nation* of Israel, a state of affairs that only materializes in the Book of Exodus.[11]

The notion that the *kedushah* of Israel stems from its covenant with God is reiterated in several other passages. Deuteronomy 7:6–9 states: "For you are a *kadosh* people to the Lord your God: of all the peoples on earth the Lord your God chose you to be His treasured people . . . know, therefore, that only the Lord your God is God, the steadfast God who keeps His gracious *covenant* to the thousandth generation of those who love him and keep His commandments." The appellation *am kadosh* stems from the fact that we have entered into a collective covenantal bond with the Almighty. The content and form of that designation manifests itself through the commandments, which set us apart and differentiate us from the rest of the nations of the world.

The link between covenant and the *kedushah* of Israel is found again in Deuteronomy, chapter 28, one of the final stages of Moses' valedictory address. He says in chapter 28, verse 9, "The Lord will establish you as His holy people, as he swore to you if you keep the commandments of the Lord your God and walk in His ways." In chapter 28, verse 69, which follows the section on rebuke if the commandments are not heeded, it is summarized, "These are the terms of the covenant which the Lord commanded Moses to conclude with the Israelites in the land of Moab, in addition to the covenant which He had made with them at Horeb." Once again, we see that the Jewish People are an *am kadosh* because they have entered into a covenantal relationship with God.

This conception of *kedushah* is of enormous importance for understanding the first mention of *kedushah* in the affairs of men. This occurs during the episode of the burning bush. Moses wandered with his flock to Horeb—which is synonymous with Sinai—and was told there: "Do not come closer. Remove your sandals from your feet, for the place on which you stand is holy ground" (Exodus 3:5). Note that as Moses receives his charge to lead the children of Israel out of Egypt, the site is set apart as *kadosh* through restrictions—Moses must remove his sandals and keep his distance. This is precisely the site at which we would expect the introduction of the concept of *kedushah*, for at that very moment Moses was informed that the Children of Israel would come to Sinai to worship God (Exodus 3:12), and it is at Sinai, of course, that the Torah was given to the Jewish people and the covenant with God was consecrated. The midrash is sensitive to this point as well: "'For the place on which you stand is holy ground'—The Holy One Blessed be He said to him, 'Moses, Moses! hold your place, for at this site I will give the Torah to Israel,' as it says, 'do not come closer. Remove your sandals from your feet, for the place on which you stand is holy ground.'"[12]

The understanding of *kedushah* as segregated by regulation for the service of God explains why pious individuals are rarely described as *kadosh*. A righteous individual may be close to God, but this does not make him *kadosh* in the biblical sense that we have here defined. To his spiritual stature inhere no further legal restrictions than to any other Jew. It is, of course, true that an individual may be termed *kadosh*; an individual *priest* may possess *kedushah*—but not as a comment on his character or personal qualities. His *kedushah*, rather, is a reflection on his genealogical status and manifests itself through the restrictions that apply to all priests. Likewise, the Torah refers to the individual nazirite as *kadosh*—"throughout his term as nazirite he is *kadosh* to the Lord" (Numbers 6:8)—as a comment on the status binding him in extra obligations, and not as a comment on his righteousness.[13]

Why is it that the entities dedicated to the service of God bear restriction and limitation? On *mikra'ei kodesh*—occasions of *kedushah*—such as the Sabbath and festivals, the range of our activities is highly proscribed. *Kadosh* objects, such as tithes, first fruits, and sacrifices, may be eaten only by certain people, in proscribed locations, and for limited periods of time. As a member of an *am kadosh*, the Jew is restricted in his diet and must abstain from a range of sexual relationships. What is the implicit message about dedicating an entity to God that mandates that it bear restrictions as well?

The identity between covenant and the establishment of limits may be interpreted homiletically. A covenant implies a partnership and a bond. As partners in a covenant with God, we cannot function in the world as if we were its total masters. Partnership implies partial sacrifice, as well as subjugation to the other. In nearly every sphere of human existence—our experience of the passage of time and the expanse of space, or our encounter with the natural and social orders— we are called upon to recognize representative elements as *kadosh*— separated for the service of God. The time, space, and objects that are limited to us through the agency of *kedushah* are signs that as God's covenantal partners, we must relinquish some control in every sphere of our existence and reserve those elements for His service.[14]

To summarize, the meaning of the word *kedushah* cannot be arrived at by simple translation. Upon inspection, we were able to arrive at a biblical definition: *kedushah* implies dedication to God, and it is expressed through regulation and restriction. It is a term that emerges only with the emergence of the Jewish people as a nation, and it only has meaning within the activities of its members.

COVENANTAL TIME AND SPACE

As we noted, time, space, objects, and persons all can be endowed with *kedushah*. However, within each of these realms, there are hierarchies of *kedushah*. The High Priest bears a higher level of *kedushah* than do the other priests, and Yom Kippur has a higher level of *kedushah* than do the other holidays.

When we examine the pinnacles of *kedushah* in time and space— the Sabbath and the Temple—an enlightening observation can be made. Like all entities endowed with *kedushah*, the Sabbath and the Temple are highly proscribed and are dedicated to the service of God. However, as the pinnacles of *kedushah* in their respective realms, they each stand as a sign and symbol of the covenantal bond between God and the Jewish people.

While the status of the Sabbath as the first entity endowed with *kedushah* lies hidden until the time when the children of Israel cross the Red Sea, from that moment on it emerges in the Bible as the preeminent symbol of the covenant between God and the Jewish people. This is most evident in Exodus 31:13–17:

> You must keep My Sabbaths, for this is a sign between Me and you throughout the generations, that you may know that I the Lord have consecrated you. . . . The Israelite people shall keep the Sabbath, observing the Sabbath throughout the generations as a covenant for all time: it shall be a sign for all time between Me and the people of Israel. For in six days the Lord made heaven and earth, and on the seventh day He ceased from work and was refreshed.

The Sabbath is not only a commemoration of God's rest following creation. The Sabbath also constitutes a sign of the covenant "between Me and the people of Israel."

The notion that the Sabbath constitutes a memorial to the covenant is further buttressed by the subsequent passage. When two narratives or two sets of commandments appear in juxtaposition, a conceptional relationship should be discerned between them. The preceding passage is followed by the narrative of the giving of the tablets (Exodus 31:18): "When He finished speaking with him on Mount Sinai, He gave Moses the two tablets of the Pact, stone tablets inscribed with the finger of God." The final commandment Moses hears before receiving the tablets is the commandment of the Sabbath, and it is here that the Sabbath is first described as a sign of the covenant. The placement of this commandment immediately prior to the giving of the tablets of the covenant is no coincidence. At Mount Sinai, the Jewish people enter into a covenant with God. At the conclusion of his stay on Mount Sinai, Moses is given two vehicles to perpetuate the memory of that event. First, Moses is told that the Sabbath will become a temporal shrine bearing witness to the covenant; and second, he is given the tablets that record the Decalogue, the essential responsibilities entailed by the covenant.

Isaiah also highlights the status of the Sabbath as the preeminent sign of the covenant. Addressing the eunuchs and converts who fear that they will not be accepted by God as full members of the Jewish people, Isaiah declares (Isaiah 56:4–6):

As regards the eunuchs *who keep my Sabbaths*,
Who have chosen what I desire
And hold fast to My covenant—
I will give them in My House
and within My walls,
A monument and a name . . .
As for the foreigners . . .
All who keep the Sabbath and do not profane it,
And who hold fast to My covenant
I will bring them to My sacred mount.

The Sabbath is the first entity to be declared *kadosh*, the first among the festivals (Leviticus 23:2–3), and it is the festival that receives more attention in the Torah than any other. As the apex of *kedushah* in the temporal sphere, it stands as a unique symbol, commemorating the covenant between God and the Jewish people.

The apex of *kedushah* in the spatial realm—the Sanctuary—also stands testimony to the covenantal bond between God and the Jewish people. What lies at the center of the realm of spatial *kedushah*? At the spiritual center of the land of Israel lies the Sanctuary. Within the Sanctuary, the most sacred place is the Holy of Holies, and within the Holy of Holies—the site endowed with the greatest *kedushah*— rests the Ark of the Covenant, bearing the tablets of the covenant. The Sanctuary is the apex of *kedushah* in the spatial realm. At its center lies the preeminent symbol of the covenant between God and Israel.

The centrality of the notion of covenant to the concept of spatial *kedushah* is evident in the very structure of the Sanctuary. It is also verbally recognized by Solomon in the concluding note of his oratory to the entire nation of Israel at the dedication of the First Temple (1 Kings 8:20–21): "I have built the House for the name of the Lord, the God of Israel; and I have set a place there for the Ark, containing the covenant which the Lord made with our fathers when he brought them out from the land of Egypt." For Solomon, the Temple was not only a temple to God; it was a center that stood testimony to the covenantal bond between God and the Jewish people.

LINKING SABBATH AND TEMPLE

Thus far we have examined how the Sabbath and Temple—the pin-nacles of *kedushah* in the realms of time and space—serve as potent symbols of the covenant. As such, they are not independent institu-tions but are integrally related. To fully grasp the biblical significance of each, the Sabbath and the Temple need to be examined in light of one another and their interrelationship must be explored.

On a surface level, the link between the two is an explicit one as the Torah calls for their safeguarding in a single command: "You shall keep My Sabbaths and venerate My Sanctuary: I am the Lord" (Leviticus 19:30, 26:2).

On a far wider scale, however, the relationship between Sabbath and Sanctuary can be seen as a preeminent theme in the section out-lining the construction of the Tabernacle in the Book of Exodus.[15] The account of the conclusion of the work of the Tabernacle bears a striking resemblance to the biblical description of the completion of the universe at the end of the sixth day of creation in Genesis:

Genesis 1–2	Exodus 39–40
And God saw all that he had made and behold it was very good. (1:31)	Moses saw all of the skilled work and behold they had done it; as God had commanded it they had done it. (39:43)
The heavens and earth and all of their array were completed. (2:1)	All the work of the Tabernacle of the Tent meeting was completed. (39:32)
And God completed all the work that He had done. (2:2)	And Moses completed the work. (40:33)
And God blessed . . . (2:3)	And Moses blessed . . . (39:43)
And sanctified it. (2:3)	And you shall sanctify it and all its vessels. (40:9)

Here we encounter a biblical passage that is laced with imagery and language from an earlier section. We will assume that the presence of those elements is meant to elucidate the meaning of the passage at hand. What is the significance of the parallel between the conclusion of the account of creation and the conclusion of the Tabernacle works?

On one level, creation ended on the Sabbath. On a second level, however, it only truly concluded once the Tabernacle work was completed. The composite parts of the physical world were completed on the sixth day of creation, but the ultimate purpose of these elements—to be dedicated to the service of God—is only realized once the Sanctuary is built, to serve as a universal focal point for the service of God. To be certain, the mere act of constructing the Sanctuary will accomplish nothing if the spiritual climate of the times is inappropriate for such activity. The conditions that create such a climate will be elucidated in chapter 4. When these conditions prevail, however, the presence of the Sanctuary represents the spiritual completion of the times and symbolizes the completion of the creation of the universe.

The integral relationship between Sabbath and Sanctuary implied by the closing chapters of Exodus sheds light on the Temple narrative of 1 Kings as well. Just as language from the Sabbath narrative of Genesis, chapter 2, is present in the Tabernacle sections of Exodus, chapters 39 and 40, Sabbath imagery is likewise present in the narrative of the completion of the Temple in 1 Kings. The biblical notion that the number seven represents wholeness and completion begins with the sanctification of the seventh day as the Sabbath following the completion of the universe in Genesis, chapter 2. The number seven figures prominently throughout the Temple narrative of 1 Kings. The Temple took seven years to complete (1 Kings 6:35) and was dedicated on the festival of Sukkot, a holiday of seven days that occurs during the seventh month of the year (1 Kings 8:2). Finally, Solomon's dedication address is composed of seven petitions (1 Kings 8:12–53).

The notion that the erection of the Sanctuary completes the process of creation is conveyed explicitly in the midrash concerning the completion of the First Temple:

"All the work [that King Solomon had done in the House of the Lord]
was completed (1 Kings 7:51)"—scripture does not say *the work*, but *all
the work*, which refers to the work of the six days of creation, as it says,
"[And God] completed all the work that He had planned to do" (Genesis 2:2). Scripture does not say [*that He*] *had done*, but, [*that He*] *had planned
to do*, implying that there was yet more work to do. When Solomon completed the Temple, God proclaimed: "Now the work of the heavens and
the earth are complete (*shelemah*)." [When it says] "All the work was completed (*va-tashlem*)," it indicates why he was named Solomon (*Shelomoh*),
for God completed (*hishlim*) the work of the six days of creation through
him.[16]

When the Bible writes that Solomon completed "all the work," the
context mandates that *work* here be understood as the work of the
Temple's construction. The midrash seems to be abandoning any effort
to relate to the biblical text itself, and rather claims that the work here
is the work of the world's creation. Nonetheless, its reading is in consonance with the leitmotif of the Sabbath–Temple connection that
is thread throughout the text of the Bible itself. This midrash relates,
then, not to the local meaning of 1 Kings, chapter 8, but to a second-
ary level of meaning of the entire story, which can be derived from a
close reading of the passages throughout the Bible relating to the
Tabernacle and Temple.

A second interpretation of the presence of Sabbath and creation
imagery within the Tabernacle and Temple may be offered. While the
physical universe was created by God alone, the Tabernacle, the pinnacle of creation, must be built by man. When man establishes a perfected society, which culminates with the building of a Sanctuary for
God, he becomes a partner in the process of creation.

The notion that man is a partner in the process of creation when
he engages in the construction of the Tabernacle can be seen in the
description of the capacities ascribed to Bezalel, chief artisan of the
Tabernacle. Describing the creation of the universe, Proverbs 3:19–20
reads:

The Lord founded the earth by *wisdom*;
He established the heavens by *understanding*;
By His *knowledge* the depths burst apart.

When God tells Moses that Bezalel is to oversee the Tabernacle works, He says: "See, I have singled out Bezalel the son of Uri the son of Hur of the tribe of Judah. I have endowed him with a divine spirit of *wisdom, understanding* and *knowledge* in every kind of craft (*melakhah*)" (Exodus 31:2–3). As we assumed previously, the presence of terminology from one biblical section in another may be seen as intended to elucidate the meaning of that passage. When the author of Proverbs borrows terminology that, in another context, describes Bezalel's creative capacities and ascribes those same virtues to God as he created the universe, it may be read as a statement that Bezalel's creation of the Tabernacle is tantamount to God's creation of the universe.[17] These parallels are reflected in the Talmud's statement that Bezalel knew how to create the heavens and the earth.[18]

Another concept that links Sabbath and Sanctuary, the pinnacles of *kedushah* in the temporal and spatial realms, is the concept of *menuchah*, which is loosely translated as "rest." R. Ovadiah Seforno, the sixteenth-century Italian biblical exegete, wrote in his commentary to Exodus 20:11 that the word *menuchah* implies, not the cessation of rigorous activity, but a state of being that stems from completion. Thus, when the Bible states in that verse that God rested (*va-yanach*) on the seventh day, the anthropomorphism is not to be taken literally, but rather is to be understood as a statement that on the Sabbath, God had completed the creation.

This sense of *menuchah* as completion is exhibited with reference both to the Tabernacle and to the Temple. When David moves the Tabernacle to Jerusalem, and the Ark of the Covenant with it, he declares to God, "Advance, O Lord, to Your resting place (*li-menuchatekha*)" (Psalms 132:8), to which God replies, "This is My resting place (*menuchati*) for all time; here I will dwell for I desire it" (Psalms 132:14). When Solomon brings the Ark to the Holy of Holies, he similarly invokes the image of rest: "Advance O Lord God, to Your resting place (*le-nuchekha*)" (2 Chronicles 6:41). From the time when the Children of Israel entered the land of Israel, the Ark had migrated from location to location. When it was brought to Jerusalem by David, and then installed in the Temple by Solomon, the process of God's migration finally reached completion. Its terminus, the Temple in Jerusalem, is thus called *menuchah*, a place that symbolizes completion.[19]

The final interrelationship between Sabbath and Sanctuary concerns the concept of *melakhah*.[20] In this chapter we have already encountered the term *melakhah* twice. When God concluded the act of creation, the activity from which He desisted on the Sabbath was termed *melakhah* (Genesis 2:2–3). We have also seen that the skilled craftsmanship executed by Bezalel and the artisans who assembled the Tabernacle and its vessels was likewise called *melakhah*.[21] The *melakhah* of the Sabbath and the *melakhah* of the Sanctuary are linked in explicit terms in the Tabernacle section in the Book of Exodus. In chapters 25 through 30, Moses is issued directions concerning the construction of the Tabernacle and its vessels. Chapter 31, which opens with the appointment of Bezalel to execute the *melakhah*, concludes with an admonition about the Sabbath: "Six days work (*melakhah*) may be done, but on the seventh day there shall be a Sabbath of complete rest, holy to the Lord; whoever does work (*melakhah*) on the Sabbath day shall be put to death" (Exodus 31:15). The command to execute the *melakhah* of the Tabernacle, then, concludes with a command to desist from *melakhah* on the Sabbath.[22] The juxtaposition of the two concepts calls on us to interpret the connection between them. The implication that emerges from the juxtaposition is that one may not engage in Tabernacle building on the Sabbath.[23] This juxtaposition is the basis of the talmudic understanding that the definition of *melakhah*—work that is forbidden on the Sabbath—is based on the specific activities that were carried out in the construction of the Tabernacle.[24]

In summary, we have seen the conceptual link between Sabbath and Sanctuary on a number of levels. The Sabbath caps God's completion of the *melakhah* of the physical order. The Sanctuary, built by God's covenantal partner, Israel, is also a process of *melakhah* and represents the completion of the spiritual order.

We conclude with a homiletic observation about the *halakhot* that bind Sabbath and Sanctuary together. The Sanctuary, we saw, is in a sense bounded by the Sabbath—for work on the Sanctuary must cease on the Sabbath. However, the Sabbath is also conversely bounded by the Sanctuary—for the very definition of prohibited work is derived from the activities of the construction of the Sanctuary.

We have discussed the concept of covenantal partnership at some length and wish to conclude by contrasting two paradigms of partnership. The first involves, say, a couple that chooses to renovate their home. They agree to split the work, with each one taking a different room. When finished, their partnership will result in a renovated home. However, their partnership will be deemed even stronger if each partner is mindful of the tastes and work of the other, for then they will have not only split the work, each will have carried out the tasks in a way that recognizes the contribution of the other.

The covenant at Sinai established God and the Jewish people as partners in the process of creation. The Sabbath—covenantally commemorative time—recalls the creation of the universe through the *melakhah* of God. The Sanctuary—covenantally commemorative space—represents a completion of the process of creation through the *melakhah* of the Jewish people. On the surface it would seem that the partners operate in a thoroughly independent fashion. God created the world without the aid of man, and later, man is called on to finish creation by erecting the Sanctuary.

However, the halakhic parameters guiding the realms of spatial and temporal *kedushah* demonstrate that, in fact, the partners are continually mindful of the contribution of the other. The *kedushah* of the Sabbath—which commemorates God's hand in creation—calls for the cessation of work. However, the very definition of prohibited work is derived from the activities of the Jewish people in their part in the process of creation, the construction of the Sanctuary. The form of the Sabbath—prohibited work—is defined by the work of the Sanctuary. The temporal commemoration of God's creation, then, receives its form solely from the creation of the Jewish people. It is as if God says: "The Sabbath commemorates My act of creation. And how will My Sabbath be observed? By being mindful of the contribution toward the completion of creation made by the Jewish people."

This consideration is symbolically exhibited in the converse direction as well. The Jewish people are called on to complete the process of creation through the building of the Sanctuary—but they do not engage in this activity on the Sabbath. The establishment of spatial *kedushah* is proscribed by the demands of temporal *kedushah*. Even as they execute their contribution to the completion of creation, the Jewish people desist from this task on the Sabbath, as they stand in commemoration of the beginning of that process, the creation wrought by their covenantal partner, the Holy One Blessed Be He.

2

Temple as Garden of Eden

When one thinks of the Temple, the garden of Eden is not one of the first associations that comes to mind. Nonetheless, both language and imagery borrowed from the garden of Eden narratives of Genesis, chapters 2 and 3, permeate many of the Bible's references to the Tabernacle and Temple. A prominent example of this concerns the presence of *cherubim* in both the garden of Eden and in the Sanctuary. Following the expulsion of man from the garden, the Bible says (Genesis 3:24), "He drove the man out, and stationed east of the garden of Eden the *cherubim* and the fiery ever-turning sword, to guard the way to the tree of life." The cherubim reappear in only one other context in the entire Pentateuch, and that is in the Holy of Holies in the Sanctuary (Exodus 25:20–21, 26:1, 26:31). The fact that the cherubim appear in only two places in the entire Torah implies an analogy between the two contexts. What is the relationship between Eden and Sanctuary?

MAN IN GOD'S DOMAIN

The position of the Eden narrative as the first story about man mandates that we interpret it as a seminal statement about his nature, perhaps even on several levels. The relationship between Eden and Sanctuary can be understood if we perceive the garden narrative as a postulate concerning the environment in which *man can enter into communion with the divine.*

The notion that man can relate to God only by entering His province stands in contrast to popular Western conceptions of the relationship between man and God. Many will claim that they believe in God and relate to him on their "own terms." Within this conception, one's relationship with God is analogous to one's relationship with a friend or relative. One generally construes such a relationship as something that exists independent of the particular setting or environment, which is powered solely by the dynamics of the two personalities in interaction. The Bible, however, posits that man can only truly relate to God through delicately orchestrated circumstances. Man cannot encounter God simply by willing the encounter to take place. Rather, man must fortify himself spiritually by entering into an environment conducive to communing with Him. Thus, when the psalmist tells of his yearnings to commune with God, he typically speaks of man entering the domain of God: "One thing I ask of the Lord, only that do I seek: to live in the *house of the Lord*" (Psalms 27:4); "The righteous bloom like a date-palm; they thrive like a cedar in Lebanon; planted in the *house of the Lord*, they flourish in the *courts of our God*" (Psalms 92:13–14). The garden of Eden narrative, which is seminally situated at the outset of the Bible, may be seen as a prototype of the conditions and environment in which man can intimately encounter God.[1] It is here that man first enters into a relationship with God. Thus, while the story of the garden and its characters is a brief one, it has ramifications for the entire biblical record and can be construed as a paradigm for subsequent discussions concerning the setting in which man encounters the divine presence. When the Bible depicts an environment in which man cultivates his relationship with God, we should expect to find the Eden prototype reemerging on both the thematic and linguistic planes.

What were the characteristics of the garden of Eden, in which Adam lived in God's presence? Several cornerstones emerge:

1. The garden was not meant to ensure a life of leisure that was devoid of responsibility. The substance of Adam's relationship with God was based on an obedience of commandments. Just as the Bible later delineates the responsibilities of the Jewish people through positive commandments and prohibitions, Adam was given two commandments, one positive and one a prohibition: "And the Lord God commanded the man saying, 'You are to eat from any of the trees of the garden; but as for the tree of knowledge of good and bad, you must not eat of it'" (Genesis 2:16–17).

2. The privilege of living in God's presence was something that Adam would have to continually merit. If he disobeyed, he would be punished with death (Genesis 2:17). Disobedience would also disrupt the balance and harmony of the natural order. The punishment issued to Adam and Eve for their transgression dictated that from then on, childbearing would be painful (Genesis 3:16) and fieldwork, arduous and taxing (Genesis 3:17–18).

3. Most significantly, defiance would result in banishment from the garden, which is to say, banishment from the privilege of living in immanent intimacy with God.

ISRAEL AS EDEN

In light of these characteristics of Eden, the land of Israel can be construed as a conceptual expansion of the garden of Eden. The account of Eden in Genesis, chapters 2 and 3, is a universal one. It heralds the capacity of all men to enter into communion with the Almighty, for all men are the descendants of Adam. However, following the Flood

(Genesis 6–7) and the Tower of Babel (Genesis 11), God elects to limit his most intimate relationship with mankind to a single people, the descendants of Abraham. The Eden paradigm resurfaces in the account of the Covenant of Circumcision between God and Abraham (Genesis 17:7–8): "I will maintain My covenant between Me and you . . . to be God to you and to your offspring to come. I give the land you sojourn in to you and your offspring to come, all the land of Canaan, as an everlasting possession. I will be their God." Here God offers to sustain an intimate relationship with the descendants of Abraham. The milieu in which this bond will flourish is in a defined locale, the land of Israel. The land of Israel represents a conceptual expansion of the garden of Eden. The garden was the environment in which Adam related to God and lived by His dictates. The message of Genesis, chapter 17, is that the land of Israel is uniquely suited as an environment in which the descendants of Abraham can establish a relationship with the Almighty.

The conceptual parallel between Eden and the land of Israel is borne out in the language describing the conditions under which the Jewish people commune with God in the land of Israel that is used in Leviticus 26:3–12:

> If you follow My laws and faithfully observe My commandments (4) I will grant your rains in their season, so that the earth shall yield its produce and the trees of the field their fruit. (5) Your threshing shall overtake the vintage, and your vintage shall overtake the sowing; you shall eat your fill of bread and dwell securely in your land. (6) I will grant peace in the land, and you shall lie down untroubled by anyone. . . . (9) I will look with favor upon you, and make you fertile and multiply you; and I will maintain My covenant with you. . . . (11) I will establish My abode in your midst, and I will not spurn you. (12) I will be ever present in your midst: I will be your God, and you shall be My people.

Here we find the ideal realization of the covenant between God and the Jewish People. In many respects it may be seen as a simulation of the garden of Eden. It is predicated first and foremost on the observance of commandments (verse 3), just as Adam's tenure in the garden was dependent on the fulfillment of commandments. In the garden of Eden account, the most manifest evidence of God's presence comes when we are told that God's voice was *mithalekh*—that it moved about—in the garden. Using the same language, God promises (verse 12) that His presence will be intimately felt within the land of Israel (*ve-hithalakhti be-tokhekhem*).[2] The narrative of Genesis, chapter 2, emphasizes God's activity for the sake of man; He planted the garden, made the rivers, and created man's mate. In Leviticus, chapter 26, God's involvement and concern are highlighted through twelve separate actions that He vows to perform for the sake of the Jewish people if they observe His commandments—I will grant rains, I will grant peace, I will look with favor upon you, etc. . . . [3] The idyllic conception of Israel as Eden, where the Jewish people live faithfully under God's protection, is the driving force behind Isaiah's redemptive vision (Isaiah 51:3):

Truly the Lord has comforted Zion,
Comforted all her ruins;
He has made her wilderness like Eden,
Her desert like the Garden of the Lord.
Gladness and joy shall abide there,
Thanksgiving and the sound of music.

As we noted, Eden was not an unconditional haven for Adam, nor is the land of Israel a haven for the Jewish people. When Adam defied God's command concerning the tree of knowledge, he became destined to work the land laboriously and was told that his efforts would bring weeds and thorns. The continuation of Leviticus, chapter 26, reveals that the same conditions occur in the land of Israel after the Jewish people defy God's commandments: they are told that "you shall sow your seed to no purpose" (verse 16) and that "your land shall not yield its produce, nor shall the trees of the land yield their fruit" (verse 20). Finally, defiance results in the expulsion from God's presence. Just as disobedience led to the banishment of Adam from the garden of Eden, disobedience leads to the exile of the Jewish people from the land of Israel (verse 33). The Eden-like environment of intimacy with God is available to the Jewish people when they establish a society in accordance with God's will in the land of Israel. However, just as Adam was banished from Eden, so, too, the Jewish people are banished from their land when they defy that will.[4]

TEMPLE AS THE IDEAL OF EDEN

If the laws concerning life in the land of Israel are designed to create an environment in which the children of Israel can encounter God, the Temple represents this environment at its apex. Within the land of Israel as a whole, the entire nation lives a collective, Eden-like existence in God's presence. The Temple, however, represents the spiritual center of the country. Here, at the site where God's presence is most immanent, the representatives of the Jewish people execute commandments and rites that symbolize the service of the nation as a whole. Here, too, the garden of Eden serves as a paradigm for the parameters of this encounter.

Throughout the Bible, the Sanctuary is described via language and terms that are borrowed from the Eden narrative of Genesis, chapters 2 and 3. In Eden, the voice of God was *mithalekh*—moving about (Genesis 3:8). The same term *mithalekh* is used to describe God's presence in the Sanctuary (Leviticus 26:11–12). In Eden, man's responsibilities are *le-ovedah u-le-shomerah*—to work the garden (*avodah*) and to preserve or guard the garden (*shemirah*). The activities of the Priests and Levites in the Sanctuary are likewise referred to as *avodah* and *shemirah*.[5] Ezekiel 28:11–19 contains a rebuke to the King of Tyre that is laced with intertwined imagery from both the garden of Eden and the Temple. Specifically, Ezekiel 28:13 endows the garden of Eden with nine of the twelve stones that the High Priest wore on his breastplate to symbolize the twelve tribes, as depicted in Exodus 28:17–20. The waters of Eden appear in conjunction with the Temple in two contexts. Psalms 36:9 reads, "They feast at the rich fare of Your Temple; you let them drink at Your refreshing stream." In the Hebrew, the phrase, "Your refreshing stream" reads, "the stream of *adanekha*"— "Your Edens"—implying that the bounty that flows forth from the Temple is reminiscent of the rivers of Eden. Second, the spring that supplied Jerusalem with water was named Gihon, (1 Kings 1:33, 38, 45; 2 Chronicles 32:30; 33:14), which was the name of one of the four rivers that flowed from Eden (Genesis 2:13).[6] The aggregate of all these allusions heightens the notion that the Temple is reflective of the garden of Eden, the first environment in which man encountered God.

Eden serves as a paradigm for communion with God in the Sanctuary in terms of man's strict accountability for his misdeeds. When man enters into the domain of the divine, his accountability increases. Infractions are judged more severely, precisely because they are committed within the intimate presence of the Almighty. In the garden of Eden, Adam is told that if he eats of the tree of knowledge, death will follow (Genesis 2:17). According to R. Saadiah Gaon and Nachmanides, this was not to say that Adam would be smitten on the spot if he ate of the tree of knowledge; rather, his life would be shortened. Nachmanides points out that the divine sentence of having one's life shortened is later found with regard to Temple officiants who violated cultic prohibitions, such as officiating while intoxicated (Leviticus 10:9) or while not adorned with the priestly garments (Exodus 28:43).[7] The meaning of this comparison is manifest. In the Temple, as in Eden, God's presence is immanent, and thus, the slightest infraction incurs capital punishment from God Himself.

All these are parallels that imply an identity between Eden and Sanctuary as environments wherein man enters the realm of the divine and resonate with a midrash that likewise equates the two: "*So the Lord God banished him from the garden of Eden*" (Genesis 3:23)—He revealed to him the destruction of the Temple."[8]

The biblical citations and midrashim cited thus far have implied a spiritual *congruence* between the environment of Eden and that of the

Sanctuary. In both, God's presence is imminently felt. Man serves God by observing positive commandments and prohibitions. In each, man is highly accountable for his actions and faces expulsion from God's presence if he transgresses His will.

TEMPLE AS EDEN AFTER THE SIN

Other biblical passages and rabbinic comments, however, imply a somewhat different correlation between Eden and Sanctuary. Accordingly, the Sanctuary resembles Eden because the Sanctuary *replaces* Eden after the fall of man as the venue through which man can aspire to commune with God. This point is explicitly expressed in the midrash: *"The Lord God banished him from the garden of Eden, to till the soil from which he was brought"* (Genesis 3:23)—"He took him from the garden of Eden and placed him on Mount Moriah to serve God until the day of his death."[9] The midrashic statement that God placed man (*hinicho*) on Mount Moriah echoes Genesis 2:15, when God placed man (*va-yanichehu*) in the garden of Eden. Man cannot return to the garden of Eden, but by serving God on Mount Moriah—the site of the Temple—man can strive to relate intimately with God, recalling the environment of Eden where man first communed with Him.

Since the Sanctuary represents a de facto substitute for the spiritual climate of Eden following the fall of man, we should expect Eden iconography in the Sanctuary to reflect the portrayal of Eden after the sin, as depicted in Genesis 3. Perhaps the most significant difference between Adam's spiritual standing before the sin and his standing afterward concerns his capacity to attain eternal life. Prior to his defiance, he was free to eat of the tree of life, but afterward he is denied this opportunity (Genesis 3:22), for eternal life in the literal sense would be incommensurate with man's fallibility.[10]

In place of eternal physical life offered by the tree of life, in the post-Eden era, God offers spiritual life in the form of the Torah (Deuteronomy 30:15–18): "See, I set before you this day life and good, death and evil. For I command you this day, to love the Lord your God, to walk in his ways, and to keep His commandments, His laws, and His norms, that you may live and increase . . . but if your heart turns away . . . you shall certainly perish." The Torah is portrayed here as a source of life. Its depiction as the difference between good and evil and between life and death may be a deliberate reference to the tree of good and evil and the tree of life in the Eden narrative and an indication that the Torah supplants them in the aftermath of man's sin. The Book of Proverbs refers to the wisdom of God's ways as a tree of life: "She is a tree of life for those who grasp her" (Proverbs 3:18). The midrash employs this verse to demonstrate that the Torah is a substitute for the tree of life of Eden:

> God hid the tree that granted eternal life to all who ate from it and in its place He gave us His Torah. This is the tree of life, for it says, "She is a tree of life for those who grasp her" (Proverbs 3:18). When a man beholds it, and sees in it God's wisdom, and His righteous and just laws and statutes, he is immediately induced to adopt a new mind, and observe them. In so doing he acquires for himself reward in this world and in the world to come, as it says, "the Lord commanded us to observe all these laws for our lasting good and to grant us life" (Deuteronomy 6:24).[11]

The analogy of the Torah as the tree of life is particularly striking when we examine the respective focal points of the garden of Eden and the Temple. Just as the tree of life stood at the conceptual center of the garden of Eden, the tablets of testimony, symbolizing the Torah as a whole, rest at the focal point of the Temple in the Holy of Holies, or *Kodesh Kodashim* (Exodus 26:33). Thus, the motif of a life-giving source at the center of Eden is preserved in the form of the tablets of testimony in the Temple.

In this light, the synagogue practice of returning the Torah to the Ark after its public reading takes on new light. The synagogue represents a simulation of, or substitute for, the Temple, a notion that will be probed in the final chapter of this book. As the Torah scroll is re-

turned to the Ark, the congregation recites Proverbs 3:18, in which
the Torah is characterized as a tree of life. The focal point of the garden of Eden was the tree of life. As an environment in which man
encounters God, the synagogue is reflective of the garden of Eden.
The Torah scroll emerges as the tree of life of the synagogue, and its
repository, the Ark, the focal point of the modern day Eden, the synagogue.

The presence of a "tree of life" at the center of the Temple takes
on remarkable significance in light of the fact that cherubim were
molded on to the Ark of testimony that bore the tablets (Exodus
25:20–21) (see fig. 1). As we noted at the outset, cherubim appear in
only one other context in the Torah, and that is with reference to the
original tree of life (Genesis 3:24): "He drove the man out, and stationed east of the garden of Eden the cherubim and the fiery ever-
turning sword, to guard the way to the tree of life." The cherubim of
Eden act as sentries guarding the most important element of the garden—the tree of life. The presence of cherubim atop the Ark of testimony is a telling sign, then, that the tablets of testimony—representing the Torah as a whole—are the post-Eden tree of life.

The cherubim are also instructive of the nature of man's encounter with the divine presence in the wake of the sin. The cherubim
guard the garden's entrance and prevent Adam from returning because immediate and full access to God's presence is no longer possible. The cherubim in the Sanctuary serve a similar function. Within
the Tabernacle and later the Temple, Priests were allowed access to
the outer chamber, the Kodesh, where they performed the rituals that
involved the candelabra and the table of shewbread. The inner chamber, or Kodesh Kodashim, contained the Ark of testimony and was the
holiest point in the Sanctuary. No one was permitted access to the
Kodesh Kodashim except for the High Priest on the Day of Atonement.
Separating the Kodesh Kodashim from the Kodesh was a partition, a
curtain with a design of cherubim worked into it (Exodus 26:31) (see
fig. 2). Just as the cherubim outside the garden of Eden served as a
notice that man could no longer achieve complete access to God's

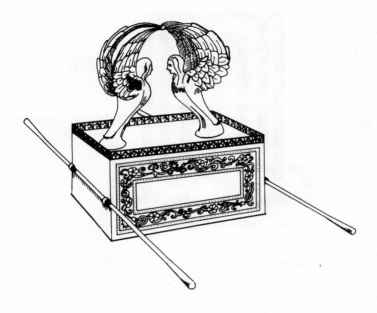

Figure 1. The Ark of the Covenant and its poles, covered by the cherubim with wings spread face-to-face. (From *The Holy Temple Revisited* by Rabbi L. Reznick, copyright © 1990 by Leibel Reznick; Jason Aronson Inc., publisher; artist, David Wilkes.)

presence, the cherubim embroidered on the curtain reminded the priests that access to the *Kodesh Kodashim*, the seat of God's presence, was forbidden to them.

On the Day of Atonement, when the High Priest entered the *Kodesh Kodashim*, he would encounter the cherubim stationed on the cover of the Ark, which bore the tablets of testimony. The wings of the cherubim were spread out, shielding the Ark (Exodus 25:20) which, if touched, caused death (2 Samuel 6:7). Thus, even the most intimate encounter between man and God, the visit of the High Priest

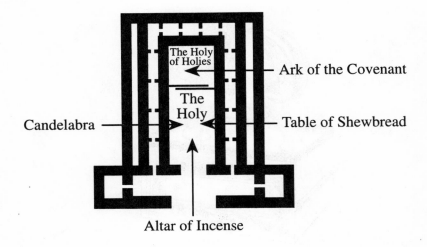

Figure 2. The division between the outer sanctum of the Sanctuary, the Holy, and the inner sanctum, the Holy of Holies.

to the *Kodesh Kodashim* on the Day of Atonement, was permeated with a sense of distance and inaccessibility. Cherubim symbolized the inaccessibility of man to the inside of the Ark of testimony,[12] just as cherubim prevented Adam from returning to God's immanent presence in the garden of Eden.[13]

The casting of the Torah in language suggestive of the tree of life implies a double message. While man may find the world around him devoid of spirituality, the Torah as a tree of life allows him to achieve an intimate encounter with the Almighty, much as Adam experienced in the garden of Eden. Conversely, however, the substitution of the Torah for the tree of life and the presence of cherubim guarding the *Kodesh Kodashim* remind man that the divine encounter of Eden can only be partially simulated and that man stands permanently outside the original garden in the wake of Adam's sin.

In the garden of Eden of chapter 2, Eden is given proscribed boundaries but there is no sense that it has an entrance or exit. Under the
idyllic conditions of that chapter, there was no need to elaborate on
Eden's gateway since man had no need to pass through it. When man
is expelled, however, God places the cherubim to the east of Eden in
order to prevent him from gaining access to the garden and the tree
of life (Genesis 3:24). Eastward, then, is the direction out of the garden. Just as the gateway to the garden of Eden was on the east, so,
too, the entrance to the Tabernacle was on the east (Exodus 27:13 –
16, Numbers 3:38).

Invoking the talmudic dictum that the divine presence dwells in
the west,[14] Maimonides deduces that eastward represents the direction away from God. He cites Ezekiel 8:16, where Ezekiel is witness
to idolaters in the Temple courtyard, who turn their backs on the
Temple and prostrate themselves eastward toward the rising sun.
Pagan worship, Maimonides concludes, was oriented eastward in service of the rising sun, and therefore, the Torah calls on the Jewish
people to direct their service of God in the Temple westward, in symbolic rejection of foreign theological impulses.[15]

A similar aspect of the Eden encounter with God that influences
our relationship with God in the Temple concerns the phenomenon
of death. In the garden of Eden, death is portrayed as the consequence
of disobedience of God's command: "As for the tree of knowledge of
good and bad, you must not eat of it; for as soon as you eat of it, you
shall be doomed to die" (Genesis 2:17). Likewise, when God decrees
the punishments to be suffered in the wake of the sin, death is the
crowning penalty and the ultimate sign of man's disobedience (Genesis 3:17–19): "To Adam he said, 'because you heeded your wife and
ate of the tree about which I commanded you saying, "You shall not
eat of it," . . . by the sweat of your brow shall you get bread to eat,
until you return to the ground, for from it you were taken: for dust
you are, and to dust you shall return.'"

If the phenomenon of death is reflective of spiritual failure, then
there can be no place for death within the precincts of the Temple.

Indeed, all forms of death, or even associations with death, are proscribed from the Temple complex. The Torah addresses these within the laws of ritual impurity, laws whose halakhic relevance is exclusively within the context of eligibility to enter the Temple complex. The things that render a person ritually impure and unfit to enter the Sanctuary nearly all involve things that have died or are associated with death, such as contact with a dead insect, carcass (Leviticus 11:24–31, 39–45), or corpse. A leper may not enter the Sanctuary; his skin is considered dead, as the Torah contrasts it to live skin (Leviticus 13:9–16), and he himself is considered partially dead, as reflected by the mandate that he observe the rites of mourning (Leviticus 13:45). Priests, the officiants of the Temple, may not come into contact with a dead body except for immediate relatives (Leviticus 21:1–4), while the high priest may not become impure, even to attend the funeral of his immediate relatives (Leviticus 21:11). Because death is the antithesis of the spiritual perfection that reigns in the Temple, priests are enjoined even from displaying public signs of mourning (Leviticus 10:6).

With the election of Israel, Eden—as a symbol of dwelling in God's domain—is accessible only to the Jewish people in the land of Israel, and, at its apex, in the Temple. In the depiction of the end of days in Zechariah, however, the Temple is portrayed through Eden imagery, with reference to a universal audience (Zechariah 14:8–9): "In that day, fresh water shall flow from Jerusalem, part of it to the Eastern Sea and part to the Western Sea, throughout the summer and winter. And the Lord shall be king over all the earth; in that day there shall be one Lord with one name." Just as rivers flowed in all directions from the garden of Eden (Genesis 2:10–14), so too water shall flow from Jerusalem to the farthest reaches, eastward and westward. In that age, when there will be one Lord with one name, the entire world will constitute a domain in which all men encounter God, even as Adam did in the garden of Eden.

3

Sinai and Sanctuary

In chapter 1, we demonstrated the integral connection between the terms *"kedushah"* and "covenant." The Ark of the Covenant, bearing the Tablets of the Covenant, was the focal point of the Sanctuary, the apex of *kedushah* in the spatial realm. The relationship between covenant and Sanctuary is a far-reaching one and has its roots in the final third of the Book of Exodus. Seminal for a discussion of the concept of covenant, of course, is the Sinai narrative of Exodus, chapters 19 and 24. The first chapters that explicitly address the Sanctuary are found in Exodus, chapters 25 through 40. In this chapter, we probe the Sinai narrative and its relationship to the Tabernacle chapters at the end of Exodus. The Sinai paradigm that will emerge provides a theological basis for understanding much of the minutiae of the Sanctuary vessels and their rites.

SINAI—AN UNCOMMEMORATED EVENT

The Exodus from Egypt and the Revelation at Sinai are milestones that cast the deepest imprint for collective identity amongst subse-

quent generations of Jews. The Bible, however, calls upon us to remember and commemorate these two events in dramatically different ways.

The Exodus is an event commemorated through commandments.
Immediately familiar are the many rites of the Passover *seder*: the eating
of matzah, the telling of the story of the Exodus, and, in the time of
the Temple, the partaking of the paschal lamb. However, these constitute only the *annual* celebration of the anniversary of the Exodus.
The bringing of the firstfruits to Jerusalem,[1] the obligation to don
phylacteries,[2] and the weekly observance of the Sabbath[3] are several
of the commandments that the Torah enjoins upon us year-round to
raise our consciousness about the liberation from Egypt and to emphasize our people's eternal connection to that event. The centrality of
the Exodus is preserved in rabbinic thought as well: "Ben Zoma ex-
pounded: 'So that you may remember the day of your departure from
the land of Egypt all the days of your life' (Deuteronomy 16:3). The
days of your life—this alone would imply during the daytime. All the
days of your life—this refers to the nighttime as well."[4] Based on this
dictum, the Rabbis determined that a Jew is biblically mandated to
recall the Exodus in the recitation of the Shema, the reading of Numbers 15:37–41 twice daily, every day of the year.[5]

While the Torah is replete with commandments and exhortations
concerning the Exodus and the commemoration of its anniversary,
the opposite is true concerning its approach to the Revelation at Sinai.
Nowhere does the Bible state the date of the theophany. Exodus,
chapter 19, the chapter that describes the events leading up to the
receiving of the Torah, begins, "In the third month of the Children
of Israel's departure from the land of Egypt, *on this day*, they came to
the wilderness of Sinai." However, the phrase "on this day" is ambiguous, and the Bible's obfuscation of the chronology of the subsequent
events leading to the Revelation makes it impossible to pinpoint the
date of the giving of the Torah from the biblical text.[6] Nor was there
unanimity within the Oral Tradition of the Mishnah; according to
R. Yossi, the Torah was given on the seventh of *Sivan*, while the accepted position, that of the Rabbis, is that the Revelation took place

on the sixth.[7] The popularly assumed connection between the holiday of Shavu'ot and the giving of the Torah is not mentioned explicitly in the Bible.[8] Perhaps more astonishing is the fact that there is not a single commandment in the Torah whose express purpose is to commemorate the giving of the Law at Sinai.[9]

Why does the Bible enshrine the Exodus in our collective consciousness with an array of rituals while obscuring the date of the giving of the Torah and leaving no ceremony to commemorate the event? By obscuring the date of the Revelation, by refusing to commemorate the event through ritual, the Torah's implicit message may be that Sinai is not a historically bound event. Every generation of Jews must feel that it has entered into a covenant with God. Every generation of Jews must feel that God's words at Sinai were spoken to them, no less than to earlier generations. To celebrate the anniversary of the Revelation—of the consecration of the covenant between God and Israel—would be to identify it as a single moment in history. To enact rituals that recall or recreate the giving of the Torah would impinge upon the timeless quality of that event.[10] The metahistorical dimension of the Sinai Revelation is expressed in the midrash to the opening verse of Exodus 19, the chapter that recounts the prelude to the Revelation: "Ben Zoma said: The verse does not say, 'In the third month . . . on *that* day [they came to the wilderness of Sinai],' rather, it says, 'on *this* day'—as if on this day, they came to the wilderness of Sinai. Each day that you involve yourself in Torah, it is as if 'on this day' you received it from Sinai."[11] The manner in which the Bible itself regards the Exodus and the Revelation at Sinai is thus paralleled in the thought of Ben Zoma in the midrash. It was Ben Zoma in the mishnah in *Berakhot* who declared that the verse "so that you shall remember the day of your deliverance from the land of Egypt all the days of your life" meant that the Exodus was a singular event in history and had to be recalled every day and night. Moreover, it is the same Ben Zoma who teaches us that the children of Israel came to Sinai not "on that day," but today, "on this day," and who taught that Sinai must not be *remembered*, but *perpetuated*.

However, without commemorative ritual, how is the Sinai experience to be perpetuated? What vehicle is to sustain the feeling of that encounter in the consciousness of the Jewish people from generation to generation? When the event of Revelation concluded, the Sinai experience—of covenantal meeting with the Almighty—was sustained in a new location: the Sanctuary.

EXODUS, CHAPTERS 24 THROUGH 40: FROM SINAI TO SANCTUARY

The relationship between Sinai and Sanctuary unfolds over the last seventeen chapters of Exodus. In this section, we will probe this relationship by examining the overall structure of these chapters. The end of Exodus can be summarized:

24—Moses ascends to receive the tablets and consecrates the covenant between God and the Children of Israel.

25–31—God commands Moses concerning the Tabernacle, its vessels, and its officers, the Priests.

32–34—The narrative of the Golden Calf and the restoration of the covenant between God and the Children of Israel in its aftermath.

35–40—Moses transmits God's commands concerning the Tabernacle, et al., and the people faithfully execute them. The divine presence returns to the people through the agency of the Tabernacle.

Our examination will assume the chronology of events at the end of the Book of Exodus to be precisely as listed.[12] That is, Moses received the tablets, at the end of chapter 24, and was immediately commanded to erect the Tabernacle. While God was relaying the details of the Tabernacle, the people sinned. Moses descended, attended to the crisis that had erupted, and returned to the Mount to ask forgiveness. Following Israel's atonement, Moses informed the people of God's desire for a Tabernacle, in chapter 35, and the repentant people faithfully executed the divine will. In the words of Nachmanides:

Once the Holy One Blessed Be He became enamored with them again, he gave them the second set of tablets, and consecrated a new covenant with them, that he would dwell within their midst. This signaled that they had returned to their original state as a beloved and betrothed companion. And with the knowledge that God would be willing to dwell among the people, Moses commanded them concerning all that he had heard previously.[13]

According to this conception, the Tabernacle was a culmination and natural extension of the covenantal bond that had been forged at Sinai. The sin of the Golden Calf only delayed its execution. However, having returned to their position of grace, the people were commanded to erect the Tabernacle as had been originally planned. Nachmanides' position that the Sanctuary represented an extension of the covenantal process echoes a voice in the midrashic tradition: "At the moment that the Children of Israel accepted the Kingdom of Heaven with joy and declared 'all that God has said we will do and we will heed' (Exodus 24:7), God immediately said to Moses, 'Speak unto the Children of Israel and gather for me an endowment' (Exodus 25:2)."[14]

The literary bridge between the close of the revelation narrative and the opening of the Tabernacle chapters supports Nachmanides' understanding. Exodus, chapter 24, depicts the finale of the Revelation narrative, the call to Moses to receive the tablets (Exodus 24:12–18):

God said to Moses, "Come up to me upon the mount, and be there, and I shall give you the Tablets of stone, and the law and the commandments which I have written to teach them. . . . (15) Moses went up to the Mount, and the cloud covered the mount. (16) God's presence dwelled on Mount Sinai, as the cloud cloaked it for six days. He called to Moses from amid the cloud on the seventh day. (17) The appearance of God's presence was like that of a consuming fire atop the Mount, beheld by the Children of Israel. (18) Moses entered the cloud and ascended the Mount. Moses was on the Mount for forty days and forty nights.

Moses ascended the Mount, ostensibly, to receive the tablets (Exodus 24:12). However, a continuous reading of the verses reveals that upon his ascent, Moses first receives the commandments of the Tabernacle, and only later the tablets: Moses entered the cloud and ascended the Mount. Moses was on the Mount for forty days and forty nights (Exodus 24:18). God spoke to Moses saying, "Speak to the Children of Israel and take for me an endowment (Exodus 25:1) . . . and make me a sanctuary and I shall dwell in their midst" (Exodus 25:7). Only a full *six chapters later*, following the lengthy sections of the Tabernacle, does the narrative of the tablets continue: "He gave to Moses, when He had finished speaking with him upon Mount Sinai, the two Tablets of testimony, Tablets of stone, written with the finger of God" (Exodus 31:18). The presence of the Tabernacle sections embedded in the narrative of the tablets indicates that they are an integral part of the theophany finale. The tablets represent one component of the finale, for they bear witness to what was said at Sinai. They are called the Tablets of the *Covenant* (Exodus 25:16, 21) for they bear the essential responsibilities engendered by the covenantal bond. The Tabernacle, however, represents a second, but equal, component, for it is the vehicle that will perpetuate the Sinai experience. It is the vehicle that will continually allow the Israelites to approach God in covenantal closeness as they did at Sinai.[15]

Nachmanides' contention of a link between Sinai and Sanctuary is buttressed by the structure of the end of the Book of Exodus as a whole. Virtually every law and commandment listed from Exodus, chapter 25, until the consecration of the Tabernacle in Leviticus, chapter 10, pertain directly to the Sanctuary.[16] Significantly, Moses is told to construct the Tabernacle vessels in accordance with the prototype he had seen of each while convening with God on Mount Sinai.[17] The sustained and focused attention to the Tabernacle laws immediately following the theophany narrative is a sign of a connection between the Revelation at Sinai and God's continued presence among the people in the Sanctuary. The meaning of this connection is explained by Cassuto:

In order to understand the significance and purpose of the Tabernacle, we must realize that the children of Israel, after they had been privileged to witness the Revelation of God on Mount Sinai, were about to journey from there and thus draw away from the site of the theophany. So long as they were encamped in the place, they were conscious of God's nearness; but once they set out on their journey, it would seem to them as though the link had been broken, unless there were in their midst a tangible symbol of God's presence among them. It was the function of the Tabernacle [literally, "dwelling"] to serve as such a symbol. Not without reason, therefore, does this section come immediately after the section that describes the making of the Covenant at Mount Sinai. The nexus between Israel and the Tabernacle is a perpetual extension of the bond that was forged at Sinai between the people and their God.[18]

Finally, it is worth noting a parallelism that highlights the role of the Tabernacle as a site for covenantal convocation. A string of correlations exists between the finale of the Sinai Revelation, as portrayed in Exodus 24, and the closing stages of the Tabernacle's construction and consecration:

Exodus 24:15–18	The Erection of the Tabernacle
Moses went up to the Mount and the cloud covered the Mount	The cloud covered the tent of meeting
The presence of God dwelled on Mount Sinai	The presence of God filled the Tabernacle (Exodus 30:34).
And the cloud covered it for six days	Moses could not come to the tent of meeting for the cloud dwelled on it (40:35).
He called to Moses on the seventh day from amid the cloud	He called to Moses . . . and God spoke to him from the tent of meeting (Leviticus 1:1).

Exodus 24:15–18	The Erection of the Tabernacle
and the appearance of the Glory of God was that of a consuming fire upon the Mount.	The glory of God appeared to the entire nation (Leviticus 9:23). Fire went out from before God and consumed upon the altar.
beheld by the Children of Israel	and the nation beheld and rejoiced (Leviticus 9:24).
Moses went into the cloud and ascended the Mount.	Moses and Aaron came into the tent of meeting (Leviticus 9:23).

What is the meaning of this parallelism? Both passages depict the climax of covenantal processes: Exodus, chapter 24, tells of the conclusion of the original pact between God and the Jewish People, while Leviticus, chapter 9, relates the climax reached after the consecration of the renewed covenant in the wake of the sin of the Golden Calf. Both at Sinai and throughout the chapters of the Tabernacle, much of the interplay is between God and Moses alone. However, in both episodes, the story peaks when the encounter shifts from God–Moses to God–nation. In Exodus, chapter 24, at the end of the theophany, the people triumphantly enter into the covenant and God, in turn, reveals himself "before the Children of Israel" (verse 17) in a consuming fire.[19] In the closing chapters of the Book of Exodus (Exodus 35:20–29), the people exuberantly fulfill God's desire that they build Him a Sanctuary to perpetuate the Sinai experience. Following this supreme gesture of loyalty by the Children of Israel, God once again responds by displaying His Glory before the entire people, consuming the sacrifices in a spectacle of fire. The lesson of the parallelism is that the latter event bears the overtones of the former because it perpetuates it. Thus, Sinai gives way to Sanctuary.

We have seen how the structure of the end of Exodus underscores the idea that the Sanctuary perpetuates the Sinai experience, yet little attention has been paid to the minutiae of the Tabernacle sections of Exodus and the passages that describe the Temple service in the Book of Leviticus. These passages often seem dry, detailed, and uninspiring. However, the motif highlighted thus far, of Sinai symbolism in the Sanctuary, can also shed much light on the details of the Tabernacle and its rites. The Sinai theophany, an experience of the senses—both aural and visual—is described vividly in several passages in the Book of Exodus, and again in the Book of Deuteronomy. Each of these experiences is laden with theological meaning, and each is perpetuated in the vessels and rites of the Sanctuary.

THE ARK—THE DIVINE VOICE CONTINUES

At Sinai, the Jewish people underwent a singular experience—they heard the voice of God. The notion that God continues to "speak" to the Jewish people is perpetuated in the Sanctuary. When Moses recounts the giving of the Ten Commandments, he describes the theophany experience as follows (Deuteronomy 5:19): "God said these commandments to your entire assembly at the mount, amid the fire, the cloud, and the cloak of mist, in a *great voice* that would never be heard again, and He inscribed them on two tablets of stone and gave them to me."

The divine voice, or *kol*, was the source of the commandments that were inscribed on the tablets. At Sinai it represented the way in which God communicated his instructions and directives. In the Tabernacle, the element of the *kol* is perpetuated in the Ark (Exodus 25:21–22): "Deposit inside the Ark the Tablets of Testimony which I will give to you. There I will meet with you and I will impart to you from above the cover, from between the two cherubim which are on top of the Ark of Testimony—all that I will command you concerning the Israelite People." The Ark symbolizes the Sinaitic element of the *kol* in two ways. First, it is the receptacle of the tablets which, as shown in Deuteronomy 5:19, were a transcript of what had been uttered by the *kol*. The relationship between the Ark and the Revelation is further highlighted by the use of the phrase, "of Testimony" concerning the Ark (verse 21) and the tablets (verse 22). The Ark and the tablets are "of Testimony" because they bear eternal witness to the *kol* that was uttered at Sinai.

However, many more commandments and instructions were to be given as the Israelites traversed the wilderness, and a venue would need to be established where Moses would continue to receive God's word.[20] In verse 22, the past gives rise to the future as the Ark is designated as the site from which God will tell to Moses, "all that I will command you concerning the Israelite People," even as He had at Mount Sinai. Thus, the receptacle of the *kol* from Sinai, the Ark, is the vehicle through which the *kol* will continue to be transmitted. As such, it assumes preeminent status among the vessels of the Tabernacle. This is reflected literarily through the fact that the section that describes the Ark is the first and longest of the passages that depict the vessels of the Sanctuary.[21]

Within a biblical theology of the Tabernacle, the Ark is not merely a composite part of the Sanctuary complex. It is, rather, a vessel whose character defines the purpose of the Tabernacle as a whole. At the Ark, we said, Moses would receive convocation from God. The language of the Torah hints that this is the broader purpose of the Tabernacle as a whole. Following its lengthy description of the vessels and the consecration of the priests, the Bible summarizes the purpose of the Sanctuary in Exodus 29:42–43: "There *I will meet with you*, and there I will speak with you, and there *I will meet with the Israelites*, and it shall be sanctified by My presence." The Hebrew verb for "to meet" (*iva'ed* in verse 42, and *ve-no'adti* in verse 43) appears in only one other place in the Tabernacle narrative, the opening phrase of Exodus 25:22, in the verse that describes the function of the Ark: "There I will meet with you (*ve-no'adti lekhah*)." By borrowing a phrase whose original context is from the section of the Ark, the Torah is stating that the Ark is the vessel that characterizes the nature of the Tabernacle as a whole. It is from the cherubim atop the Ark that the *kol* emanates to

Moses, transmitting guidance and commands. From the perspective of the nation encamped around the Tabernacle complex, the Tabernacle as a whole is the site at which God communicates his instructions to the Jewish people and a conduit of divine instruction, just as Mount Sinai had been at the event of Revelation.

No figure after Moses received God's word from atop the Ark. Nonetheless, the Sinai symbolism of the Holy of Holies can be seen as a permanent aspect of the Sanctuary iconography. The fact that Moses received the *kol* from amid the cherubim was a sign that God's presence was most immanent within the Holy of Holies. Even though no later figure was privy to hear the *kol*, the seat of God's presence remained atop the Ark. Thus, just as the peak of Mount Sinai represented the location at which God's presence was most immanent at the Revelation, the Ark within the Holy of Holies assumed this stature within the precincts of the Tabernacle, and later, the Temple.

THE ALTAR OF INCENSE— IMMANENCE AND TRANSCENDENCE

Though the offering of incense is discussed in several passages (Exodus 30:1–10, 30:34–38, Leviticus 16:12–13), the Bible offers no explicit explanation of this rite. When the Sanctuary is understood as a vehicle to perpetuate the Sinai Revelation, the incense emerges as a powerful theological symbol.

One biblical postulate about the relationship between man and God is that man cannot see God and survive. When Moses requests to see God, God replies, "You cannot see My face, for man may not see Me and live" (Exodus 33:20).[22] Why is this?

Man is indeed meant to strive for a close relationship with God. He is to perceive himself as individually called by God, and he is to feel that God observes him and is mindful of his situation. However, man must also have a sense of the great distance that exists between himself and his Maker. If man only perceives the intimacy of his relationship with God, he will lose sight of God's omnipotent and almighty attributes. An excess of intimacy perforce comes at the expense of awe. In short, man must possess, at one and the same time, a sense of God's immanence in the world and also a sense of His transcendence above it. Were man allowed to, as it were, "see" God, he would lose sight of the fact that God's true essence is boundless in every respect.

The notion that God's presence is intimately present yet ultimately inaccessible is fundamental to an understanding of the Sinai theophany. The narrative of Exodus, chapter 19, revolves around this tension. In the opening verses of the chapter, God informs Moses that He is about to embrace the Jewish people as His chosen people. However, in verses 12 and 13, Moses is warned to limit access to the Mount while God's presence rests on it. Then, even after Moses complies, God warns him a second time (verse 21) as the people are led to their encampment around the Mount. Finally, just prior to the utterance of the Ten Commandments, God issues a final warning (verse 24), to both the priests and the nation at large, forbidding access to the Mount.[23] As the Children of Israel approach both the *moment* of Revelation, and the *site* of Revelation, they are given ever sterner warnings not to ascend the Mount. As God's immanent nature becomes apparent, a counterbalance must be placed to buoy His transcendent quality as well.

Limited accessibility is also a cardinal principle concerning the relationship between the nation and the Tabernacle. Israelites are forbidden entry into the Tabernacle complex altogether, while the Levites can enter only to fulfill a limited role. Even Priests must be careful not to trespass certain boundaries within the Sanctuary. God's presence among the people, as manifested by the Sanctuary, creates a sense of intimacy with the divine and puts an emphasis on God's immanent nature. God, however, is not only immanent, but transcendent. The laws that limit access to the Tabernacle as a whole, and to its inner precincts in particular, highlight God's transcendent nature. Nachmanides describes this phenomenon allegorically: "All of these laws accent the exalted nature of the Temple, as they said 'One cannot compare a royal palace that has no guards to one that is surrounded by guards.'"[24]

The same principle of intimacy tempered by inaccessibility governs Moses' encounter with God at Sinai as well. While Moses convocates with God "face to face" (Deuteronomy 34:10), it is done amid the shroud of what the Bible calls the *anan*, or "cloud." Hence, when Moses meets God atop Mount Sinai to receive the Decalogue, the Bible states: "And the Lord said to Moses, 'I will come to you in a thick *anan*, in order that the people may hear when I speak with you' (Exodus 19:9)." Likewise, when Moses ascends the Mount to receive the Tablets of Testimony at the close of the theophany narrative, it states: "When Moses had ascended the mountain, the *anan* covered the mountain. The Presence of the Lord abode on Mount Sinai, and the *anan* hid it for six days. On the seventh day He called to Moses from the midst of the *anan*." (Exodus 24:15–16). The Zohar explains that the cloud was a necessary component for the Revelation to occur: "*Moses went inside the cloud and ascended the mountain* (Exodus 24:18)—we learn from this that he shrouded himself in the cloud. And once he was shrouded by the cloud, only then [could Scripture write] *and he ascended the mountain*; before he shrouded himself in it, he would not have been able to enter into God's presence."[25]

At Sinai, man was shielded from God's presence behind the veil of an *anan*. This protective veil is preserved in the Sanctuary in the offering of the incense. In biblical terms, the offering of incense is not termed the "*offering* of incense" or the '*service* of incense.' Rather, it is termed the *anan ha-ketoret* (Leviticus 16:13), literally, the "cloud of incense," and thereby it echoes a term from Moses' encounter with God at Sinai. Once again, we can see how the vessels of the Sanctuary focus on the notion that in the Sanctuary, like at Sinai, man *meets* God. Concerning the positioning of the Altar of Incense within the Tabernacle, the Bible says (Exodus 30:6): "Place it in front of the curtain that is over the Ark of the Pact—in front of the cover that is over the Pact—*where*

I will meet with you." The Torah reiterates the fact that the Ark is the site at which God will meet with Moses. Because of this, says the Torah, the Altar of Incense must be aligned with the Ark. In light of these points, the *anan ha-ketoret* may be seen as the Sanctuary parallel to the *anan* of Sinai. Just as the *anan* served as a veil between Moses and God's presence at Sinai, so, too, the *anan ha-ketoret* is a symbolic buffer between the priests serving in the outer chamber of the Sanctuary and the divine presence in the Holy of Holies.

The *anan ha-ketoret* plays an acute role in the depiction of the Temple service of the high priest on the Day of Atonement in Leviticus 16. When the high priest enters before the Ark in the Holy of Holies on the Day of Atonement, it is the most direct encounter between man and God to occur during the course of the entire year. The high priest's entrance into the Holy of Holies begins as he is called upon to offer a bull to atone for priests who may have entered the Sanctuary while in a state of impurity (Leviticus 16:11). He is then instructed to sprinkle the blood of the bull on the cover of the Ark, but before he approaches the Ark he is required to execute the following ritual (Leviticus 16:12–13): "and he shall take a censor of glowing coals scooped from the altar before the Lord [i.e., the Altar of Incense], and two handfuls of finely ground aromatic incense, and bring this behind the curtain. He shall put the incense on the fire before the Lord, so that the cloud from the incense screens the cover that is over the [Ark of] the Pact lest he die." Only with the protective screen of the *anan ha-ketoret*, the symbolic perpetuation of the *anan* at Sinai, can the high priest enter into God's Presence.[26]

THE ALTAR OF BURNT OFFERINGS—
BEHOLDING REVELATION

For the people standing at the foot of Mount Sinai, the only visible evidence of God's Presence was the great consuming fire, or *aish*, that engulfed the Mount (Exodus 24:17): "Now the Presence of the Lord appeared in the sight of the Israelites as a consuming *aish* on top of the mountain." This is likewise highlighted in Moses' retelling of the event in Deuteronomy (5:20–22): "While the mountain was ablaze with *aish* you came up to me, all your tribal heads and elders, and said, The Lord our God has just shown us His majestic Presence and we heard His voice out of the *aish*. . . . Let us not die, then, for this fearsome *aish* will consume us." Although man cannot see God, there is a visual component to revelation, and that is fire. At the burning bush, the Torah writes that the angel of God appeared to Moses from amid the bush (Exodus 3:2)—God Himself was not visible, but His revelation to Moses was visibly perceptible through the agency of the fire.

Why is revelation visually represented by fire? This symbolism is explored by a midrash on the verse that tells of the fire that descended onto Mount Sinai as the children of Israel prepared to receive the Torah:

> The words of Torah can be metaphorically represented by fire. Fire is critical to sustain life, and so too are the words of Torah critical to sustain life. If one nears a fire he is singed, while one who strays from fire becomes cold. It is the same with the words of Torah. One who comes too near is singed, while one who strays too far becomes cold.[27]

Man's relationship to fire bears a duality. Man is drawn toward it as a source of heat. If he comes too close, however, he is burnt. Man must therefore keep his distance. In doing so, however, he cannot stray too far, lest he become cold. Revelation bears this same duality. The spiritually sensitive individual yearns for an intimate relationship with the divine. For this he lives. As we pointed out in our discussion of the *anan ha-ketoret*, however, man cannot come too close to the divine, for he will be consumed. Conversely, he who is distanced from God lives a spiritually frigid existence.

This understanding of fire as symbolic of revelation is evident in two biblical narratives. At the burning bush, Moses is initially drawn near to the fire (Exodus 3:3). Yet once God speaks to him, he shrinks in fear of being consumed (Exodus 3:6). The same duality is exhibited at the revelation of Sinai. In Exodus 19:21–24, God repeatedly insists that the people be restrained in their eagerness to scale the Mount while the revelation takes place. Once God has revealed himself, however, the people shrink back in terror (Exodus 20:15–16).

A primary motif of the Sanctuary is that God's revelation and presence amid the Jewish people continues even after they depart from Sinai. The image of the *aish* existed as a permanent feature of the Tabernacle in the Altar of Offerings, the site where all sacrifices were consumed by fire. The Bible emphasizes that the fire upon this altar was not only for the burning of sacrifices but was to remain lit at all times (Leviticus 6:5–6): "The fire on the altar shall be kept burning, not to go out: every morning the priest shall feed wood to it. . . . A perpetual fire shall be kept burning on the altar, not to go out."

The Altar of Offerings was situated at the entrance to the Sanctuary courtyard. For the people encamped surrounding the Tabernacle, the Ark, the Altar of Incense, indeed, all the Tabernacle vessels were hidden from view. The only vessel that was visible to the nation from outside the Tabernacle was the Altar of Offerings (see fig. 3). Once again, the Sinai paradigm is preserved; the visible evidence of revelation was seen only in the great conflagration that surrounded the Mount. From outside the Tabernacle—the site of God's perpetuated presence among the people—the nation could see only the Altar of Offerings, whose fire is perpetual and does not go out.

A fascinating pattern emerges when the Ark of the Covenant, the Altar of Incense, and the Altar of Offerings are examined together. The Bible describes them all as integral to the process of man *meeting* God in the Tabernacle. We have already seen how the Ark and the Altar of Incense serve symbolically in the convocations between man and God in the Tabernacle. We have noted that the descriptions of the Ark and of the Altar of Incense employ the same term, *le-hiva'ed*, meaning "to meet" (Exodus 25:22 concerning the Ark, and Exodus 30:6 concerning the Altar of Incense), to depict these encounters. The only other passage about vessels where this term appears is the section that describes the daily service on the Altar of Offerings (Exo-

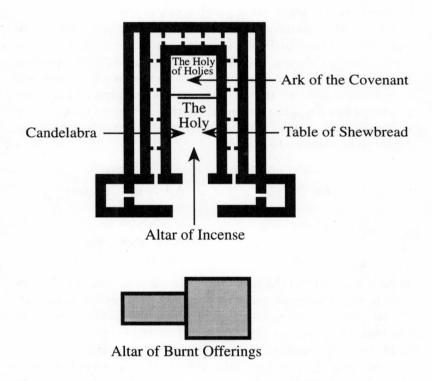

Figure 3. The courtyard of the Temple. The Ark resided in the Holy of Holies. The Altar of Incense was situated in the outer chamber, or the Holy, and was visible only to the Priests who served there. The closest the nation at large could come to the Temple was to offer a sacrifice on the Altar of Burnt Offerings, located in the courtyard (bottom of diagram). Thus, the only symbolic element of the Sinai Revelation that the nation could see in the Sanctuary was that of fire, which was represented by the perpetual fire that burned atop the Altar of Offerings.

dus 29:42): "It shall be an eternal offering for all your generations at the entrance to the Tabernacle, before the Lord, *the place where I shall meet with you,* the place where I shall speak to you."

The Torah reiterates that the Tabernacle is the place where God will meet with the Children of Israel in conjunction with the service on the Altar of Offerings. The Altar of Offerings, the Altar of Incense, and the Ark of the Covenant, then, may be seen as a triad of vessels that simulate different aspects of the Sinai experience and are integral to the identity of the Tabernacle as the site where God convenes with the Jewish people. Schematically, the Tabernacle and Mount Sinai can be compared as follows:

Sinai	Tabernacle
kol	Ark of the Covenant
anan	*anan ha-ketoret*
Moses	Moses/high priest
aish	Altar of Offerings
nation	nation

In both, the center of the encounter is the point at which God's presence is most immanent, and from which the *kol* emanates. In each, the representative of the nation is shielded from God's presence by the *anan.* However, just as the meeting between God and Moses was hidden from the view of the people, the Ark and Altar of Incense are located inside the chamber of the Tabernacle and are not visible to the nation at large. The tribes encamped around the perimeter of the complex can view only the fire of the Altar of Offerings, which rests in the courtyard outside the Tabernacle itself, even as the Jewish people saw only fire as they observed the theophany at Sinai.

PILGRIMAGE—RELIVING SINAI

The chapters that portray the Ark, *anan ha-ketoret,* and the Altar of Burnt Offerings highlight the Tabernacle as a convocational venue, or meeting point, between God and His covenantal partner, the Jewish people. Later biblical commandments also attest to the role of the Sanctuary as the perpetuation of the Sinai experience.

The first is the obligation of a thrice-annual pilgrimage. What is the central idea of a pilgrimage? Most telling about the purpose of the pilgrimages to the Temple is the language used by the Bible to describe this endeavor. In rabbinic terminology, the pilgrimage is referred to as *aliyat regel*, literally, the ascent by foot. It refers to the spiritually elevated status of Jerusalem and to the trek involved in making the trip. In Islam, pilgrimage to Mecca is called *hajj*, which comes from the verb for "to encircle" and refers to the central ceremony of the pilgrimage, the seven circumambulations around the Ka'bah.[28] When the Bible speaks of pilgrimages, it commands every male to "be seen before the face of the Lord God" (Exodus 23:17, 34:23; Deuteronomy 16:16). The phrase "to be seen before the face of God" has a very distinct antecedent. "Face to face God spoke with you on the Mount from amid the fire" (Deuteronomy 5:4) is the way Moses characterizes the Revelation at Sinai. When the Children of Israel are commanded to appear before God at the Temple, it is to renew the sense of direct, collective encounter between God and the Jewish people.

This connection is buttressed when we examine the places where the Bible records this obligation. The commandment to ascend to the Sanctuary during the festivals appears in nearly identical language in three places. The first is in Exodus, chapter 23, as one of the closing commandments of the Revelation at Sinai. The second mention is in Exodus, chapter 34, as one of the final commandments issued after the reconsecration of the covenant between God and the Jewish people, following the sin of the Golden Calf. The location of this commandment twice at the conclusion of covenantal passages highlights its purpose. It is intended to create a forum in which Israel can come directly before God, as they did when the covenant was first formed at Sinai. The Talmud records a practice in the Temple that underscores the notion of pilgrimage as a face-to-face encounter: "When Israel would ascend for the festival pilgrimage, they would roll back the curtain dividing the outer chamber [of the Temple] from the Holy of Holies, and they would display before [the nation] the cherubim, whose stance was that of a young couple enamored one with the other, and they would declare to [the nation], 'Behold the adoration the Almighty has for you—it is even as the adoration between man and woman.'"[29]

Of all the commanded pilgrimages one in particular stands out as a cyclical simulation of the entire Sinai experience. It is the pilgrimage of *Hakhel* (Deuteronomy 31:10–13):

> Every seventh year, the year set for remission, at the Feast of Booths, (11) When all Israel comes to appear before the face of the Lord your God in the place which He will choose, you shall read this Torah aloud in the presence of all Israel. (12) Congregate the nation, the men and the women and the children, and the stranger within your midst, so that they may hear and that they may learn to fear God, your Lord, and will come to keep and fulfill all the words of this Torah. (13) And their children, who will not know, will hear and learn to fear God your Lord.

There are several elements that set the *Hakhel* pilgrimage apart from the normal one associated with the three festivals. Not only males attend this pilgrimage, but every man, woman, and child in Israel. This convocation, therefore, calls for the entire nation to appear before God. Further, at this site where the nation appears before the Face of God, the king is to read from the Torah before the entire assembly. The image of the entire people coming to the place of God's dwelling and hearing the Torah read en masse distinctly recalls the Revelation at Sinai. Moreover, the passage that describes the purpose of the convocation (verses 12–13) employs language nearly identical to Moses' description of the purpose of the Revelation at Sinai:

Deuteronony 31:12–13	**Deuteronony 4:10**
Congregate (*hakhel*) the nation,	Congregate (*hakhel*) to me the nation
the men, and the women and the children, and the stranger that is in your gates	

Deuteronony 31:12–13	Deuteronony 4:10
so that they may hear	and I shall make them hear my words
and so that they shall learn	so that they shall learn
and they will fear your Lord God	to fear me
and shall dutifully keep all the words of this Torah.	
And their children, who do not know, will hear and learn to fear your Lord all the days that you live in the Land.	all the days that they live in the Land, and their children they shall make learn.

In Deuteronomy, chapter 4, Moses retold the story of the Revelation at Sinai. When the Torah echoes that language in Deuteronomy, chapter 33, it is to demonstrate that the *Hakhel* convocation is a re-living of the Sinai experience. The concept of *Hakhel* as a simulation of the Revelation at Sinai gains halakhic expression as well in the writings of Maimonides: "Converts who have not learned must prepare themselves to listen attentively with trepidation and awe, with joy, yet with fear, as was the spirit on the day that [the Torah] was given on Sinai."[30]

In summary, the Torah did not wish to commemorate the Revelation at Sinai, for Sinai constituted an event that is not to be associated with a particular moment in time. The structure of the end of the Book of Exodus showed us that the Sanctuary was an extension of the Sinai Revelation. Through the Ark, the Altar of Incense, and the Altar of Offerings, the elements of *kol*, *anan*, and *aish* reveal the Sanctuary to be a perpetuation of Sinai as a conduit for divine instruction and guidance. By coming to the Sanctuary during the festivals in order to appear before the face of God, the people are able to renew the sense of collective covenantal encounter with God along lines similar to those of Sinai. Through the commandment of *Hakhel*, the people simulate the stand at Sinai, experiencing it for themselves, and thus bringing the Revelation experience out of the past and into the present.

4

Political Prominence—
The Prerequisite
to Solomon's Temple

The previous chapter focused on the meaning of the Tabernacle by analyzing its roots at the close of the Book of Exodus. As the site at which God's presence dwelled, the Temple represents a continuation of the Tabernacle. In many important ways, however, the Temple represents a progression beyond the Tabernacle. We turn now to probe the meaning of the Temple itself. What were the conditions prevalent in Solomon's time that warranted the construction of the First Temple?

The Tabernacle was never meant to be a permanent structure, but rather, a precursor to a more lasting and fixed structure, the Temple. This premise rests on the Torah's description of the Tabernacle in the books of Exodus and Numbers. The Tabernacle section of Exodus, chapters 25 through 30, and 35 through 40, describes a structure made of skins and linens, supported by posts, and devoid of any solid walls. It is a structure designed for a nation on the move. The collapsible and portable nature of the Tabernacle is further evident in Numbers, chapters 3 and 4, where the Levites are issued detailed instructions concerning the dismantling of the Tabernacle and the manner in which its composite parts were to be transported in the wilderness.

Many assume that the transportable nature of the Tabernacle was simply a technical necessity of circumstance. The migration of the Children of Israel through the wilderness mandated that the structure of the central shrine be transportable as well. Once in the land of Israel, however, the need for portability would be obviated and the time would be ripe for erecting a permanent structure. The Temple, accordingly, should have been erected upon entry into the land of Israel, or, at the latest, upon completion of the conquest, fourteen years later.

Nonetheless, when we review the chronicle of the early prophets, we discover that, in fact, over four centuries elapsed before the construction of the Temple! The only event in the entire prophetic record explicitly dated to the Exodus from Egypt is the construction of the Temple by Solomon (1 Kings 6:1): "In the four hundred and eightieth year after the Israelites left the land of Egypt, in the month of Ziv—that is, the second month—in the fourth year of his reign over Israel, Solomon began to build the House of the Lord." Why did four centuries elapse before the Temple was built? The fact that the Temple was not erected upon entrance into the land of Israel suggests that the settling of the Children of Israel in their land was not a sufficient condition for the erection of the Temple. To grasp the religious meaning of the events that culminated with the building of the Temple, we need to investigate the roots and meaning of a particular nomenclature often used by the Bible to refer to the Temple. In the Book of Deuteronomy, with an eye toward entry into the land of Israel, God speaks of the central shrine in the land as *the place I shall select to establish My name*. This term is first used in Deuteronomy 12:5, and it appears another twenty times throughout the book as the exclusive label for what we term the Temple. In 1 Kings, this nomenclature is likewise employed by Solomon as he constructs the Temple. In his lengthy address to the people at the dedication of the Temple, Solomon refers to the Temple nine times, exclusively, as the *House of God's name.* What is implied by a "place," or "house" for "God's *name*"? The connotation of this term is the key to understanding the transition from Tabernacle to Temple and, indeed, is one of the most crucial points for understanding the biblical meaning of the Temple itself.

BABEL—EXALTING THE NAME OF MAN

The notion that the Temple is a house dedicated to God's *name* can be understood when the Temple is seen as the climax of a religio-historical process that begins with the Tower of Babel.

What was the failing of the builders of Babel? The Torah explicitly labels the generation of the Flood as wicked and corrupt (Genesis 6:3–12), but at first glance, Genesis, chapter 11, gives no overt description of the evil of the builders of the tower:

All the earth had the same language and the same words. (2) And as men migrated from the east, they came upon a valley in the land of Shinar and settled there. (3) They said to one another, "Come *let us* make bricks and *let us* bake them hard."—Brick served them as stone, and clay served them as mortar. (4) And they said, "Come, *let us* build us a city, and a tower with its top in the sky, and *we shall make a name for ourselves*; else we shall be scattered all over the world." (5) The Lord came down to look at the city and tower which man had built, (6) and the Lord said, "If as one people with one language for all, this is how they have begun to act, then nothing that they may propose to do will be out of their reach. (7) Let Me, then, go down and confound their speech there, so that they shall not understand one another's speech." (8) Thus the Lord scattered them from there over the face of the whole earth; and they stopped building the city. (9) That is why it was called Babel, because there the Lord confounded the speech of the whole earth; and from there the Lord scattered them over the face of the whole earth.

The builders of the tower displayed unity and common purpose. This desired state stood in contrast to the generation of the flood when

morality had ebbed and men had become incapable of living in brotherhood. However, the builders of the tower were united for the sake of
an unholy end. A close reading of the passage reveals the repeated
use of the first-person plural: "Let *us* build *us* a city, and a tower with
its top in the sky, and *we* shall make a name for *our*selves." Their repeated self-references point to an agenda of self-aggrandizement and
worship of man's capacities and powers. The very projects they
planned emphasized man's dominion and strength. In the biblical
frame of reference, cities are not metropolitan centers, nor are towers
merely a favored form of architecture. They are structures that represent impregnability and strength.[1] No natural materials such as wood
or stone were to be used. Employing, again, the first-person plural,
they wished to show these structures to be the achievements of man
alone: "Let *us* make bricks and let *us* bake them hard." The narrative
comment at the end of verse 5 emphasizes the self-serving nature of
their endeavor by echoing their self-reference: "Brick served *them* as
stone, and clay served *them* as mortar." When the Torah describes
God's first impression of these activities, it says, "the Lord came down
to look at the city and tower which man had built." Written from the
perspective of God, Who is all-knowing, it is an almost cynical remark
on the activities of mortal, finite beings who held themselves to be all
powerful. The tower, "which man had built," was to be so high that it
would reach the sky. However, in reality it was so low, so removed
from the realm of God, that God had to "come down" to see it.[2]

What was the sin of the builders of Babel? The builders of the Tower
of Babel violated a rule that is cardinal to all theistic religions. As
creator of the universe, God and God alone is worthy of glory and
stature. Man is a servant whose ultimate purpose is the faithful service of God. The essence of their failing was contained in their declaration that "we shall make a name for ourselves." By devoting all their
energies to self-aggrandizement, the builders of the Tower of Babel
failed to comprehend their proper ontological place within the order
of being. In setting out "to make a name for themselves" that would
be remembered by all future generations of man, they not only failed

to devote themselves to the name of God, they removed Him from the picture altogether.

In one sense, their failure was more tragic than was the failure of the generation of the Flood. The generation of the Flood, the Bible reports, was corrupt. Men gave in to their baser inclinations. However, in the social climate of Babel, men had overcome personal self-interest and were bonded in unity. When God exclaims, "If as one people with one language for all, this is how they have begun to act," it is out of profound disappointment. Men had risen to their moral best—total brotherhood—only to be consumed by a spirit of radical anthropocentrism, in which they aimed "to make a name" for themselves.

ABRAHAM—EXALTING THE NAME OF GOD

It is directly out of the ruins of Babel that the Torah leads us to Abraham. The sixteen verses that separate the Babel account and the birth of Abraham are a condensed chronology whose literary aim is to build up to the arrival of Abraham on the biblical stage. Thus, God's prophecy to Abraham (Genesis 12:1) that he will give rise to a great nation should be understood as a reaction to the failing of the generation that would have built the Tower of Babel. What characterizes Abraham's career is that he consistently prevails over the surrounding powers and wins their respect—for himself, and more important, for God. In different terms, he makes a name for God. At three points in his career Abraham called in God's name—*vayikra beshem Hashem*: when he entered the land of Israel for the first time (Genesis 12:8); when he returned from Egypt laden with riches, having humiliated Pharaoh (Genesis 13:4); and upon entering into a pact with the Philistine king, Abimelech (Genesis 21:33). The meaning of these declarations is commented upon by Nachmanides: "He cried out the name of God in a great voice before the altar and declared His sovereignty to all of mankind."[3] Calling out in God's name was a public declaration designed to establish God's *reputation* in the eyes of men. The Torah's choice of language here is significant. Abraham's act "and he proclaimed the *name* of God"—*vayikra be-shem YHWH* (Genesis 12:4) stands in contrast to the motive of the builders of the Tower of Babel—"and we shall make a *name* for ourselves"—*na'aseh lanu shem*. The Hebrew word *shem* bears the same multiple layers of meaning as does the word *name* in English. In its most common usage a name is the designation of a specific entity as in, "his name is Joe." However, the word *name* can also mean "distinguished reputation," or "renown," as in, "he is worthy of his family's name."[4] The two meanings are intricately related. When a person's name is mentioned, it is not merely his physical presence that comes to mind, but his traits and character as well.

The biblical word *shem* functions in the same way.[5] When the builders of Babel set out to make a *name* for themselves, it was to heighten their own majesty and magnificence in their eyes, and in the eyes of future generations. When Abraham proclaimed the *name* of God in the presence of the Canaanites, it was precisely with the meaning that Nachmanides ascribed to it—as a proclamation of God's greatness and glory. To call out in God's *name* was to proclaim His *reputation*.[6] The advent of Abraham is juxtaposed with the Babel narrative because Abraham represents the beginning of a redress to the anthropocentric spirit of Babel. This insight, which is built upon literary insights from the text of the Torah itself, is conceptually echoed in the *midrash* as well:

[The builders of the Tower] approached Abraham and said: "You are strong; come and assist us and we shall build a tower with its top in the sky." He replied: "Desist! 'The *name* of the Lord is a tower of strength (Proverbs 18:10)'—and you proclaim, 'let us make a *name* for ourselves.'" What did The Holy One blessed Be He do to them? He dispersed them, as it says (Proverbs 11:8): "And God dispersed, etc."[7]

On its own, the *midrash* could be understood, simply, as a contrast between Babel, a tide of heresy, and Abraham, a bulwark of belief.

However, in light of this presentation, one can understand that the midrash and the deeper meaning of the biblical text converge toward the same point: Abraham represents the antithesis of Babel. At Babel, men called in their own name, while Abraham proclaimed the name of God.

"A HOUSE FOR GOD'S NAME"

No matter how great his fortunes, Abraham was but a single individual. His efforts initiated the process of declaring God's sovereignty in the world. Nonetheless, while some neighboring powers may have come to respect him, and through him, God, his impact could only be limited. God's acclaim can only be recognized broadly by the nations of the world if His providence is evidenced in the affairs of an entire nation.

This brings us to the designation of the Temple in the Book of Deuteronomy. Consistently, it refers to the Temple as "the place that God will select to establish His name." When the Torah refers to the Temple as the place where God's *name* will be established, it is a telling statement of the Temple's purpose: *the Temple—a "house for God's name"—symbolizes a public declaration of God's sovereignty.* The ambition of declaring God's sovereignty in the world, which was initiated by Abraham, is the calling of the Jewish people on a wider scale.

Now we can begin to understand the significance of the events that culminated with the construction of the First Temple. God's acclaim in the world is a direct function of how Israel is perceived. The events that culminated with the building of the First Tem-ple need to be seen in light of the following question: under what conditions would a nation—any nation—command broad respect? In this regard, we need only look at the hallmarks of a great country today. A great country should possess political stability at home and should be at peace with its neighbors. It should possess a strong economy and should be home to a culture that boasts strong virtues.

The criteria by which we would judge a country favorably today are the same criteria that constitute the biblical conditions necessary for the construction of the Temple. Fittingly enough, the broad definition of the conditions that warrant the building of the Temple are laid out the first time the Torah speaks of "the place I shall select to establish My name" (Deuteronomy 12:9–11): "(9) You have yet to come to the place of rest and the place of inheritance that the Lord your God is granting you. (10) When you cross the Jordan and settle the land that the Lord God is granting you, *and He grants you safety from all your enemies around you and you live in security,* (11) then you must bring everything that I command you to the site where the Lord your God will choose to establish His name." Why should the establishment of the Temple as the central shrine be tied to the political stability of the country?

If the Temple is perceived as a house for God's reputation as sovereign, the reasoning becomes clear. When Israel is in a state of persecution or constant war, its condition does little to sanctify, or magnify, the divine name. The prerequisite of security laid down in Deuteronomy, chapter 12, is only one of the conditions that warrant the erection of a symbol of God's name. To identify the others, we need to turn to the earliest episode in which the construction of the Temple is discussed—David's request to build the Temple in 2 Samuel 7.

SECURE BORDERS AND STABLE RULE

David's request to build the Temple and God's response to that request are contained in a passage that bears sufficient nuances to warrant citing it in full. The passage should be read with an eye toward identifying the preconditions for the Temple's erection:

> When the king was settled in his palace and the Lord had granted him safety from all the enemies around him (2) the king said to the prophet Nathan: "Here I am dwelling in a house of cedar, while the Ark of the

Lord abides in a tent!" (3) Nathan said to the king, "Go and do whatever you have in mind, for the Lord is with you."

(4) That same night the word of the Lord came to Nathan: (5) "Go and say to My servant David: Thus said the Lord: Are you the one to build a house for Me to dwell in? (6) From the day that I brought the people of Israel out of Egypt to this day I have not dwelt in a house, but have moved about in a Tent and Tabernacle. (7) As I moved about wherever the Israelites were, did I ever reproach any of the tribal leaders whom I appointed to care for My people Israel: Why have you not built Me a house of cedar?

(8) Further, say thus to My servant David: Thus said the Lord of Hosts: I took you from the pasture, from following the flock to be ruler of My people Israel, (9) and I have been with you wherever you went, and have cut down all your enemies before you. Moreover, I will give you great renown like that of the greatest men on earth. (10) I will establish a home for My people Israel and will plant them firm, so that they shall dwell secure and shall tremble no more. Evil men shall not oppress them any more as in the past, (11) ever since I appointed chieftains over My people Israel, I will give you safety from all your enemies.

"The Lord declares to you that He, the Lord, will establish a house for you. (12) When your days are done and you lie with your fathers, I will raise up your offspring after you, one of your own issue, and I will establish his kingship. (13) He shall build a house for My name, and I will establish his royal throne forever. (14) I will be a father to him, and he shall be a son to Me. When he does wrong, I will chastise him with the rod of men and the affliction of mortals; (15) but I will never withdraw My favor from him as I withdrew it from Saul, whom I removed to make room for you. (16) Your house and your kingship shall be ever secure before you; your throne shall be established forever."

The passage is an enigmatic one. Does God approve of the idea of a Temple or not? In verses 4 through 7, God seems to imply that the Tabernacle, which had served as the central shrine for four centuries, was quite adequate, while in verse 13 he tells David that his son will build the Temple. This immediately leads to a second question: if God approves of the idea of a Temple, why is David's son the one to erect it rather than David himself? Why does God grant David and his progeny dynastic rule over Israel at precisely the moment when David requests permission to build the Temple?

A final question emerges about this passage: in 1 Chronicles 22, David claims that he was denied the right to build the Temple because he was a man of war. However, in this seminal text concerning the preconditions for the Temple's construction, there is no hint of this notion. In light of the following discussion, we will return later to probe the full meaning of that critical passage.

Each of these questions touches on points that are central to the meaning of the Temple. To unravel these issues, we must begin at the outset of the passage. Verse 1 opens with an introductory clause concerning the timing of David's request—"When the king was settled in his palace and the Lord had granted him safety from all the enemies around him." What is the import of the fact that God had granted David safety from all the enemies around him? This is of immense significance in light of the conditions for erecting the Temple set down in Deuteronomy, chapter 12, and the state of affairs prevailing in the Jewish state during the previous four centuries.

The language of Deuteronomy 12:10 is clear. Offerings will be brought to the place God selects to establish His name when "you cross the Jordan and settle the land that the Lord God is granting you, and *He grants you safety from all your enemies around you.*" When the Bible writes that David made the request when "the Lord had granted him safety from all the enemies around him," it is a deliberate reference to the terms of Deuteronomy 12:10, and a sign that in David's eyes, the times were right to erect the Temple.

The fact that God had granted David "safety from all the enemies around him" is particularly salient for a discussion of the conditions necessary to build a Temple, in light of the history of the Israelites during the period of the Judges. The Book of Judges is a chronicle of a three-century period in which Israel entered a recurring cycle of disobeying God's commandments and of servitude and subjugation by foreign powers, separated by intermittent periods of redemption. When David defeated the Philistines (2 Samuel 5)—the perennial foe of the Israelites during the period of the Judges and the reign of Saul—it marked the fulfillment of the prerequisite of Deuteronomy 12:10 for the first time in three centuries. For the first time, Israel would not be the subject of scoff and derision among its neighbors. For the first time, Israel would be perceived as strong, and as a direct result, God Himself also would be seen as strong. Under these circumstances, thought David, the time could be ripe for building a house for the establishment of God's name—His reputation as universal sovereign.

However, what of God's response in the ensuing verses? Broadly, it seems to be an endorsement of David as king, yet David's request to build the Temple is denied. Rather, for reasons that are unclear, only his son, we read, will be eligible to build the Temple. The key to understanding God's response revolves around the meaning and various usages of the word *bayit* literally, "house" in this section. David desired to build a *house* for God's name. But God demurs: "Are *you* the one to build a house for Me to dwell in?" Indeed, says God, in 2 Samuel 7:8–10, you have achieved a level of acclaim unknown in Jewish history, but I must build a *bayit*—meaning a dynastic ascension to the throne—for you before you can build a *bayit*—meaning the Temple—for Me. Why is the establishment of dynastic rule a precondition for the building of the First Temple?

The answer highlights another critical condition that was necessary for the building of the First Temple. David thought that he had consolidated his rule over Israel. The ultimate mark of domestic stability, however, rests not with the effectiveness of any single leader. Even the most able leader can lead his people for several decades at most. Stability in domestic affairs can only be ensured for the long term if guidelines are established and accepted by all for the transition of power from one ruler to the next. In modern democracies, that is achieved by constitutional dictates. Within the biblical framework, however, the orderly transfer of rule was attainable in one primary fashion alone: dynastic ascension to the throne. David thought that he had achieved the degree of domestic stability necessary to warrant the building of the Temple. God's response is that indeed, a measure of stability had been achieved, but permanent stability can only be the by-product of dynastic ascension—the orderly transfer of rule from one leader to the next.

God's response is now understood. Far from discouraging David in his quest to build the Temple, God's response is a vindication of David and of his request. David asks to build a *bayit*—a House for God's Name. God, in return, vows to establish David's "house"—the Davidic line—as the sole rulers of Israel. The reward itself constitutes the political stability that is a necessary condition for the Temple's erection.

The import of dynastic stability for the construction of the Temple also explains why David himself could not erect the Temple: "The Lord declares to you that He, the Lord, will establish a house for you. (12) When your days are done and you lie with your fathers, I will raise up your offspring after you, one of your own issue, and I will establish his kingship. (13) He shall build a house for My name, and I will establish his royal throne forever." David is promised dynastic rule, but the realization of that promise will only take place with the ascension of David's son to the throne. Not a single leader of Israel had seen his progeny successfully assume the mantle of power. The stability inherent in the ascension of a son of David to the throne would be without precedent. Such a measure of stability would represent a political maturity that would lead to the respect of Israel and of God in the eyes of her neighbors. Under such circumstances, a public symbol of God's reputation as sovereign could be recognized as valid.

The necessity of the implementation of dynastic rule as a prerequisite for the construction of the Temple was explicitly recognized by Solomon as well. At the dedication of the Temple, Solomon addressed the people as follows (1 Kings 8:17–19):

> Now my father David had intended to build a House for the name of the Lord, the God of Israel. (18) But the Lord said to my father David, "As regards your intention to build a House for My name, you did right to have

that intention. (19) However, you shall not build the House yourself; instead, your son, the issue of your loins shall build the House for My name."

And the Lord has fulfilled the promise that He made: *I have succeeded my father David and have ascended the throne of Israel as the Lord promised and I have built the House for the name of the Lord, the God of Israel.*[8]

The fact that Solomon would erect the Temple, and not David, says Solomon, was not an inherent rejection of David. On the contrary, it was a recognition of him. Solomon is the one who builds the Temple for in Solomon dynastic order and stability are realized.

WELCOMING NON-JEWS TO THE TEMPLE

The process of attaining a climate in which God's name is acclaimed throughout the nations reaches its apex in the early years of Solomon's reign. Prior to depicting the construction of the Temple in 1 Kings 6–8, the Bible sees it fit to portray a general picture of Solomon's kingship. As the chapter that immediately precedes the account of the construction of the Temple, 1 Kings, chapter 5, can be seen as a depiction of the conditions that needed to be in place before a house could be built for God's name.

Solomon had complete hegemony over the entire land of Israel (1 Kings 5:1). He had a flourishing and prosperous economy (verses 2–4), peace with all his neighbors (verses 4–5), and a large army (verses 6–8). All these constitute achievements that earn a nation respect—then as well as today. The most detailed account of Solomon's kingship, however, concerns his wisdom, and the impression it made on the neighboring rulers (verses 9–14):

> The Lord endowed Solomon with wisdom and discernment in great measure, with understanding as vast as the sands on the seashore. . . . He was the wisest of all men. . . . He composed three thousand proverbs, and his songs numbered one thousand and five. He discoursed about trees, from

the cedar in Lebanon to the hyssop that grows out of the wall; and he discoursed about beasts, birds, creeping things, and fishes. Men of all people came to hear Solomon's wisdom, [sent] by all the kings of the earth who had heard his wisdom.

Solomon's repute among the nations had already been evidenced in his marriage to the daughter of Pharaoh (1 Kings 3:1), demonstrating affinity between the kingdoms of Egypt and Israel. Now, his acclaim spread to all the nations of the world. Solomon's acclaim and its importance as an extension of God's acclaim reaches its pinnacle in Solomon's dealings with Hiram (1 Kings 5:15–26):

> King Hiram of Tyre sent his officials to Solomon when he heard that he had been anointed king in place of his father; for Hiram had always been a friend of David. (16) Solomon sent his message to Hiram: (17) You know that my father David could not build a house for the name of the Lord his God because of the enemies that encompassed him, until the Lord had placed them under his feet. (18) But now the Lord my God has given me respite all around; there is no adversary and no mischance. (19) *And so I propose to build a House for the name of the Lord my God, as the Lord promised my father David, saying, "Your son whom I shall set on your throne in your place, shall build the House for My name."* (20) Please, then, give orders for cedars to be cut for me in the Lebanon. My servants will work with yours, and I will pay you any wages you may ask for your servants; for as you know there is none among us who knows how to cut timber like the Sidonians.

The passage highlights many of the points that have been developed in this chapter. The fact that Hiram initiates the contact with Solomon is itself a sign of foreign recognition. Solomon's reply in verses 17 through 19 stresses the need for political stability discussed earlier. A House for God's Name could not be built while relations with neighboring nations were strained. Now, Solomon says, peace reigns and the Davidic dynasty is firmly established, and so the House for God's Name can be built. The end of the passage (verses 21–26) is the most significant:

(21) When Hiram heard Solomon's message, he was overjoyed. "Praised be the Lord this day," he said, "for granting David a wise son to govern this great people." (22) So Hiram sent word to Solomon: "I have your message; I will supply all the cedar and cypress logs you require. . . . " (24) So Hiram kept Solomon provided with all the cedar and cypress wood he required, (25) and Solomon delivered to Hiram 20,000 *kors* of wheat as provisions for his household and 20 *kors* of beaten oil. . . . (26) The Lord had given Solomon wisdom, as He had promised him. There was friendship between Hiram and Solomon, and the two of them made a treaty.

The theological significance of this passage as a comment concerning the relationship between Jews and non-Jews cannot be underestimated. The House for God's Name would be made of materials donated by a neighboring nation, thereby symbolizing that acclaim. David had initiated amicable relations with Hiram, but when Solomon and Hiram made a pact, it was the first time that a treaty had been established between Israel and a neighboring power. Immediately after delineating the details of the treaty between Hiram—who praises God and His great nation—and Solomon, the Bible proceeds to begin the account of the construction of the House for God's name.

The universal relevance of the Temple as a symbol of God's name is given special stress in Solomon's prayer at the Temple's dedication (1 Kings 8:41–43):

If a foreigner who is not of Your people Israel comes from a distant land for the sake of Your name—(42) for they shall hear about Your great name and Your mighty hand and Your outstretched arm—when he comes to pray toward this House, (43) oh, hear in Your heavenly abode and grant all that the foreigner asks You for. Thus all the peoples of the earth will know Your name and revere you, as does Your people Israel; and they will recognize that Your name is attached to this House that I have built.

The function of the Temple as a symbol for God's acclaim in the world reaches its apex with the visit of the queen of Sheba to Solomon's court (1 Kings 10:4–9):

When the queen of Sheba observed all of Solomon's wisdom, and the
palace he had built (5) . . . and the burnt offerings which he offered at
the House of the Lord, she was left breathless. (6) She said to the king,
"The report I heard in my own land about you and your wisdom was true.
(7) But I did not believe the reports until I came and saw with my own
eyes that not even the half had been told me; your wisdom and wealth
surpass the reports that I heard. . . . (9) Praised be the Lord your God,
who delighted in you and set you on the throne of Israel. It is because of
the Lord's everlasting love for Israel that He made you king to administer
justice and righteousness."

Solomon emerges as a figure commanding universal respect, but because he is only an extension of God's kingship, the respect he commands immediately converts into acclaim for God himself.

We opened our discussion of the concept of declaring God's name
by probing its origins in the Book of Genesis. Abraham, who declared
God's name, began the process of reversing the spirit of the builders
of Babel, who toiled for the glorification of their own name. The Book
of Deuteronomy spoke exclusively of the Temple as the place where
God shall establish His name. For 480 years following the Exodus, that
designation went unrealized due to Israel's failures. Only for a brief
time under David and Solomon did Israel truly bring acclaim to God's
name, thereby warranting the building of the First Temple. The final
redress of the spirit of Babel is the vision that animates the eschatology
of Isaiah (2:1–3):

This is the prophecy of Isaiah son of Amotz concerning Judah and Jerusalem: (2) And it will come to pass at the end of days that the mountain of
God's house will be firmly established, even higher than the peaks and all
the peoples will flow toward it as a river. (3) And many nations will go
and will cry, "Let us go up toward the mountain of God's house, to the
house of the Lord of Jacob, and we will learn from His ways and walk in
His paths, for out of Zion goes forth the Torah and the word of God from
Jerusalem."

Literarily and conceptually, Isaiah's image of the end of days represents a reversal of the social and spiritual climate of the builders of
Babel. The nations that were dispersed across the entire earth (Genesis 11:9) will now flow as one toward a central point. At Babel they
were centered in a valley (Genesis 11:2)—a topographic feature sunk
in the earth, the realm of man. In Jerusalem they will gather toward a
hilltop, a topographic symbol pointing heavenward, which is indicative of fealty toward God. The scattered dialects will now speak in
one voice, just as they did before the tower was conceived, but now
they will speak in one voice that declares God's greatness, not their
own. At Babel they erected a tower whose top reaches the sky, but in
Jerusalem, they will migrate toward God's house, higher than the tops
of hills. At Babel they looked only inwardly for direction concerning
the conduct of their affairs, but in Jerusalem, they will look toward
God. The city of Babel and its tower were symbols of the desire of man
to make a name for himself, but in the end of days, these will be re-
deemed as the city of Jerusalem and the Temple will emerge as site
and symbol of the endeavor of proclaiming the name of God.

THE INCOMPATIBILITY
OF TEMPLE AND BLOODSHED

A well-known notion concerning the building of the First Temple is
that David was disqualified as its builder because he was a man of war.
As we have seen, the narrative of 2 Samuel 7 makes no mention of
this. To grasp the full meaning of this disqualification, we need to
examine the source of this conception, in David's words to Solomon
as he hands over the reigns of power in 1 Chronicles 22:7–10:

> David said to Solomon, "My son, I wanted to build a House for the name
> of the Lord my God. (8) But the word of the Lord came to me, saying,
> 'You have shed much blood and fought great battles; you shall not build

a House for My name for you have shed much blood on the earth in
My sight. (9) But you will have a son who will be a man at rest, for I will
give him rest from all his enemies on all sides; Solomon [Shelomoh] will
be his name and I shall confer peace [shalom] and quiet on Israel in his
time. (10) He will build a House for My name; he shall be a son to Me
and I to him a father, and I will establish his throne of kingship over
Israel forever.'"

It is important at the outset to establish that the Bible is not register-
ing here a pacifistic view of conflict, nor even a condemnation of
David's wars. Nowhere in the Bible is David criticized for any of the
wars that he waged. His wars were just, fought on behalf of God and
in defense of the Jewish people. Rather, the passage needs to be seen
as a comment on the spiritual ramifications of killing another human
being. The act of killing another human being may be justified, and
even necessary at times. Nonetheless, as the ultimate destructive act,
killing—even when justified—leaves an individual spiritually tainted.
It is in this vein that the Torah declares, concerning the construction of the altar: "If you make for Me an altar of stones, do not build
it of hewn stones; for by wielding your sword upon them you have
profaned them" (Exodus 20:22).

The prohibition of carving stones for the altar applies to all metal
tools. However, by using the word *sword*, the Torah lends insight into
the rationale of the prohibition. Metal tools resemble a sword, and a
sword, as an instrument of death, is antithetical to the spiritual perfection symbolized by the altar. The construction of the Temple can
take place only when the spiritual standing of the Jewish people is on
the highest plane. David's wars were just and necessary, but in an age
of warfare, the Jewish people cannot attain the high spiritual standing necessary for the Temple's construction.

By contrast, Solomon will build the Temple, says God, because he
"will be a man at rest, for I will give him rest from all his enemies on
all sides; Solomon [Shelomoh] will be his name and I shall confer peace
[shalom] and quiet on Israel in his time." David's generation, while

secure in an unprecedented fashion, was one embroiled in foreign conflicts, while Solomon's rule was to be punctuated by full peace. Only when Israel is at full peace can God's name be acclaimed by its neighbors. Only when Israel is at full peace do the times warrant building a House for God's name.

These words need to be seen in conjunction with the narrative of David's request earlier in his career, as portrayed in 2 Samuel, chapter 7. David thought his kingship was sufficiently established to warrant affiliating God's reputation to it, as symbolized by the erection of the Temple. However, God's response was that he was mistaken in his premise. The rule of a king is deemed strong, not by the mere presence of a palace, but through continuity into the following generation. David's wars go unmentioned because there was at issue a more fundamental precondition for the erection of the Temple, that of stable leadership. At the end of his career, however, as he passed the reins of a secure kingdom to his son Solomon, David underscored the importance of maintaining full peace as a condition that must exist before the times are ripe to build the Temple.

BETWEEN TABERNACLE AND TEMPLE— PARTICULARISIM VERSUS UNIVERSALISM

At the outset of this chapter we asked why four centuries elapsed from the conquest of Joshua before the Tabernacle was superseded by the Temple. Thus far, we have attempted to answer this question by concentrating on the purpose of the Temple as a symbol of God's name— but what of the Temple's precursor, the Tabernacle? What was the symbolic role of the Tabernacle, and how did it differ from that of the Temple? To answer this we will need to examine the terminology used by the Bible to describe the Tabernacle, and then contrast it with what we have already seen in this chapter concerning the Temple.

The Book of Deuteronomy, in looking toward the entry of the Children of Israel into their land, refers to the Sanctuary in the land of Israel as "the place I shall select to establish My name." Nowhere prior to the Book of Deuteronomy, however, does the Torah refer to the Tabernacle by that name. It would seem, then, that only in the land of Israel was the central shrine intended to become a public symbol of God's acclaim in the world. This is readily understood in light of the conditions necessary to warrant the erection of this symbol. During their trek through the wilderness, the Israelites were victorious over several opponents and were feared by neighboring powers, but never did they earn the amicable respect and admiration that the Jewish people attained during the time of Solomon. Because the Israelites were only feared as a military power and not venerated as a nation, the Tabernacle, prior to entry into the land of Israel, did not warrant the standing as a symbol for God's acclaim in the world. What, then, did the Tabernacle symbolize?

The Tabernacle was a potent symbol of the unique relationship between God and the Jewish people. In the previous chapter we noted that the Tabernacle was born out of the Sinai experience and, in its minutia, represented a perpetuation of that event. It represented God's exclusive revelation to the Jewish people, in which the Jewish people alone served God. At its inception, it is heralded as a symbol of God's affinity to the Jewish people (Exodus 25:8): "Make Me a sanctuary that I may dwell among them."

To be sure, the Sinai imagery and iconography present in the Tabernacle were integral to the Temple as well. The Temple, however, bears an additional symbolic dimension. It was erected in an age when Israel and God were esteemed by the surrounding nations. It was open to worship for gentiles as well as for Jews. The Temple, declared Isaiah, would be the focal point for the collective worship of all of humanity. The primary distinction between the symbolic functions of the Tabernacle and those of the Temple can be drawn as follows: the scope of the Tabernacle as a shrine for the service of God was *particularistic*, exclusively serving the Jewish people, whereas the scope of the Temple was *universal*, a shrine with its doors open to the entire congregation of mankind.

To understand the relationship between Israel's particularistic shrine—the Tabernacle—and Israel's more universal and ecumenical shrine—the Temple—we need to grasp a cardinal point concerning the dynamics of the relationship between God and the Jewish people. The covenant between God and the Jewish people is not a static relationship, created at a singular moment in time at Sinai and remaining a constant thereafter. While we posit that the covenantal relationship is ultimately an immutable one, over time, it can gain expression as a stronger or weaker bond in proportion to Israel's behavior as a covenantal partner. Utilizing the symbolism of the prophet Hosea, rabbinic literature often casts the covenantal bond between God and Israel as the relationship between man and wife, an image that is instructive for our purposes. The marital bond is initiated by the wedding rite, and thereafter, the couple remains husband and wife. However, the quality of that relationship is continually changing and dynamic. A couple will be drawn closer as their behavior and mutual sacrifice reflect the commitment they have made to one another, and in like fashion, Israel's relationship with God grows closer as the nation executes its covenantal calling.

The process of transition from Tabernacle to Temple serves as a reflection of Israel's ontological and spiritual ascent—a strengthening of the covenantal bond. When God descended onto Mount Sinai, His immanent nature—what the rabbis termed the divine presence (hashra'at ha-shekhinah)—attained its greatest manifestation until that moment in history. However, the consecration of the covenant represented only the commencement of the mission of the Jewish people, which was to be a nation called upon to devote itself to proclaiming God's name in the world. That mission saw increasingly greater fulfillment as the Jewish people perfected a society that would be worthy of God's open association. Such a society would, in turn, proclaim God's acclaim in the world. When the Jewish people reached the zenith of that covenantal process, during the time of Solomon, the covenantal bond was at its strongest and, as a result, God's immanence was at its greatest.

As stated in the introduction, religious symbols provide us with a vocabulary through which metaphysical and divine reality gain concrete expression. Now, when the Jewish people fulfill their covenantal calling, their bond with God is strengthened, and God responds by making His immanent nature more manifest.

The contrast in design and structure between the Tabernacle and the Temple is reflective of this dynamic nature of God's immanence. The Tabernacle—even after entry into the land of Israel—was a portable structure, bounded by skins and linens (Exodus 26–27). Accordingly, it is almost always referred to as an *ohel*—a tent. By contrast, the Temple was triple the size of the Tabernacle, had stone walls and a roof (1 Kings 6), and is consistently referred to as a *bayit*—a house. In the Tabernacle, God dwelled with the Jewish people, but in the desert, Israel had not yet created a social and spiritual order worthy of God's fullest association. His bond with the Jewish people was not yet complete. Thus, while God allied Himself with the Jewish people, it was only in quarters that were temporary and transient.

With this in mind, we can now understand why the Tabernacle—an *ohel*—remained the central shrine following entry into the Promised Land, even though the technical necessity of a transportable shrine had been obviated, as the Israelites were no longer on the move. The Book of Deuteronomy speaks of the central shrine in the land as the place where God will establish His name. The blueprint of Deuteronomy calls for the Israelites to establish a perfected society in the land of Israel, based on justice and fealty toward God. Had the Israelites executed the plan faithfully, they would have merited God's bounty and protection. With a just society, one that was secure and prosperous, a setting would emerge in which God's full and open manifestation would be warranted. During the turbulent period of the Judges, however, Israel failed to fulfill its mission to establish a society that would inherently proclaim God's name. Though the people failed in their calling, God continued to openly associate himself by allowing the Sanctuary to remain standing, but the Sanctuary could only take the form of the Tabernacle—a transient and temporary structure—

which was the appropriate symbol of an underdeveloped bond between God and the Jewish people. It is no surprise, then, that while the Book of Deuteronomy refers to the central shrine as the place God will select to establish His name, this terminology was almost never used by the prophets with reference to the Tabernacle during the four centuries prior to the building of the Temple. Because Israel failed in its mission, the Tabernacle was never superseded by the Temple. When Israel behaves contrary to her covenantal calling, the central shrine fails to serve its symbolic purpose of acclaiming God's reputation in the world.

Under David and Solomon, however, Israel lived up to her covenantal calling. An environment had been created in which the divine presence could become manifest to a higher degree than ever before. Now it became appropriate to erect a symbol that would symbolize the strength and vitality of the covenantal bond; it became appropriate to symbolize God's immanent presence with the Jewish people through the durable structure of a house.

The progression in God's association with the Jewish people, as witnessed in the transition from Tabernacle to Temple, is also reflected in the status of the cherubim in each period. In several pre-Temple references, the Bible refers to God as "He who dwells on the cherubim,"[9] indicating that within the Tabernacle, God's presence was most immanent atop the cherubim. Regarding the Temple, however, no explicit mention is made of the cherubim atop the Ark. Rather, it is on the floor of the Holy of Holies that Soloman erects two enormous cherubim, whose wings spread open from wall to wall (1 Kings 6:23–28).

The contrast between the location of the cherubim in the Tabernacle and those in the Temple is symbolically significant. As long as Israel's bond with God was not fully realized, God's presence remained, figuratively, a passenger atop the cherubim of the Ark. However, after that bond was maximized, the only cherubim mentioned are the ones planted on the floor of the Holy of Holies, symbolizing the rootedness of God's presence.

This is further symbolized by the placing of the Ark into the Holy of Holies in the Temple. When the details of the Ark's design are delineated in Exodus, chapter 25, the Torah states that the poles of the Ark must not be removed from the rings that bear them (Exodus 25:15). The function of the poles, of course, was to allow the Ark to be carried from place to place. When Solomon deposited the Ark into the Holy of Holies, however, the poles of the Ark were drawn forward (1 Kings 8:8), symbolizing that God's presence would no longer travel from place to place but had reached its terminus.[10]

If the process of transition from Tabernacle to Temple needed to be summarized in a single phrase, it would be described as a process of *consummation*. As we saw in the first chapter of this book, R. Ovadiah Seforno, in his commentary to Exodus 20:11, said that when a process is consummated, the ensuing state of wholeness and completion is referred to as *menuchah*—literally, "rest." The notion that the Temple symbolizes the consummation of the relationship between God and the Jewish people is seen in the centrality of the word *menuchah* in many of the biblical passages that discuss the Temple. We earlier saw this word as one of the key conditions necessary for the Temple's construction. The Torah spoke of the offerings that would be brought "when you cross the Jordan and settle the land that the Lord God is granting you, and He grants you safety (*ve-hini'ach lekhah*) from all your enemies around you and you live in security" (Deuteronomy 12:10). Recall that the notion of *menuchah*—rest from surrounding enemies—is presented as the backdrop for David's request to build the Temple in 2 Samuel 7, and as part of David's valedictory to Solomon (1 Chronicles 22:7–9):

> David said to Solomon, "My son, I wanted to build a House for the name of the Lord my God. But the word of the Lord came to me, saying, 'You have shed much blood and fought great battles; you shall not build a House for My name for you have shed much blood on the earth in My sight. But you will have a son who will be a man at rest, (*ish menuchah*) for I will give him rest (*menuchah*) from all his enemies on all sides.'"

The word *menuchah*, in this context, therefore, is indicative of completion: completion of the political preconditions necessary for the Temple's erection. However, within the context of the Temple, *menuchah* is not only a political state of affairs toward which the Jewish people must strive. *Menuchah* also reflects the consummation of Israel's development as a perfected order. The psalmist, in describing the dynamics of David's overture to construct the Temple, portrays David's desire to build the Temple by saying (Psalms 132:8), "Advance, O Lord, to your resting place (*li-menuchatekhah*)." In David's eyes, the time had come for God to fully consummate His relationship with the Jewish people. God affirms David's impulse by distinguishing a particular site as the focal point for His intimate presence among the Jewish people: "This is My resting place (*menuchati*) for all time; here I will dwell for I desire it."

In summary, we have seen how the Temple reflects the apex of an evolutionary process: Israel's calling to magnify the name of God. Abraham initiated this process in the wake of the anthropocentrism of Babel. The Tabernacle, an *ohel*, stood in the infancy of Israel's covenantal relationship with God. The full maturation of that bond would come as Israel created a great society that would be worthy of having God's reputation associated with it. The Temple, a *bayit*, reflected that maturation. As the site affiliated with God's acclaim, the Temple serves, for Jews and non-Jews alike, as the spiritual focal point of mankind.

5

A Multifaceted Center and Its Problems

One of the primary identities of the Temple is that it is the place of *hashra'at ha-shekhinah*, the site at which God's presence is most manifest. It is no surprise, then, that the Temple is the focal point of prayer. Nonetheless, as the site at which God's presence is most intimately manifest, the Temple is also the *center* of the nation in several major spheres of collective life. This is exhibited in the structure of the Book of Deuteronomy. Chapters 12 through 26 depict commandments that are to be the social and religious frame of life in the land of Israel. Within this section, the central shrine, "the place in which God shall establish His name," is mentioned nearly twenty times. The Temple is cast as the center for sacrifices (chapter 12), the consumption of tithes (Deuteronomy 14:23–25), the celebration of the festivals (chapter 16), and the center of the judicial system (chapter 17). In this chapter, we will explore how the Temple constitutes the national center for social unity, education, and justice. The concentration of activity and jurisdiction at the Temple, however, renders it prone to abuse, and in the second half of this chapter, we will probe the social and religious ills that emerged as an endemic part of the Temple's existence.

SOCIAL UNITY

A reading of the commandments enumerated in the Book of Deuteronomy reveals that the Temple was a central gathering point for the Jewish people. On the one hand, the Torah paints a picture of the demography of the land of Israel: each of the twelve tribes of Israel is to inherit its own tribal territory, within the land (Numbers 33:53–54), thereby bolstering tribal identity. Indeed, nearly all biblical figures are introduced by tribal identification, as in, "There was a *man of Benjamin* whose name was Kish son of Abiel . . . " (1 Samuel 9:1). Tribal identity, however, needs to be balanced by collective national identity. The Temple serves as the forge toward that end. Several commandments performed at the Temple highlight its social significance in particular, as a force for unity and brotherhood within the nation. The commandment of *ma'aser sheni*—the second tithe—is an example. Tithes are usually thought of as a kind of tax, presented either to the Priest or to God. *Ma'aser sheni*, however, is different. Deuteronomy 14:22–26 commands us to take a tithing of one's produce and bring it to "the place where God shall choose to establish His name." This tithe is to be consumed by the owner and anyone else he wishes to include. A tenth of a farmer's produce could amount to quite a hefty load, and so the Torah makes the provision that the produce may be sold and the money used instead to buy goods in Jerusalem, to be consumed there. The consumption of the *ma'aser sheni* is depicted in festive terms (Deuteronomy 14:26): "Spend the money on anything you want—cattle, sheep, wine or ale, or anything you may desire. And you shall feast there, in the presence of the Lord your God, and rejoice with your household." Maimonides highlighted the social component that was an inherent part of the commandment of *ma'aser sheni*: "As for the second tithe, it is commanded that it should be spent exclusively on food in Jerusalem. For this leads of necessity to giving some of it in alms; for as it could only be employed on nourishment, it was easy for a man to have others have it little by little. *Thus it was necessarily brought about a gathering in one place, so that brotherhood and love among the people were greatly strengthened.*"[1]

In similar fashion, the Torah calls for the fourth yield of a tree's life to be brought to Jerusalem so that it could be consumed amid jubilation (Leviticus 19:24). The reality of every household in Israel coming to the Temple on an annual basis and celebrating with great feasts rendered the Temple nothing less than a national meeting place, where families from all over Israel would convene in a singular fashion.

For many, this pilgrimage was probably done in conjunction with the pilgrimages of the three festivals, Pesach, Shavuot, and Sukkot. In chapter 3 we claimed that these pilgrimages—whereby the entire House of Israel convened before God—represented a perpetuation of the Sinai encounter. However, the festival pilgrimages, by their nature, also bore a social component as well. In coming before God, the tribes of Israel also came together as one. This point animates the psalmist in his reflections on the ascent to Jerusalem for the festival pilgrimage (Psalm 122):

> A song of ascents. Of David.
> I rejoiced when they said to me,
> "We are going to the house of the Lord."
> (2) Our feet stood inside your gates, O Jerusalem.
> (3) Jerusalem built up, a city knit together,
> (4) to which tribes would make pilgrimage,
> the tribes of the Lord,
> —as was enjoined upon Israel—
> to praise the name of the Lord.
> (5) there the thrones of judgment stood,
> thrones of the house of David.
> (6) Pray for the well-being of Jerusalem:
> "May those who love you be at peace.
> (7) May there be well-being within your ramparts, peace in your citadels."

(8) For the sake of my kin and friends,
I pray for your well-being;
(9) for the sake of the house of the Lord our God
I seek your good.

The first point that emerges is that Jerusalem, with the Temple at its center, is a potent force for Jewish unity; the psalmist stands at its gates not in solitude but with his fellow pilgrims: "*Our* feet stood inside your gates, O Jerusalem" (verse 2). He lauds the fact that all the tribes of Israel gather there (verse 4) and concludes by praying for the well-being of his kin and friends, who are bound together by the common endeavor of pilgrimage to Jerusalem (verse 8). The unifying aspect of Jerusalem and the Temple is borne out in halakhic writings as well: with all of Israel coming to Jerusalem for the festival, lodging would be at an expensive premium. The rabbis determined, however, that no boarding fees could be collected from festival pilgrims, as the land of Jerusalem belongs equally to all.[2]

EDUCATION

An examination of the role of the Priests and Levites—those who officiated in the Temple—highlights their identity as educators. In tracing the scope of activity in the Temple, an appropriate focus falls on the role of the Priests and Levites as officiants in the Temple, and on their role in society at large. For the sake of simplicity, we will refer to them collectively as Levites; the Priests were but a subset of the tribe of Levi, and, apart from their ritual responsibilities, they served in similar capacities.

The Levites constitute a brigade. Just as an army brigade executes the wishes of a ruler or government, the Torah casts the Levites in quasi-military terms, indicating that they constitute a special brigade devoted to the service of the King of Kings. Numbers 8:24 states that from the age of twenty-five and up, the Levites shall join the *legion* of the service of the Tent of Meeting. In his valedictory blessings to the tribes of Israel, Moses blessed the tribe of Levi: "May the Lord bless His *corps* and favor his undertaking" (Deuteronomy 33:11).

What were the tasks performed by the Levites? The primary duties that immediately come to mind are the various and sundry activities associated with the rites of the Temple. However, this impression, which is easily garnered from a cursory reading of the Torah and references to the Levites in the traditional prayers, is, in fact, misleading.

Only a small portion of a Priest's or Levite's time was dedicated to service in the Temple. The rotations worked by the families of Levites in the Temple are listed in 1 Chronicles 23–24. Both the Priests and the Levites were divided into twenty-four families, each of which was responsible for a tour of duty in the Temple. According to 2 Chronicles 23:5–8, each tour of duty consisted of one week's work in the Temple. This means that a typical Priest or Levite would serve in the Temple for only slightly more than two weeks out of any year! What, then, occupied the members of God's corps during the better part of the year? For what purpose were they being supported by the tithes of the Jewish people?

While the Torah focuses on the role of the Levites as Sanctuary officiants, they served in a second capacity that gains greater amplification in the later books of the Bible: their role as *educators*. Explicit references to this role already appear in the Torah. When the Priests are commanded to abstain from entering the Sanctuary while intoxicated, the Bible writes (Leviticus 10:8–11): "And the Lord spoke to Aaron saying: (9) Drink no wine or ale, you or your sons with you, when you enter the Tent of Meeting, that you may not die—it is a law for all time throughout your generations—(10) for you must distinguish between the sacred and the profane, and between the unclean and the clean. (11) *And you must teach the Israelites all the laws which the Lord has imparted to you through Moses.*" Verse 11, identifying the Priests as teachers, is not an independent command but is related to the prohibition of entering the Sanctuary while intoxicated. The censure against officiating while inebriated underscores the need for dignity during preformance of the sacred rites. This same dignity must be maintained when the Priests attend to their further responsibility of imparting God's laws to the Jewish people. The role of the Levites as educators is also central to the blessing given the tribe of Levi by Moses in his valedictory address (Deuteronomy 33:10): "They shall teach Your norms to Jacob and Your instructions to Israel."

The later books of the Bible contain numerous references to the Levites as educators, both in the poetic passages of the latter prophets and in the prose narratives of 2 Chronicles. When the Judean king Jehoshaphat wanted to fortify the religious awareness of the people, it was to the Levites that he turned (2 Chronicles 17:7–9):

> In the third year of his reign he sent his officers Ben-hail, Obadiah, Zechariah, Nethanel, and Micaiah throughout the cities of Judah to offer instruction. (8) With them were the Levites, Shemaiah, Nethaniah, Zebadiah, Asahel, Shemiramoth, Jehonathan, Adonijah, Tobijah, and Tob-adonijah the Levites; with them were Elishama and Jehoram the priests. (9) *They offered instruction throughout Judah, having with them the Book of the Teaching of the Lord. They made the rounds of all the cities of the Lord and instructed the people.*

A similar reform took place later during the reign of Hezekiah, shortly before the destruction of the First Temple. Once again, the key to educating the people was the involvement of the Levites (2 Chronicles 31:4): "He ordered the people, the inhabitants of Jerusalem to deliver the portions of the Priests and the Levites, so that they might devote themselves to the Teaching of the Lord." From this passage we see that in Hezekiah's eyes, the primary purpose of the tithes and priestly gifts was not to support them in their role as Sanctuary officiants, but to enable them to devote themselves to the study and dissemination of the Torah.[3] The notion that the Levites, inclusive of the Priests, constitute God's corps, a brigade dedicated to the service of God in the Temple and to the dissemination of His word amidst the Jewish people, is succinctly summarized by Maimonides:

And why did not Levi partake of the patrimony of the land of Israel and its spoils with his brethren? Because he was set apart to serve God, to worship Him and *to teach His just ways and righteous ordinances to the masses.* As it is stated, "They shall teach Your norms to Jacob and Your instructions to Israel." Therefore, they have been set apart from the ways of the world; they do not wage war like the rest of Israel, nor do they inherit or acquire unto themselves by physical force. They are, rather, the Lord's corps, as it is stated, "Blessed, O Lord, his corps;" and He, blessed be He, vouchsafes them, as it is stated, "I am thy portion and thine inheritance."[4]

The dual role of the Levites as Sanctuary officiants and as educators is apparent. Less clear, however, is the interrelationship between these roles. If we think in terms of the modern-day synagogue, the roles of officiant and educator are usually distinct. Broadly, the rabbi serves as an educator, while the prayer services will be led by a cantor. Was the Priest—the officiant/educator of old—performing two distinct and separate roles or working in capacities that integrally related to one another?

The blessing to the tribe of Levi at the end of the Book of Deuteronomy provides one approach to this question. Moses blessed the tribe of Levi, saying (Deuteronomy 33:9–10):

[Levi] said of his father and mother,
"I consider them not."
His brothers he disregarded,
Ignored his own children.
Your precepts alone they observed,
And kept Your covenant.
(10) They shall teach Your norms to Jacob
And Your instructions to Israel.
They shall offer You incense to savor
And whole-offerings on Your altar.

Verse 9 lauds the courage displayed by the Levites in the aftermath of the sin of the Golden Calf. When Moses called for the faithful to gather, the tribe of Levi answered the call and at Moses' behest summarily killed three thousand Israelites, in effect "disregarding his brothers, and ignoring his own children." By displaying such devotion, the Levites proved themselves as the appropriate bodies to execute God's most sacred callings—the transmission of His teachings and the service of the Temple. Within this conception of the relationship between the Levites' roles as officiants and educators, their two functions are essentially distinct. Each task was awarded to them in recognition of their devotion, but the tasks are not necessarily related to one another.[5]

Another perspective on the relationship between these two roles of the Levites stems from *Ta'anit* 16a. What is the derivation of the name of the Temple Mount as Mount "Moriah"? One opinion in this tractate maintains that it is called "Moriah" because *hora'ah*—instruction—stems from that point to all of Israel. Rashi comments:[6] "[This] opinion says a mountain from which *hora'ah* goes out—meaning the Torah to all of Israel, 'for out of Zion shall go forth the Torah (Isaiah 2:3)'; 'They shall teach Your norms to Jacob (Deuteronomy 33:10).'" The second verse cited by Rashi is, of course, the blessing to the tribe of Levi to the effect that they will serve as the educators of the Jewish people. The implication of the talmudic passage, according to Rashi, is that this capacity is integrally related to the service of the Temple. It is precisely from their point of service at the Temple that the Levites go out to all of Israel, taking the word of God—the *hora'ah*—with them from Mount "Moriah."

Amplifying on Rashi's understanding of the talmudic passage in Tractate *Ta'anit*, we may posit the relationship between the two capacities as follows: even though the role of the Priest or Levite as Temple officiant is quantitatively dwarfed by his primary role as educator, the Temple nonetheless serves as the foundation point for that role. In the Temple, the Priest or Levite encounters the divine. It is from that encounter that he then takes God's Torah and transmits it to the rest of Israel. The paradigm of chapter 3 of this book, that the Sanctuary perpetuates the experience of Sinai, can again prove illustrative. At

Sinai, Moses (himself a Levite) encountered God in His sacred precincts and then brought the Torah to all of Israel. The Levites reenact that process by serving semiannually in the Temple—the place God chooses to establish His name—and then taking *hora'ah* to all of Israel.

The notion that the Temple represented the educational hub of the country is recognized by the thirteenth-century *Sefer Ha-Chinukh*:

> As every man would take up the tithe of all his cattle and flocks year after year, to the location where the occupation with wisdom and Torah was to be found, namely Jerusalem, where the Sanhedrin were—those who had cognition and understood knowledge. . . . As we know, the second tithe (*ma'aser sheni*) was eaten there. Then, in any event, the owner of the stock would either go there himself to learn Torah or he would send one of his sons there, that he should study there and be sustained by that produce.[7]

The various commandments to bring produce to Jerusalem—to the place God chooses to establish His name—were seen before to highlight the nature of the Temple as a force for social unity. As the Israelites would consume their produce at the Temple, the occasion also took on an educational dimension with exposure to Israel's greatest judges in the Sanhedrin.

JUSTICE

When tracing the role of the Temple in the life of Israel as prescribed in the Bible, attention must be drawn to its function as the focal point of the judiciary system. In modern bureaucracies, the government ministries that are devoted to education and to the administration of justice are distinct. The administration of justice attends to the adjudication of the competing rights of citizens. It has little to do with the endeavor of teaching the young how to function in society, or any of the other aims of a ministry of education. Within the biblical conception, however, the two realms are inextricably bound.

From a biblical perspective, the judicial and educational realms both stem from the same source—the authority of the Torah. When the Levites teach the masses, the course of study is God's laws. When the courts adjudicate, whether it is a question of torts or of ritual law, their criteria are likewise God's laws. Because the Temple represents a perpetuation of Sinai—the point at which God's laws were originally transmitted—the Temple becomes the natural center for the adjudication of those laws.

Let us examine the dynamics that govern the relationship between the judiciary system and the Temple. The primary source for this relationship is Deuteronomy 17:8–10:

> If a case is too baffling for you to decide, be it a controversy over homicide, civil law, or assault—matters of dispute in your courts—*you shall rise and ascend to the place which the Lord your God has chosen*, (9) and come before the levitical priests, or the magistrate in charge at that time, and present your problem. When they have announced to you the verdict in the case, (10) you shall carry out the verdict that is announced to you from the place which the Lord chose, observing scrupulously all their instructions to you.

This passage is the basis for two fundamental concepts concerning the relationship between the judicial system and the Temple: the role of the Levites within this system and the significance of God's presence in the Temple for the execution of proper judgment.

Verse 9 implies that the members of the high court are, in some fashion, Levites. The designation of the Levites as judges is akin to their designation as teachers. The tithing system creates a system of support for the Levites which allows them to devote themselves to the mastery of God's laws. As masters of God's laws, it follows that they should serve, not only as the teachers of those laws, but as their adjudicators as well. The Bible attests to the degree to which the Levites served in this capacity. At the end of his reign, David divided the Levites into units. Of the 38,000 Levites numbered, 6,000 were set aside to be judges and officers (1 Chronicles 23:4).

The notion that judges were to be drawn, largely if not exclusively, from the ranks of the Levites, gains expression in the Oral Law as well. The *Sifrei* to the phrase in Deuteronomy 17:9 "and you shall come before the levitical priests" states: "It is a commandment that the high court contain members who are Priests or Levites. This does not mean, however, that the court is disqualified if it has no such members—for the verse says, 'and you shall come before the levitical priests *or the magistrate in charge at the time.*'"

The second concept that stems from Deuteronomy, chapter 17, pertaining to the relationship between the judicial system and the Temple concerns God's presence in the Temple. As we noted, the Book of Deuteronomy consistently refers to the Temple as the place where God chooses to establish His name. It is no surprise, then, that when the Torah locates the high court in the Temple, in verse 8, it uses this terminology. However, the phrase is repeated redundantly two verses later, in verses 9 and 10: "When they have announced to you the verdict in the case, you shall carry out the verdict that is announced to you *from the place which the Lord chose.*" The repetition of this phrase is instructive—not of the site of the court, but of the nature of its authority. As R. Yehuda Ha-Levi writes in the *Kuzari*,[8] the ruling of the judges of the high court is to be heeded because they are endowed with divine inspiration symbolized by their presence at the site where God's immanence is at its highest degree.

This concept should not be simplistically mistaken. The inspiration that R. Yehuda Ha-Levi mentions is not some power magically invested in the judges by their mere presence in the Temple complex. We posited in the previous chapter that God's presence in the Temple is reflective of the strength of the covenantal bond between God and the Jewish people. Conversely, then, the removal of God's presence from the Temple or the Temple's destruction would reflect a weakening of that bond. This axiom bears directly on the authority of the entire court system. Because the authority of the court is a function of God's inspiration, the court accordingly loses some of its authority when God distances himself from the Jewish people. The very highest power of the Jewish court—indeed, of any court—is the power to render capital decisions. The license to put a man to death is a power associated with God himself, as the One who naturally grants and takes life as He wishes. The high court only has this power when the covenantal bond is strong and the Sanhedrin resides in God's presence in the Chamber of Hewn Stone in the Temple. Basing himself on *Sanhedrin* 52b, Maimonides describes this function as follows: "Capital offenses are adjudicated only when the Temple is standing, and the high court resides in its chamber in the Temple; . . . when the priests offer sacrifices upon the altar, capital cases are heard, providing that the high court is situated in its place."[9]

Until this point, our portrayal of the Temple has emphasized its positive aspects; its power as a multilayered symbol and its multipurpose function within the life of the nation. We saw how the Temple's identity as the place of *hashra'at ha-shekhinah* made it also the national center for social unity, education, and welfare.

The Temple, however, engendered several social ills by the very virtue of its existence. Without losing track of all its symbolic and functional value in the life of the nation, we can only gain a full understanding of the Temple's implications by probing the social problems attendant to its existence.

OVEREXPANSION

As we pointed out in the preceding chapter, the Temple was the culmination of a long historical evolution. It was the climax of processes of change in the religious, social, political, and economic realms. It is quite tempting to read the opening chapters of the Book of Kings and conclude that Solomon's age represented a plateau of bliss and that all the people needed to do now was live off the fat of the land.

However, for all it accomplishments, the age of Solomon was subject to the same social and political dynamics that face any culture in

any era. Nearly every positive social force can bring in its wake un-
desired consequences, and indeed, in our time, critics of capitalism
will point out that while capitalist societies encourage the entre-
preneurial spirit and a healthy work ethic, they often breed greed
and devolve into cultures of materialism. Pluralism, a hallmark of contemporary Western culture, is heralded as the foundation of tolerance
and social stability. Many will say, however, that the pluralism of our
times has begot a culture of moral relativism and an effacement of
values.

By their very nature, the evolutionary processes that culminated
with the Temple's construction were dynamic ones. No society ever
reaches a climax and then stands still. Unless the entire gamut of social
and political forces is carefully and continuously monitored, even a
great society can quickly find itself thrown out of kilter, hurtling down
a dangerous course. The political and social progress of Solomon's age
brought about the Temple's construction, yet it was precisely those
currents that later engendered pitfalls that would plague the Jewish
people for centuries to come.

Less than twenty years after Solomon completed work on the
Temple and palace, the Jewish state found itself torn asunder between
the kingdoms of Judea and Israel. The dissolution of Solomon's empire can be seen as an unintended result of the forces that led to Israel's
greatness and the Temple's construction in the first place.

Perhaps the dominant impression one gets from a reading of Solomon's reign in 1 Kings 5–10 is the incredible scope of his building
projects. The work of constructing the Temple and palace took twenty
years (1 Kings 9:10). Following those achievements, he embarked on
a project to build a citadel and wall around Jerusalem and erected
seven major fortresses across the country and an unspecified number
of garrison towns, chariot towns, and cavalry towns (1 Kings 9:15–19),
which were home base to 1,400 chariots and 12,000 horses (10:26).
To bolster his contacts aboard, Solomon erected a separate palace for
the daughter of Pharaoh in proximity to the Temple (1 Kings 9:24)
and built a fleet of ships at the port of Eilat (1 Kings 9:26).

While these projects manifested Solomon's strength and were undoubtedly recognized by the surrounding nations, they constituted an enormous burden on the country and engendered dramatic changes in the fabric of the society. To build the Temple and palace, Solomon conscripted 30,000 laborers, who were sent to Lebanon in rotating shifts of 10,000 workers on a trimonthly basis (1 Kings 5:27–28). For his later projects, Solomon again conscripted men broadly, to serve as warriors, attendants, officials, and commanders and to man his army and oversee the gargantuan construction efforts (1 Kings 9:22). Solomon's projects may have magnified his greatness, and even God's—but it came at the expense of the people.

The dissolution of Solomon's empire, then, may be analyzed from a social and political perspective. When we look to the arguments put forth by Jeroboam to stir revolt, we can discern their roots in the social upheaval caused by Solomon's expansion. When Solomon's son, Rehoboam, ascended the throne, God turned to Jeroboam the son of Nebat to be the catalyst that would split the kingdom (1 Kings 11:31–39). Jeroboam had directed the work efforts of an entire tribe (1 Kings 11:28) during Solomon's expansion and was keenly aware of the toll it had taken in human terms. His challenge on behalf of the people to Rehoboam highlighted the popular discontent that Solomon's expansion had aroused (1 Kings 12:4): "Your father made our yoke heavy. Now lighten the harsh labor and the heavy yoke which your father laid on us and we will serve you." When Rehoboam rejects the request of the people, they secede. Their statement to Rehoboam is a telling one about the origins of the conflict:

> We have no portion in David
> No share in Jesse's son!
> To your tents, O Israel!
> *Now look to your own House, O David.*

Recall from the previous chapter that the term *bayit*—house—bears multiple connotations. It refers to the Davidic dynasty, but it also refers to a physical structure and may be understood as a scornful rebuke concerning the labor expended in building the king's palace or, as Rashi understood it, a rejection of the Temple—the House the Davidic line built for God. Immediately after the succession, the people executed Adoram, who had been Solomon's chief officer for work projects, thus venting all their anger at the person who most directly symbolized the disruption of life that had been wrought by the expansion.

While Solomon's expansion produced ill effects socially, the period was one of great cultural upheaval as well. Recall that the Temple was universal in its scope; it was a place where gentiles were welcome to pray alongside Jews and a symbol designed to broadcast God's name to the entire world. The cultural ramifications of this openness were that under Solomon, Jerusalem became a cosmopolitan center, which was accessible to peoples from many different cultures. While the notion that the Temple is an ecumenical center for the whole of mankind is a lofty ideal, its implementation on the plane of reality brings with it the risk of cultural dilution. When a host country opens its doors to an influx of foreigners, the danger lurks that foreign influences will overwhelm or corrupt the indigenous host culture. When the Bible depicts Solomon's marriage to the daughter of Pharaoh, it offers no objections. Her entry into the Jewish king's court was a sign of political achievement; this was a royal marriage indicative of a political alliance. With time, though, Solomon became distracted from executing God's will, having been influenced by the women he had married from all the neighboring countries (1 Kings 11:1–4). The influence of foreign culture on the court had repercussions for the nation as a whole. Israel lost its own identity as God's nation, instead falling victim to foreign influence (1 Kings 11:33): "Thus says the Lord, the God of Israel: I am about to tear the kingdom out of Solomon's hands . . . for they have forsaken Me; they have worshipped Ashtoreth the goddess of the Phoenicians, Chemosh the god of Moab, and Milcom the god of the Ammonites."

The lessons of the dissolution of Solomon's empire, then, are two. Ideally, the Temple is to be universal in its scope, but in welcoming the nations of the world to Jerusalem, the Jewish people must post a vigilant watch to maintain the purity and authenticity of Jewish values. The second lesson that emerges is that in the aspiration to build a great society—which is a healthy aspiration in and of itself—the Jewish people must maintain a sense of proportion to safeguard themselves against the social burnout that plagued Israel as a result of Solomon's expansion.

PERSONAL EXPRESSION AND
CENTRALIZED WORSHIP

The ensuing struggle between Jeroboam and Rehoboam highlights another aspect of the socioreligious dynamics of the Temple. We have seen that the Temple served as the site for collective worship at a centralized location, contributing to the cohesiveness of the nation. However, centralized worship also bears inherent difficulties—it deemphasizes individual religious expression. Speaking in the terms of that period, the debate centered around the conditions necessary to offer sacrifices. Could one offer a private sacrifice anywhere and anytime he wished, or was he mandated to bring his sacrifice to the Temple in Jerusalem, where priests would perform the ritual for him?

The answer to this question has a biblical history that begins with the Book of Deuteronomy. Because the Sanctuary is the site where God's presence is most immanent, sacrificial worship is proscribed to within its limits upon entry into the land (Deuteronomy 12:8–14). Private sacrifice must give way to a higher value inherent to centralized worship: the Jew wishing to offer a sacrifice must recognize that God's immanence at the Sanctuary is a function of His covenantal relationship with the *entire* nation of Israel. He approaches God at the Sanctuary, therefore, as a member of the entire Jewish people, and not merely as an individual.

Nonetheless, in numerous episodes throughout the pre-Temple period, we read of righteous individuals who offered sacrifices *outside* the Sanctuary (Judges 13:19, 1 Samuel 9:12, 1 Kings 3:2, 2 Chronicles 1:3). How could these sacrifices be brought outside the site where God's presence is most immanent? The Jerusalem Talmud hints at the answer. Sacrifices were proscribed to within the precincts of the Sanctuary, it explains, only when the Ark of the Covenant resided within the Holy of Holies. When the Ark was outside the Sanctuary, however, private sacrifice—*heter bamot*—was permitted.[10] The Ark could be outside the Sanctuary for a variety of reasons. During war, for example, it was taken to the battlefront. In other periods, the entire institution of the Sanctuary fell into disuse. Under these circumstances, private sacrifice was permitted outside the Sanctuary as well. The mandate that sacrifice be proscribed to the Sanctuary only when the Ark resided within it is well understood. Sacrifice is proscribed to the Sanctuary because it is the site at which God's presence is most immanent. Nonetheless, recall that within the Tabernacle, the Ark was the seat of the divine presence. When the Ark was absent from the Tabernacle, therefore, God's immanence in the Sanctuary was diminished.

These guidelines continued until the erection of the Temple. Recall from the previous chapter the significance of the erection of the Temple by Solomon. God's presence would no longer be associated solely with a vessel such as the Ark, or even with the *structure* of the Sanctuary. Rather, Jerusalem itself became eternally identified as *makom ha-shekhinah*—the site at which God's presence was most immanent. The institution of private sacrifice, therefore, is permanently frowned upon once the Temple is built. Ark or no Ark, Temple or no Temple, God's presence remains a permanent fixture atop Mount Moriah and, therefore, sacrifices may not be offered anywhere else.[11] To offer sacrifices elsewhere would be to deny the immanence of God's presence at Jerusalem.

A chorus emerges in the Book of Kings condemning the monarchs for not abolishing the practice of private sacrifice (1 Kings 15:14, 22:44; 2 Kings 12:4, 14:4, 15:4, 15:35). Interestingly, it is always those kings who were noted for their piety who are reprimanded for this lapse. It would seem that while centralized sacrificial worship was the proper mandate, the earlier practice of private sacrifice had become entrenched. Even the most dedicated of kings proved unable to steer the populace toward the newer and permanent convention of a sacrificial center.

The issue of personal versus collective religious expression comes to a head during the dissolution of Solomon's empire. When Jeroboam came to power, he recognized the potency of the Temple—which was in the hands of his adversary, Rehoboam—as a force that could draw the masses to Jerusalem and undermine his own legitimacy (1 Kings 12:26–27). After consulting with his advisors, he proposed an alternative style of worship that emphasized popular ritual service and greater individual religious expression. He erected two golden calves, one in the territory of Dan and one in Bethel—the northern and southern reaches of his kingdom. In so doing, Jeroboam was rejecting the notion that God resided in one central location (i.e., the Temple). Rather, his actions declared, God was everywhere—from one end of the kingdom to the other. His appeal to the people of his kingdom, "You have been going up to Jerusalem long enough" (12:28), highlighted this point, and it played to the popular desire to participate in the Temple rites. In contrast to the caste system of Temple worship, which allowed only Levites to participate in the services, Jeroboam popularized sacrificial worship by establishing several cult places and appointing priests regardless of their descent (12:31).

While Jeroboam's strategy appealed to popular sentiment, the ensuing events demonstrate that the Bible sides with centralized worship over individual expression. Contained in 2 Chronicles, chapter 13, is a depiction of the civil war between Jeroboam and Abijah (Rehoboam's son, who succeeded the throne of Judah). On the eve of the battle, Abijah made a plea to Jeroboam not to wage war. Abijah's arguments include a lengthy portion devoted to the debate over centralized Temple worship versus popular and individual expression (2 Chronicles 13:9–12):

Did you not banish the priests of the Lord, the sons of Aaron and the Levites, and like the peoples of the land, appoint your own priests? Anyone who offered himself for ordination with a young bull of the herd and seven rams became a priest of no-gods! (10) As for us, the Lord is our God, and we have not forsaken Him. The priests who minister to the Lord are the sons of Aaron, and the Levites are at their tasks. (11) They offer burnt offerings in smoke each morning and each evening, and the aromatic incense, the rows of bread on the pure table; they kindle the golden lampstand with its lamps burning each evening, *for we keep the charge of the Lord our God*, while you have forsaken it. (12) See, God is with us as our chief, and His priests have the trumpets for sounding blasts against you. O Children of Israel, do not fight the Lord God of your fathers, because you will not succeed.

One can detect in verse 11 a tone that appeals to traditionalist values, as if Abijah were saying, "This is the way it has always been done, and therefore it is the only authentic way." Abijah's victory (2 Chronicles 13:15–20) stands as a mandate that Jeroboam was ill advised in his program to decentralize sacrificial worship from Jerusalem and from the hands of the priests.

THE KINGSHIP OF GOD—
KINGSHIP OF THE DAVIDIC KING

An issue that is critical for an understanding of the social and political dynamics surrounding the Temple is that of *kingship*. A dominant theme throughout the Bible is that God is the King of Kings. What, then, is the nature of the kingship of the Davidic king, and in what senses are both man and God "king"?

In biblical as well as contemporary times, the fame and fortune of a nation is often associated with its leadership. Within the biblical scope, this means that when the Israelites are respected, the respect and credit focus on the king. From the perspective of the Bible, of course, the true glory is that of God. However, in the eyes of men—

Israelites and gentiles alike—the hand of God is not miraculously overt, and thus, credit is given to the king. The biblical conception of a king, therefore, is that his kingship, or rule, is but an extension of the rule of the King of Kings, God himself. In this vein, 1 Chronicles 29:23 can state, "Solomon successfully took over *the throne of the Lord* instead of his father David." Clearly, the Bible does not mean to say that Solomon superseded God. Rather, Solomon sat on the throne of God because his kingship was an extension of God's rule. It is in this light that the psalmist declares that God invites the king to sit with him (figuratively speaking), saying, "The Lord said to my lord [i.e., the king], 'Sit at My right hand, while I make your enemies your footstool'" (Psalms 110:1).[12] Credit to the king, therefore, is credit to God.

When David is told, in 2 Samuel 7, that his descendants will rule dynastically, his tribute to God reflects the concept that the glory of the Jewish people and their king is only to be seen as the glory of God himself (2 Samuel 7:22–26):

> You are great indeed, O Lord God! There is none like You and there is no other God but You. . . . And who is like Your people Israel, a unique nation on earth, whom God went and redeemed as His people, winning renown for Himself and doing great and marvelous deeds for them [and] for Your land—[driving out] nations and their gods before Your people, whom You redeemed for Yourself from Egypt. You have established Your people Israel as Your very own people forever; and You, O Lord, have become their God.
>
> And now, O Lord God fulfill Your promise to Your servant and his house forever; and do as You have promised. And may Your name be glorified forever, in that men will say, "The Lord of Hosts is God over Israel; and may the house of your servant David be established before You."

The concept that the kingship of the Davidic king is an extension of the kingship of God sheds great light on the relationship between the Temple and the king. The Temple is a house for the name of God: a structure that symbolizes His acclaim as sovereign in the world. However, God's power and virtue are expressed only through the agency of His people Israel, with the Davidic king leading them. We previously explained that a strong dynasty was a precondition for building the Temple because Israel cannot attain acclaim unless the nation is politically stable. Now we see a second dimension to the integral relationship between the Davidic dynasty and the Temple: it is through David and his descendants that God is accorded glory.

The integral link between the monarchy and the Temple is also exhibited in the account of the Temple's construction in 1 Kings 6:1–7:51. Wedged within the narrative of the erection of the Temple, the Bible depicts the construction of Solomon's palace (1 Kings 7:1–12) and heralds the completion of the Temple, together with the completion of the palace, in 1 Kings 9:1 and 9:10.[13]

Because the king's glory is so integrally linked to that of God, however, a counterbalance is necessary to remind the mortal monarch of the limit of his hegemony. The king is sovereign over the entire country and all its inhabitants—with the exception of one sphere: the Temple. In many of the surrounding cultures, one of the primary roles of the king was to serve in the capacity of high priest to the local deity. In contrast, the Jewish king, who is a descendant of David, can never be the high priest and is forbidden from performing any of the rites of the Temple service.

This dynamic of the relationship between the king and the Temple is seen in the conduct of the Judean king Uzziah. The Bible casts Uzziah as a king of exemplary conduct, a devout leader who was attentive to the prophets of his time (2 Chronicles 26:4–5). In return, his campaigns to fortify the country and establish more secure borders were all successful (2 Chronicles 26:5–10). Following the account of these achievements, the Bible portrays in detail Uzziah's ensuing military buildup. It tells of Uzziah's 2,600 officers, who commanded a standing army of 307,500, and of all the armaments that were allotted to them (2 Chronicles 26:11–15). This buildup, however, had corruptive consequences (2 Chronicles 26:15–21):

His fame spread far, for he was helped wonderfully, and he became strong. (16) When he was strong, he grew so arrogant he acted corruptly: he trespassed against his God by entering the Temple of the Lord to offer incense on the incense altar. (17) The priest Azariah, with a brigade of eighty priests of the Lord, followed him in (18) and confronting King Uzziah said to him, "It is not for you Uzziah, to offer incense to the Lord, but for the Aaronite priests, who have been consecrated to offer incense. Get out of the Sanctuary, for you have trespassed; there will be no glory in it for you from the Lord God." (19) Uzziah, holding the censer and ready to burn incense, got angry; but as he got angry with the priests leprosy broke out on his forehead in front of the priests in the House of the Lord beside the incense altar. (20) When the chief priest Azariah and all the other priests looked at him, his forehead was leprous, so they rushed him out of there; he too made haste to get out, for the Lord had struck him with a plague. (21) King Uzziah was a leper until the day of his death. He lived in isolated quarters as a leper, for he was cut off from the House of the Lord.

What were the motivations that drove Uzziah to violate the sanctity of the Temple by entering its inner precincts? At first blush, it would seem that Uzziah's motivations were no different than those of the other kings who misused the Temple for the purposes of their own glory. In violating the sanctity of the Temple, Uzziah wished to demonstrate that he was above the law. Indeed, there are several indications in the passage that support this reading. His actions, according to verse 15, were motivated by haughtiness in the wake of his great military buildup. It is also evident that Azariah saw personal distinction as the driving force in the king's actions: "Get out of the sanctuary, for you have trespassed; *there will be no glory in it for you* from the Lord God" (verse 18). On the strength of these supports the midrash contends that Uzziah desired for himself the title of High Priest.[14]

An alternative reading is possible, however, that portrays Uzziah in a more favorable light. Recall that the chapter opens by praising Uzziah for his loyalty to God. Even at the moment of infraction, the Bible hints at Uzziah's positive intentions: "he trespassed against *his* God by entering the Temple of the Lord" (verse 16). Uzziah's actions stemmed from devotion—albeit misplaced—to God. He is struck with leprosy—a most fitting punishment, for the primary law pertaining to the leper is that he may not enter the Temple complex. Uzziah unlawfully trespassed the precincts of the Temple. His punishment signals this to him by restricting his access to any part of the Temple complex while in his state of affliction. When he is struck with leprosy, the Bible notes, he rushes to leave the Temple, dutifully obeying the law of the leper, and compliantly suffers his punishment until the end of his life. If, in fact, Uzziah was acting out of misplaced loyalty, what was it that motivated his infraction? A second voice in the midrash plumbs Uzziah's motivations: "He was motivated not for the sake of personal aggrandizement, nor for the sake of personal glory, but for the sake of his Master—for he said to himself, 'It is good that a king should serve the Glorious King.'"[15] In one sense, Uzziah's sentiments were quite appropriate; he seems to have realized that God's glory is a function of how the king is perceived. Acting on this premise, he wished to publicly demonstrate by serving in the Temple that even a powerful sovereign is servile before God. What Uzziah failed to grasp was that the limits of a powerful sovereign are most sharply demonstrated by the law that a king may not serve in the Temple at all.[16]

GOD DESTROYS HIS OWN HOUSE?

Many of the religious and social problems attendant with the Temple's existence arose out of the misconceptions of the kings of the period. Perhaps the greatest risk engendered through the presence of a Temple, however, is one that stems from a misconception of the masses. As a symbol of God's acclaim in the world, the Temple can be misconstrued as inviolate, even during a period of waywardness. This is the focus of Jeremiah 7:3–12:

> Thus said the Lord of Hosts. . . . (4) Don't put your trust in illusions and say, "The Temple of the Lord, the Temple of the Lord, the Temple of the

Lord are these [buildings]." (5) No, if you really mend your ways and your actions . . . (7) then only will I let you dwell in this place. . . . (9) Will you steal and murder and commit adultery and swear falsely, and sacrifice to Ba'al, and follow other gods whom you have not experienced, (10) and then come and stand before Me in this House which bears My name and say, "We are safe"?—[Safe] to do all these abhorrent things! (11) Do you consider this House which bears My name, to be a refuge of thieves? As for Me, I have been watching—declares the Lord. (12) Just go to My place at Shiloh, where I had established My name formerly, and see what I did to it because of the wickedness of My people Israel.

Viewing the Temple through the eyes of Jeremiah, it is difficult for us to comprehend the mentality of his audience. Could they not see the hypocrisy in their actions? Further, it is evident that they were aware they were behaving contrary to God's will. Jeremiah observes that they come to the Temple and declaim, "We are *safe*"—a declaration that implies a consciousness of guilt, a knowledge that offenses have been committed. How, then, could they think that God would be desirous of their visits to the Temple?

The people of Jeremiah's time were well aware that stealing, adultery, and the like were wrong, but they assumed that their actions could be atoned for if followed by the proper remedial action. Their premise was not entirely mistaken. God may look unfavorably at one who willfully commits an infraction. Nonetheless, a wrong committed in one sphere does not cancel out the merit of a right carried out in another. It is meritorious for a person to keep kosher, for example, even if he desecrates the Sabbath.

The value of Temple worship, however, cannot be viewed in such a compartmentalized fashion, where merits and demerits stand in separate columns of the tally sheet. There is a fundamental difference between Temple worship and the fulfillment of other ritual commandments. When a Jew is called upon to fulfill a ritual obligation, he is called upon to *obey*. If he complies, he is considered meritorious, for with regard to that particular commandment, he has done his duty; he has obeyed. The commandment to worship in the Temple, however, is not merely a calling to obey. As Jeremiah expresses it here in verse 10, to worship in the Temple is to come before God in His House. It is a step beyond complying with God's commands—*to come to the Temple is to address God directly.* If a person does not display fidelity toward God or if he acts immorally, then the very basis of his relationship with God will be found wanting. Under these circumstances Temple worship not only loses its meaning; it becomes an abomination, because it is a statement that the individual has the audacity to address God directly in His house at a time when the very core of their relationship has rotted.

By contrast, Jeremiah's audience saw Temple worship, not only as a good deed that would stand unaffected by their transgressions, but as the very key to their salvation. Aware of the significance of Temple worship, they assumed that an appearance in God's house would surely be enough to atone for even the most grievous offenses. Jeremiah's message to them, however, is that one can only contemplate coming to the Temple if the total scope of one's relationship is upright. One can only appear directly before God if the totality of one's relationship with God warrants it.

Jeremiah's admonition highlights a second aspect of the Temple's presence that the people had misconstrued. What perspective stands behind their statement, "the Temple of the Lord, the Temple of the Lord, the Temple of the Lord are these [buildings]"? In the previous chapter, we asserted that the Temple had been built as a symbol of God's acclaim in the world. Jeremiah's audience took the converse to be as true as well: if the acclaim of God in the world was represented by the Temple's construction, then its destruction must symbolize God's defamation. Thus, they reasoned, the Temple could never be destroyed—for why would God ever let His name be so defamed? Taking this one step further, the people of Jeremiah's age assumed that since God's Temple could never be destroyed, Jerusalem was, therefore, inviolable to enemy attack, and that there was no need to heed the prophets, like Jeremiah, who were forecasting impending doom. It was in this spirit that the people confidently declared, "The

Temple of the Lord, the Temple of the Lord, the Temple of the Lord
are these [buildings]."

While Jeremiah's contention that the Temple can be destroyed is
apparent to us, there seems to be some merit in the claims of Jeremiah's
detractors. How can God allow the Temple to be destroyed if that will
lead to a defamation of His name? The Bible offers two approaches to
this problem. Immediately following the Temple's completion, God
appears to Solomon and says (1 Kings 6–9):

> If you and your descendants turn away from Me and do not keep the
> commandments [and] the laws which I have set before you, and go and
> serve other gods and worship them, (7) then I will sweep Israel off the
> land which I gave them; I will reject the House which I have consecrated
> to My name; and Israel will become a proverb and a byword among all
> peoples. (8) And as for this House, once so exalted, everyone passing by
> it shall be appalled and shall hiss. And when they ask, "Why did the Lord
> do thus to the land and to this House?" (9) they shall be told, "It is be-
> cause they forsook the Lord their God who freed them from the land of
> Egypt, and they embraced other Gods and worshipped them and served
> them; therefore the Lord has brought this calamity upon them."

As we saw in chapter 4, a necessary condition for the Temple's con-
struction was that Israel achieve greatness in the eyes of the nations.
Through Israel, God's reputation as sovereign would be proclaimed.
This passage reveals, however, that the converse is not always true—
Israel can be scorned and ridiculed (verse 7), without God's stature
being diminished. Rather, the nations will recognize that God has
destroyed the Temple because Israel was unworthy of having the
Temple in its midst.

Indeed, there have been episodes in history when the nations have
understood Israel's suffering as God's punishment for her sins. However, Israel's punishment has not always been interpreted according
to this formula. In many instances the nations have seen in Israel's
suffering prima facie evidence that Israel's claims of chosenness are

false and that God, as conceived by the Jewish people, does not exist. If the destruction of the Temple can lead not only to Israel's ignominy, but God's as well, we are returned to our point of departure: how could God allow the Temple to be destroyed?

This takes us to a second answer, which requires us to examine some of the basic premises we have established concerning the conditions necessary for the Temple's construction. We have posited that the Temple could only be built once Israel's actions and stature constituted a sanctification of God's name in the world, but what happens when that level of achievement begins to deteriorate? The Book of Kings is a record of how Israel failed to maintain the standards achieved during the time of Solomon, yet the Temple remained standing for over four hundred years. Apparently, then, the standards needed to sustain the Temple's existence were not as high as those needed to warrant its erection.

This was the case because Jeremiah's detractors were, in fact, partially correct in their basic premise about the implications of the Temple's destruction: when the Temple is destroyed, the name of God *does* suffer deprecation. In an age when the Temple stands but Israel sins, the Temple will not be destroyed quickly. Even if the people are no longer worthy of His presence in their midst, God will refrain from destroying the Temple because this would diminish His name among the nations. At a certain point, however, Israel's iniquity becomes so great that her actions inherently constitute a defamation of God's name.

Earlier, we saw that the prophets regarded the relationship between God and Israel as a bond of marriage. The marriage paradigm is useful in understanding why the Temple stood for so long while Israel sinned. Generally, a couple will decide to marry only once each side has become convinced of the high merits of the other. Once married, however, the couple will remain wed in spite of severe strains on the relationship. Had these strains expressed themselves during courtship, the marriage would never have been consummated, but once the marriage exists, separation and divorce will only be a measure of last resort. Only when shared life becomes entirely intolerable will the married couple move to separate.

Within this conception, we can return to the Book of Kings and offer an explanation of why the Temple stood for so long while Israel sinned. Although Israel's actions were wayward, they were not so corrupt as to warrant the Temple's destruction, which would have led to a defamation of God's name. When Israel's very behavior became the cause of God's defamation, however, no further purpose was served by allowing the Temple to stand. Whether the Temple stood or fell, God's name would be defiled by the actions of the Jewish people. Israel's highest covenantal calling is fulfilled when its actions are a tribute to God's name. Conversely, then, its greatest failure occurs when its actions lead to the deprecation of God's name among the nations. Under these conditions, God sees no purpose in the Temple's existence and leads the effort to bring about its destruction (Ezekiel 24:21): "Thus said the Lord God: *I* am going to desecrate My Sanctuary, your pride and glory, the delight of your eyes, and the desire of your heart."

6

Making Sense of Sacrifices

We come now to the feature of the Temple that is the most alien to the contemporary Western mind, the aspect of animal sacrifice.

We have cast the Temple as a recreation of the garden of Eden, as a perpetuation of the Sinai experience, and as a monument to God's sovereignty in the world. However, we have probed its theological and conceptual significance with little discussion of the primary activity that takes place there—the offering of sacrifices. Our probe of the sacrifices has been put off until this point for two reasons. The first is to challenge a popular perception concerning the Temple's function as seen in the liturgy. Virtually all references to the Temple in the traditional prayers portray the primary identity of the Temple as the site of sacrificial worship. By probing the Temple's meaning through five chapters with little mention of the sacrifices, we have attempted to dramatize the conceptual richness of the Temple as a multilayered symbol and to emphasize the Temple's significance independent of its identity as the venue for sacrificial worship.

Treatment of the sacrifices has also been held until this point to highlight the fact that the sacrifices cannot be discussed in isolation.

The theological underpinnings of sacrificial worship and the minutiae of its rites can only be properly understood as components of a
greater conceptual whole. Having laid that conceptual groundwork,
we can now probe the meaning of the sacrifices.

FOUR OBJECTIONS TO ANIMAL SACRIFICE

A discussion of this sort must, first and foremost, address the misgiv-
ings that our society harbors concerning the very notion of animal
sacrifice. Objections to sacrificial worship are raised on four accounts:

1. *The sacrifices seem mechanistic and meaningless.* The point seems
well taken—a cursory reading of the sacrificial codes of Leviticus or
Numbers reveals a litany of detail with precious little explanation of
symbolism or meaning. Take for example, the first sacrifice mentioned
in the Book of Leviticus (1:3–9):

> If his offering is a burnt offering from the herd, he shall make his offering
> a male without blemish. He shall bring it to the entrance of the Tent of
> Meeting, for acceptance in his behalf before the Lord. (4) He shall lay his
> hand upon the head of the burnt offering, that it may be acceptable in his
> behalf, an expiation for him. (5) The bull shall be slaughtered before the
> Lord; and Aaron's sons, the priests, shall offer the blood, dashing the blood
> against all sides of the altar, which is at the entrance of the Tent of Meet-
> ing. (6) The burnt offering shall be flayed and cut up into sections. (7)
> The sons of Aaron the priest shall put fire on the altar and lay out wood
> upon the fire; (8) and Aaron's sons, the priests shall lay out the sections,
> with the head and the suet, on the wood that is on the fire upon the altar.
> (9) Its entrails and legs shall be washed with water, and the priest shall
> turn the whole into smoke on the altar as a burnt offering, an offering by
> fire of pleasing odor to the Lord.

The sacrifices seem meaningless because the Torah provides little
explicit explanation of their symbolism or importance. They seem
mechanistic because the verses emphasize what is *done* when bringing

a sacrifice, and not on what is *thought* or *felt*. On this second point, the more learned reader may say to himself, "Ah, but I know better— 'True sacrifice to God is a contrite spirit' (Psalms 51:19)—the prophets all condemned sacrifice without proper intent and righteousness."[1] While this may defuse the charge that sacrifices are a mechanistic, rather than heartfelt, mode of worship, it only begs the question. If what God is really looking for is a contrite heart and an obedient spirit, why bother with sacrificial worship in the first place? In what way do the sacrifices foster or represent the feelings of contrition and devotion?

2. *The depictions of the sacrifices emphasize gore, not grandeur.* We expect the Bible to stress resplendence and dignity when portraying the environment of the Temple. Indeed, the accounts of the materials and craftsmanship employed in the construction of the Tabernacle (Exodus 35–40) and the Temple (1 Kings 6–7) bear out these characteristics. However, if we return to the passage from Leviticus 1, which is representative of many of the sections that depict the sacrificial services, a very different image emerges. The Temple officiants seem to stand knee-deep in entrails and suet while liberally sloshing blood over the altar. Such accounts of the Temple service constitute an affront to our aesthetic sense and run counter to what we consider a majestic mode of serving God.

3. *The notion that God "smells" and "eats" the sacrifices seems pagan.* The postulate that God is incorporeal is a basic tenet of Jewish belief. Thus, when the Torah describes sacrifices, as in the previous passage, as a source of "a pleasing odor to the Lord" or as God's "bread" or "sustenance" (Leviticus 21:6, 22:25; Numbers 28:2), it is jarring. It smacks of precisely the pagan conception of the gods as corporeal that the Torah repeatedly and emphatically disclaims with respect to God Himself.[2] It is insufficient to dismiss such terminology as anthropomorphic and not literal. Anthropomorphism is a device used to convey an image or idea. When the Bible says that God delivered the Israelites from Egypt with "a mighty hand and an outstretched arm," the anthropomorphism is effective because it portrays God's strength in vivid, human terms. However, what idea or message about God

emerges from statements that He "smells the odors of the sacrifices" or that they constitute His "sustenance"?

4. *It is morally wrong to kill an animal as an expression of religious feeling.* In a society that is increasingly conscious of cruelty to animals and receptive to the view that animals possess rights, the thought that an animal should be slaughtered in the service of God seems anachronistic and immoral. The predominant view in Western society is that killing animals is permissible when a constructive purpose is served, such as providing food or clothing, but that the wanton killing of an animal—swerving one's car to crush a turtle, for example—is considered unnecessary and, hence, immoral. In a post-Temple age spanning nearly two millennia, Jews have learned to give expression to their religious impulses in many ways—meditation, reflection, Torah study, song, prayer, prostration, and the hundreds of religious gestures embodied in the performance of the commandments. Seemingly, then, there is not a religious impulse whose expression is omitted within the present rubric of Jewish religious practice. Under these circumstances, it seems to many, there is no longer any need to kill an animal for the sake of religious expression. Once sacrificial worship is viewed as superfluous and expendable, the killing of an animal for ceremonial purposes begins to appear immoral.

To uncover the meaning of the sacrifices, we are going to focus on the language the Torah uses in its depiction of the sacrificial rites. We will derive the implications of the primary terms and phrases of the sacrificial sections by examining how these terms are employed in other contexts. A fuller understanding of these terms will provide us with a conceptual framework in which to analyze the composite segments of the sacrificial service.

"KORBAN"—NOT "SACRIFICE"

The natural starting point for our investigation is with the precise meaning of *korban*, the Hebrew word for sacrifice. The term *sacrifice*, both in its original Latin meaning and its modern English connotation, bears shades of meaning that belie the implications of the Hebrew term *korban*. The word *sacrifice* is a conjunction of two Latin words, *sacer*—holy—and *facere*—to make. When one offered a sacrifice in the Greco-Roman world, it was viewed as the process of making something holy by offering it to the gods.

With the rise of Christianity, the term *sacrifice* took on a new meaning. Christianity rejected the institution of animal sacrifice on two accounts. First, it contended that God had no use for them and that worship was to be expressed through piety and righteousness. Moreover, Jesus had offered the ultimate sacrifice—his own life—on behalf of mankind, rendering all further sacrifice irrelevant and unnecessary.[3] One aspect of sacrificial worship, however, did appeal to the Church Fathers, and that aspect is dominant in the contemporary meaning of the word *sacrifice*. Sacrifice, in the ancient world, had been perceived as a bilateral process. Sacrifice called upon the owner of the animal to *renounce* his ownership of the animal so that the gods could *receive* the animal in his place. While Christianity shunned the notion of a deity that accepted physical gifts, it embraced the notion of renunciation—for its own sake and even without a recipient—as a religious act. Within the Christian view of the meaning of sacrifice, vows of abstinence and even martyrdom could be described as acts of sacrifice, because they embodied the spirit of abnegation and renunciation.[4]

The connotation that the early Church Fathers gave to the word *sacrifice* has given rise to its secular meaning today, which is synonymous with *forfeiture*. In its modern, nonritual meaning, *sacrifice* implies abnegation by one party, without necessarily implying that another party receives what has been renounced. It is in this sense that we speak of a fallen soldier as one who sacrificed his life, or of an item in a budget that was sacrificed. In each case, the object that was sacrificed was not transferred from one party to another. Rather, the object experienced total negation and nullification.

To some extent, both the original Latin meaning of the word *sacrifice* and its evolved secular use accurately describe aspects of the biblical notion of sacrifice in the Sanctuary. In its original Latin meaning, *sacrifice* meant something that was made holy. Indeed, when an animal is dedicated for the purpose of being offered as a sacrifice, it is referred to as *hekdesh*—something made holy. The secular use of the word *sacrifice*, as nullification, or abnegation, is also appropriate. When an animal is dedicated to be a sacrifice, the owner may no longer use the animal for his personal use—he has renounced his claim to it. The sacrifices of the Temple, then, do bear an element of renunciation, perhaps even in the modern meaning of the word *sacrifice*, as synonymous with forfeiture and nullification.

These connotations of the term *sacrifice* do not, however, strike at the heart of the connotation of the Hebrew word for sacrifice, *korban*. Were the dominant aspect of a sacrifice the fact that it is conferred with *kedushah*, we would expect the Hebrew word for sacrifice to be derived from the root *k.d.sh*. If the renunciation of ownership were the defining feature of a sacrifice, we would expect that the Hebrew word for sacrifice would express limitation and forfeiture.

The Hebrew word *korban* bears none of these undertones. The word *korban* (pl. *korbanot*) comes from the root *k.r.v.*, meaning "close." The word *korban* literally means "that which has been brought close," and it refers to the sacrifice as something that enters into God's presence in the Sanctuary. To offer a sacrifice is termed *le-hakriv korban*—literally, "to bring the sacrifice close." Because the word *korban* bears different connotations than the word *sacrifice*, our discussion will favor the use of the term *korban* or, when need be, *offering*, in place of the term *sacrifice*. In this chapter, we will propose two general interpretations of how the *korbanot*—offerings that are brought close to God—are symbolic of the emotional and spiritual stance of the Jew as he attempts to come closer to his Maker.

SYMBOLS OF PENITENTIAL SPIRIT

The association of the *korbanot* with the process of repentance is a familiar one. However, the vocabulary of sacrificial discourse bears nuances that dramatize the symbolism of the sacrifices. As we stated earlier, our aim is not to analyze the minute laws of each and every *korban*, but rather to examine the primary terms and principal ritual components of the *korbanot*. We begin by examining the sacrificial rite of *semikhah*.

Semikhah—Transferring Identity

The first step in the offering of an animal as a *korban* is the process of *semikhah*—laying hands on the animal's head. The word *semikhah* stems from the infinitive *lismokh*, "to lean." In its sacral context, it refers to the fact that as the owner lays his hands upon the head of the animal, he effectively leans on it. The meaning of this ceremony is highlighted when we examine the practice of *semikhah*, or "leaning," as it appears in other biblical contexts. At the end of his life, Moses asks God to appoint a leader for the people to replace him and God answers (Numbers 27:18–23):

> Single out Joshua son of Nun, an inspired man, and lay your hand (*vesamakhta*) upon him. (19) Have him stand before Elazar the priest, and before the whole community, and commission him in their sight. (20) Invest him with some of your authority, so that the whole Israelite community may obey.... Moses did as the Lord commanded him.... He laid his hands upon him and commissioned him—as the Lord had spoken through Moses.

Moses' act of *semikhah*—leaning—is best understood by observing, simply, what transpires when we lean on something. By leaning on an object or another person, one transfers his weight to another support. His weight is no longer supported by his own frame, but by the object upon which he is leaning. When Moses performed the act of *semikhah* and leaned on Joshua, the transfer of his physical weight represented the transfer of the weight of his title, his responsibility, and his authority. By leaning on Joshua, Moses symbolically demonstrated that his authority now rested, both figuratively and literally, on the person of his lieutenant.

This notion is illustrated in a second instance of *semikhah*—the investiture of the Levites as auxiliary officiants in the Sanctuary. Because it is logistically unfeasible to train the entire nation to perform the detailed rituals of the sacral services, the Levites were consecrated as emissaries of the nation, a collective proxy of the entire Jewish people. Their induction as representatives of the entire nation centers around an act of *semikhah* (Numbers 8:5–11):

> The Lord said to Moses, saying: (6) Take the Levites from among the Israelites. . . . You shall bring the Levites forward before the Tent of Meeting. Assemble the whole Israelite community, (10) and bring the Levites forward before the Lord. Let the Israelites lay their hands (*ve-samkhu*) upon the Levites, (11) and let Aaron designate the Levites before the Lord as a wave offering from the Israelites, that they may perform the service of the Lord.

When the elders of the people "leaned" on the Levites through the act of *semikhah*, it symbolically empowered the Levites to perform the Temple rites on behalf of the entire people.

When a person performs the act of *semikhah* on the head of an animal designated as a *korban*, it is likewise an act of investiture. The owner leans on his designated animal, conferring an element of his identity onto it. It is no coincidence that the *Halakhah* calls for the owner to lean on the animal with both his hands, with all his force.[5] When the owner leans on the animal with the full force of his weight, he is supported by the animal alone. It is this rite that manifests the notion that the animal stands in the place of the owner himself.

The notion that the animal is seen as representative of the owner plays a critical role in the approaches of two medieval commentators concerning the symbolism of the sacrifices. Nachmanides, in his commentary to Leviticus 1:9, offers a general explanation of the *korbanot*:

> He should burn the innards and the kidneys [of the offering] in fire because they are the instruments of thought and desire in the human being. He should burn the legs [of the offering] since they correspond to the

hands and feet of a person, which do all his work. He should sprinkle the blood upon the altar, which is analogous to the blood in his body. All these acts are performed in order that when they are done, a person should realize that he has sinned against God with his body and his soul, and that "his" blood should really be spilled and "his" body burned, were it not for the loving-kindness of the Creator, Who took from him a substitute and a ransom, namely this offering, so that its blood should be in place of his blood, its life in place of his life, and that the chief limbs of the offering should be in place of the chief parts of his body.[6]

The offering of a *korban*, according to Nachmanides, is essentially an execution in effigy. Its purpose is rehabilitative. As he stands before God in the Temple and witnesses his own execution by proxy for sins he committed, the owner of the offering is meant to reach a new awareness of his obligations to God so that his breach will not be repeated.

The thirteenth-century *Sefer Ha-Chinukh* in a different vein also presents the sacrificial animal as a surrogate for the owner in a *korban*. In its comments to the commandment to build a Sanctuary, it states:

The body of a human being and of an animal are similar in every respect. They differ only in that man's body possesses a rational mind, while the animal's does not. Man should know, therefore, that when he sins he acts as if he has no rational mind, and as such, reduces himself to the status of an animal, inasmuch as it is [the rational mind] alone that separates [him from the beast]. He is therefore commanded to take a physical body like his own, and to bring it to the place most suited to foster his rational mind (i.e., the Temple) and to burn it there, and obliterate its every trace, wholly consumed it shall be with no remnant whatever. He does this in the place of his own body to impress upon him the deepest impression that the notion that the body can be divorced from the rational mind has been eradicated and obliterated entirely.[7]

For Nachmanides, the power of the *korban* as a rehabilitative force lies in its symbolism as the recipient of the punishment that the owner should have rightly received. The various rites carried out are to be viewed by the owner as *punitive measures* on his own body. While the

Sefer Ha-Chinukh also sees the animal as representative of the owner, the focus of the equation between man and beast is from a different angle. Man, in his essential being, is distinguished from the animals, and not similar to them. Only when he sins does man become likened to a beast, for his rational mind has been eclipsed. In offering a *korban*, the owner eradicates the element of his sinful persona that exhibited animalism rather than humanity. The rites of the *korbanot*, then, are not symbolically *punitive*, but *purgative and cathartic*.

The Torah enumerates five major categories of *korbanot*, each of which will receive attention in our discussion of the sacrifices. We begin by examining the three categories of *korbanot* that stand as symbols of penitence: *chatat*, *asham*, and *olah*.

Chatat—Purification

The term *chatat* is often translated as "sin-offering," implying that it is derived from the word *cheit*, meaning "sin," or "transgression."[8] The correlation between the word *cheit* and the *korban* that it engenders, a *chatat*, is substantiated by the set of circumstances that most commonly mandate a *korban chatat*: the inadvertent violation of a transgression due to inattention.

In his commentary to Leviticus, R. David Zvi Hoffman challenges the assumption that the term *chatat* is a derivation of the word *cheit*.[9] He points out that there are many circumstances when a *korban chatat* is mandated even though no transgression has been committed: with a woman after childbirth, a leper, one who has experienced an irregular emission, and a person who has come into contact with a corpse.[10] *Chatat*, he claims, comes from the word *le-chatei*—to purify through ablution. *Le-chatei* is the infinitive used in several ritual instances to denote purification through the sprinkling of a liquid. When the Priests are dedicated for service in the Tabernacle, Moses purifies (*vaychatei*) the altar (Leviticus 8:15). When a domicile is found to be halakhically leprous, the priest cleanses, or, purifies (*le-chatei*), it by sprinkling a ritual ablution on the dwelling (Leviticus 14:49). The waters sprinkled upon a person who is ritually impure due to contact with a corpse are referred to as a purification (*chatat*) (Numbers 19:9).[11]

Hoffman's thesis is well understood in the circumstances when a *korban chatat* is brought in the wake of ritual impurity. As we saw, however, the *korban chatat* is also brought following inadvertent transgression. Why must a person bring a *korban chatat*—an act of purification and cleansing—in the wake of a transgression?

The word that the Bible uses to refer to ritual impurity in the legal sense, *tum'ah*, is also used to describe the spiritual defilement of one who has sinned. The closing line of the section forbidding illicit relationships declares, "Do not defile (*ti-tame'u*) yourself in any of those ways" (Leviticus 18:24). Similarly, Ezekiel claims, "they shall bear their punishment . . . so that the House of Israel may never again stray from Me and defile itself (*yi-tame'u*) with all its transgressions" (Ezekiel 14:10–11). The meaning of this spiritual defilement in the wake of a transgression was expressed in our time by the late Rabbi Joseph B. Soloveitchik:

> This impurity makes its mark on the sinner's personality. Sin, as it were, removes the divine halo from one's head, impairing his spiritual integrity. . . . The moment a person sins he lessens his own worth, brings himself down, and becomes spiritually defective, thus foregoing his former status. . . . He is subjected to a complete transformation as his original personality departs, and another one replaces it. This is not a form of punishment, or a fine, and is not imposed in a spirit of anger, wrath or vindictiveness. It is a "metaphysical" corruption of the human personality, of the divine image of man.[12]

When a person transgresses, the *korban chatat* represents a cleansing of the spiritual defilement that his sin has engendered. This is salient in Nachmanides' explanation of the *korban chatat*: "The reason for the offerings for the erring soul is that all sins [even if committed unwittingly] produce a particular 'stain' upon the soul and constitute a blemish thereon, and the soul is only worthy to be received by the countenance of its Creator when it is pure of all sin. It is for this reason that the erring soul brings an offering, through which it becomes worthy of approaching *'unto God who gave it'* (Ecclesiastes 12:7)."[13]

Asham—Indemnity

A second category of *korbanot* brought in the wake of certain transgressions is that of *ashamot*. Once again, the derivation of the name of the *korban* and the use of that root in other contexts can prove illuminating. In a nonsacral context, the term *asham* means an indemnity or a reparation payment.[14] Numbers 5:7 states that if one confesses to a theft, he should return that which he is guilty of having stolen (*ashamo*) and also pay a fine. The word *asham*, then, bears the implication of restoring damages.

It is difficult to delineate in all cases between the violations that engender a *korban chatat* and those that engender a *korban asham*. Nonetheless, the reason why an *asham* is mandated with respect to certain infractions is clear in light of the general definition of the term as a redress of damages done. If a person inadvertently derives personal benefit from resources that had been dedicated to the Temple, a *korban asham* must accompany his restitution (Leviticus 5:14–16). When a person commits any form of larceny—such as outright theft, the failure to return a lost object or an object held for collateral, or purgery that results in undue losses, he is obligated to make restitution and offer a *korban asham*. A nazirite pledges to avoid ritual defilement during the term of his vow to be a nazirite. If he should inadvertently become defiled, he must re-serve the entire period of time; he must repay, as it were, the full term that he had originally pledged. In addition to this restitution of his pledge, he must offer a *korban asham*. The common denominator between these cases is clear. In each of these cases the *korban asham* symbolizes the act of making restitution for damages done.[15] It is important to note that the *korban asham* as symbol of reparation is offered even when the reparations are not being made to God. The *korban asham* that is brought in the wake of larceny is for an offense that is civil, rather than religious, in nature. The fact that a civil offense mandates the offering of a *korban asham* demonstrates that an offense toward another person is an offense against God as well and that restitution to the damaged party must also be followed by symbolic restitution to God.

Olah—Complete Dedication

The *korban chatat* and *korban asham* are obligatory *korbanot*. A third category of *korban*, the *korban olah*, is brought in different circumstances (sometimes obligatory and sometimes out of the volition of the owner). An individual would bring a nonobligatory *korban olah* as expiation for an infraction that did not mandate him to bring a *chatat* or *asham*.[16] A *korban olah* is also offered in conjunction with a *korban chatat* when a ritually impure individual returns to a state of *taharah*— ritual purity.

The word *olah* means "one that rises," meaning, within a sacral context, toward God above. The nature of the *korban olah* is vividly portrayed in the account of the binding of Isaac. When Abraham is commanded to sacrifice his son, he is told to offer Isaac as an *olah* (Genesis 22:2). When Abraham spotted the ram amid the brush, he offered it as an *olah* in his son's stead. God's call to Abraham dramatizes the sense of devotion that we are called upon to feel in our service of God. Our entire being—even our very lives—should be selflessly devoted to God. When an animal is offered as a *korban olah*, it functions in the same way as the ram that was offered in the place of Isaac. It symbolizes our willingness to devote our entire existence to the service of God.

The laws of most *korbanot* call for a portion of the animal to be offered on the altar and a portion to be reserved for the officiating priest. In a *korban olah*, however, no meat is reserved for the attending priest. Rather, the entire flayed body of the animal is offered on the altar. Recall the symbolism of the *korban olah* as portrayed in the account of the binding of Isaac. The *korban olah* stands in the place of its owner as a symbol of selfless and total devotion to God. When a Jew confers his identity onto an animal through the act of *semikhah* and then offers that entire animal as a *korban olah*, it is a vivid symbol of his own dedication to God in the entirety of his essence.

Blood—Symbol of the Soul

Within the popular conception, to offer a sacrifice means to kill an animal and burn it on an altar. One sacrificial rite that is often ignored is that of *zerikat ha-dam*; after collecting the blood as the animal expired, the priest would then sprinkle or splash the blood at different points on the altar, depending on the type of *korban* that was being offered.[17] In this section we examine the elaborate attention that the Torah gives to the blood rites inherent in each and every animal offering.

Once again, we must first probe the meaning or symbolism of blood generally within the Bible and then return to the narrow context of the *korbanot*. There are many biblical prohibitions relating to one's diet, most of which are not capital offenses. The penalty for the consumption of blood, however, is *karet*—spiritual excommunication. The Torah itself offers a glimpse of why the consumption of blood is considered so grievous (Leviticus 17:10–11): "And if any man of the house of Israel or of the strangers who reside among them partakes of any blood, I will set My face against the person who partakes of the blood, and I will cut him off from among his kin. *For the soul of the flesh is in the blood.*" What is the meaning of this equation? What does it mean that we cannot consume the blood of even a kosher animal because the soul of the flesh is in the blood? Nachmanides sees the status of animal blood as possessed with a soul in the following manner:

> [God] permitted man to use their bodies for his benefit and needs . . . and that their soul [i.e., blood] should be used for man's atonement when offering them up before Him, blessed be He, but not to eat it, since one creature possessed of a soul is not to eat another creature with a soul, for all souls belong to God. . . . [An animal has] in a certain sense a real soul.

It therefore has sufficient understanding to avoid harm, and to seek its welfare, and a sense of recognition towards those with whom it is familiar, and love towards them, just as dogs love their masters, and they have a wonderful sense of recognition of the people of their households.

Earlier, we saw within Nachmanides' thinking that when an animal is offered in place of man, a form of transubstantiation is at work; the animal's legs are to be perceived as the owner's legs, the animal's innards as his innards, and so forth. This passage, however, reveals that the surrogacy of the animal's blood for the owner's is of a different nature than the other examples just mentioned. It is not merely that the animal's blood is spilled in place of the owner's. All blood—human or animal—is representative of the soul of that being. Thus, when special detail is accorded to the blood of an animal within the rites of the *korbanot*, it is not merely because the blood of the animal represents the blood of the owner, but because the *soul* of the animal represents the owner's *soul*. This correlation between blood and soul is helpful for understanding other representational uses of the word *blood*. Blood is occasionally described in conjunction with human traits or characteristics. When the Torah wishes to express a person's innocence, it will refer to the person as possessing "clean blood" (Deuteronomy 19:10, 21:8). Ezekiel warns the wayward people that they will be judged with "wrathful blood" (Ezekiel 16:38). The association of human traits with blood is understood when one's blood is symbolically perceived as the seat of his essence.

This correlation between blood and soul is particularly salient for the symbolism of the *korban olah*. The sprinkling of the blood upon the altar within the iconography of the *korban olah* may symbolize, not the forfeiture of the owner's life, but the rededication of his soul in concert with the rest of his being. When a Jew designates an animal as his surrogate through the act of *semikhah* and witnesses the sprinkling of its blood—symbolic of his own essence and character—at the base of the altar, it symbolizes the spirit of penance and the rededication of the person's soul toward the service of God. This understanding of the symbolism of the *korban olah* is exhibited in the midrash as

well. The opening verse of the section that outlines the laws of the
korbanot begins, "When a person brings an offering from amongst you"
(Leviticus 1:2). The plain meaning of the verse calls for a reordering
of the words, "When a person from amongst you brings an offering."
The midrash, however, builds on the fact that the phrase, "from
amongst you," follows, and seemingly modifies, the word *offering*, and
says from God's perspective, "When you voluntarily offer a *korban*
[*olah*] and it is slaughtered and its blood is sprinkled upon the altar, I
consider it as if you have offered your very selves."[18]

Thus far we have examined the meaning of the *korbanot* as symbols of penance and expiation, an approach that later gains promi-
nence in rabbinic thought. This general explanation neatly explains
many aspects of the *korban chatat*, *asham*, and *olah*. This approach to
the *korbanot* as a *total* explanation begins to crumble, however, when
a fourth category of *korbanot*, the *korban shelamim*, is considered. The
korban shelamim is a votive or voluntary offering, and it is never alluded
to within the context of transgression or expiation. The biblical sections that outline its laws frequently refer to it as God's "sustenance,"
or as "a pleasing odor to the Lord," terms that are rarely found in
conjunction with the expiatory *korbanot*. Finally, while the owner
never partakes of the meat of the expiatory *korbanot*, he is required to
do so in abundance when offering a *korban shelamim*. In spite of all
the features that distinguish the *korban shelamim* from its counterparts,
its basic ceremonial components are the same rites that are the framework for the *korbanot* of expiation. Thus, while the rites of *semikhah*,
shechitah (slaughter), and *zerikat ha-dam* were well understood within
the rubric of an expiatory process, the *korban shelamim* presses us to
explain them within a different conceptual framework.

COVENANTAL GESTURES

Perhaps the primary concept that has resurfaced time and again
throughout these chapters has been the significance of the term *cov-*

enant as the basis for a conceptual understanding of the Temple. It is to the term *covenant* that we turn once again to offer a general understanding of the role of the *korbanot* in the Temple.

Let us recall the meaning of the term *kedushah* as defined in chapter 1 of this book. We noted that across the entire Bible, we rarely see an individual described as *kadosh*. Further, we saw that, remarkably, the term *kedushah* was never included in the discourse between God and the patriarchs, and that God first uses it when speaking to Moses at Mount Sinai, at the revelation of the burning bush. An entity endowed with *kedushah*, we said, was set aside via legal prohibitions for the service of God. The appearance of *kedushah* within the affairs of man seemed to be linked to Israel's collective bond with God as a *nation*, and is therefore not mentioned during the earlier period of the patriarchs. The pinnacles of *kedushah* in time and space, the Sabbath and the Temple, respectively, were shown to represent the covenantal bond between God and His people Israel. We then saw in chapter 3 how the encounter between God and Israel, initiated at Sinai, would be perpetuated in the Sanctuary. In chapter 4, the evolution of the Sanctuary from Tabernacle to Temple was traced, and we noted that while the covenant was established at Sinai, it was by its nature dynamic, and that the covenantal bond could wax and wane in relation to Israel's conduct.

Rededicating the Covenant

Since the covenantal bond is dynamic, it necessitates rededication on an ongoing basis. When the Jewish people declared *"na'aseh venishma"*—"we will obey and we will hear"—when offered the Torah at Mount Sinai, it entered all Jews for all time into the covenantal bond. The Sanctuary is the site where this rededication was to be played out.

Now, whenever two parties enter into a pact, there are rites or ceremonies that mark the newly established bond. Thus, when two states establish a pact or treaty, a document may be jointly signed, the national anthems of both countries will be played before their respective flags, and gifts will be exchanged between heads of state as a gesture of national good will.

If, as we have posited, the Temple is the spatial focal point of the covenant between God and the Jewish people, then we would expect the rites performed there to somehow reflect this process of perpetual covenantal celebration and reconsecration. How should this bond be celebrated? What are the customs and conventions that would be appropriate for the celebration of such a pact?

While the term for covenant—*brit*—is often given narrow application to refer to the covenant formed at Sinai, that very same word is often employed in reference to the covenants, or pacts, formed between many different parties throughout the Bible. If we wish, therefore, to understand what gestures would be appropriate to manifest and display the *brit* between God and the Jewish people, we would do well to examine the biblical protocol for other parties entering into a *brit*. When such conventions are examined, an overall theme emerges: many of the principal aspects of the sacral service in the Temple can be understood as generic covenantal gestures that have been given application to the celebration of the covenantal bond between God and the Jewish people.

Zevach—The Covenantal Feast

One of the primary words that appears in the sacrificial sections of the Bible as a synonym for *korban* is the word *zevach*. To determine its precise meaning, we will once again explore the meaning of the word within both its narrow and its broader contexts. Within the lexicon of the sacrificial sections, the word *zevach* most commonly refers to an animal that has been slaughtered for sacrificial purposes.[19] In its more general, nonsacral sense, however, the word *zevach* means a feast centered around the consumption of meat. Thus, when Adonijah attempted to usurp the throne in the waning days of David's rule, he slaughtered (*va-yizbach*) sheep and oxen and made a feast for his supporters (1 Kings 1:9). Upon joining Elijah as his attendant, Elisha took twelve oxen and slaughtered them (*va-yizbachehu*) to prepare a feast for the local people (1 Kings 19:21). The woman of Ein-Dor slaughtered a veal calf (*va-tizbachehu*) to offer Saul a feast as he departed to battle with the Philistines (1 Samuel 28:24).

If *zevach* in its more general context means a feast of meat, then the sacral connotation of *zevach* as a synonym for an animal slaughtered to be a *korban* must relate to this meaning in some way—but in what sense? Who is it that is feasting when a *zevach* is offered as part of the Temple service?

One of the most universal conventions practiced between parties who enter into a bond is that of a shared meal. In contemporary diplomatic protocol this might take the form of a "state dinner"; after the matters of diplomatic substance have been negotiated, the representatives of the two states will typically mark the newly formed bond by sharing in a lavish meal.

In biblical times, the formation of a bond between two parties was ritualized and observed in like fashion. When Abimelech the king of Gerar proposed to Isaac that they establish a *brit*—a pact or treaty of friendship—Isaac affirmed by preparing a feast at which they ate and drank together (Genesis 26:28–30). When Laban proposed to Jacob that they forge a *brit* and part ways amicably, the Bible notes that they marked the event by erecting a monument of stones and sharing a meal (Genesis 31:44–46).[20] After reaching agreement concerning the terms of the pact, Jacob initiated an even larger feast: "Jacob then slaughtered an animal on the Height, and invited his kinsmen to partake of the meal" (Genesis 31:54). The language used here is particularly instructive for the use of the word *zevach* in the sacrificial sections. In Hebrew, the phrase, "Jacob then slaughtered an animal" reads "*va-yizbach Ya'akov zevach*," where the verb, *slaughtered*, and the object, *animal*, both are derivations of the root *z.v.ch*. In commemoration of the *brit* just established with Laban, Jacob prepared a *zevach*—a great banquet of meat to be shared by the parties of the treaty. In the words of thirteenth-century exegete R. David Kimchi: "He made a celebratory feast so that they could all dine together as they took their part of one another, in commemoration and observance of the *brit*."[21]

Bearing in mind the import of the Temple as the covenantal center, we now come to a clearer understanding of why the word *zevach* is synonymous with the word *korban*. The Temple, as we have shown, is the focal point for the commemoration of the *brit*—the covenant between God and the Jewish people. Moreover, we said that in its nature, the covenant is dynamic and is renewed and rejuvenated on an ongoing basis. As the Jewish people continually rededicate themselves as covenantal partners, the notion of *korban* as *zevach* comes into play. The *korbanot* are an expression of a universal convention between partners to a *brit*. As the Jewish people continually rededicate themselves to their Covenantal Partner, they bring *zevachim* to the covenantal center to symbolize through celebratory feasts the rejuvenation of the bond between them. Classically, a true feast included wine. With this in mind, the analogy of *korban* as feast is further buttressed by the requirement that the offering of every *korban* include the presentation of loaves and wine (Numbers 15:1–14).

A God Who Eats?

The understanding of *zevach* as covenantal feast is buttressed by other aspects of the Temple service. At the outset of the chapter, we noted that one aspect of the Temple service that is troubling to some is that it seems pagan; the references to the *korbanot* as "God's bread," or statements that they are "a pleasing odor to God," belie the theological postulate of God's incorporeality. To claim that such language is figurative, we said, would prove a helpful solution only if we could find significance in the nonliteral imagery. The notion of *zevach* as covenantal feast provides that missing link. Indeed, God possesses no physical attributes whatever. When the Torah speaks of His sensual responses to the *korbanot*, however, it highlights the extent to which the *zevach* is a shared experience; man, literally, and God, figuratively, partake of the same feast.

The notion of *zevach* as covenantal feast is also central to an understanding of the site at which the *korbanot* are offered, the altar itself. Were expiation the primary purpose of the *korbanot*, we would expect the Hebrew word for *altar* to reflect that function. We would expect that the altar would be referred to as the *mekhaper*—literally, "that which brings atonement." The Bible instead refers to the altar as the *mizbe'ach*—the site at which the *zevach* is brought. The designation of the altar as *mizbe'ach* underscores the centrality of the identity of the entire institution of *korbanot* as *zevachim*—celebratory feasts.

Feasting at Sinai

Like so much of the imagery present in the Temple, the notion of *zevach* as covenantal feast has its antecedent in the narrative portions of the Sinai Revelation (Exodus 24:3–11):

> Moses went and repeated to the people all the commands of the Lord and all the norms; and all the people answered with one voice, saying, "All the things that the Lord has commanded we will do!" (4) Moses then wrote down all the commandments of the Lord. Early in the morning, he set up an altar at the foot of the mountain, with twelve pillars for the twelve tribes of Israel. (5) He delegated young men among the Israelites, and they offered *olah* offerings and sacrificed young bulls (*va-yizbachu zevachim*) as *shelamim* for the Lord. . . . (7) Then he took the record of the covenant and read it aloud to the people. And they said, "All that the Lord has spoken we will faithfully do. . . . (9) Then Moses and Aaron, Nadab and Abihu, and seventy elders of Israel ascended . . . [and] they beheld God, and they ate and drank.

The interplay between Israel's agreement to the terms of the *brit* and the meal taken to mark that agreement unfold according to the appropriate formula of "business first, celebration later." In verse 3, Moses first informs the people of the laws. Only after the people have expressed their assent does Moses commission the *korbanot* to be offered. Just as parties to a pact will finish their negotiations and then mark the treaty with a shared feast, so, too, Moses secured the people's readiness to enter into the covenant and only then began the preparations for the *korbanot* to be offered.

It is in this context that we can understand the end of the passage—that the elders of Israel ate and drank. Having accepted entry into the *brit*, the elders of Israel ate and drank—in part, presumably, from the *korbanot* they had offered. With God symbolically receiving the meat offered on the altar, and with the elders partaking of the meat as well, a veritable feast was held in which both God and Israel participated in observance of the newly established covenant. It is in this spirit that the thirteenth-century commentary, *Chizkuni*, understood the feast of the elders upon the mount: "[They ate and drank] as is the manner of those that establish a *brit* in that they descended from the mountain with joy, and partook of the *zevachim shelamim* that had been prepared as a *zevach* by their attendants."[22]

The notion that the *zevach* symbolically shared at Sinai was an integral part of the covenantal commencement is echoed in Psalms 50:5, in which God declares: "Bring in My devotees, who made a covenant with Me over a *zevach*." The degree of intimacy between God and the Jewish people, according to this verse, stemmed not only from the fact that a covenant had been formed, but also from the fact that both parties had celebrated it with a *zevach*.

It is worth noting precisely which *korbanot* were offered as the covenantal bond was forged. Verse 5 notes two types of *korbanot* offered—*olot* and *shelamim*. Recall that the *korban olah*, in which the entire animal is offered on the altar, symbolizes the owner's complete dedication to God in his entirety. As the Children of Israel committed themselves to the terms of the covenant, the *korbanot olah* symbolized the totality of their commitment to God.

What of the *korban shelamim*? What is its nature? The passage under study here is particularly instructive for the meaning of the *korban shelamim*, for its mention here marks the first biblical reference to this *korban*. As we noted earlier, the laws of the *korban shelamim* differ in one significant regard from those of the other animal offerings. The *korban shelamim* is the only *korban* where the owner of the animal partakes of the meat; in the case of the *korban olah* the meat is entirely consumed on the altar. When a *korban chatat* or *asham* is offered, sections are reserved for the officiating priests but none are kept for the owners.

The terminology used in conjunction with the *korban shelamim* is a telling sign of its nature. While the word *zevach* can refer to any animal offering, it is most frequently employed in conjunction with the *korban shelamim*. The present case is illustrative of this. After the Torah tells of the *olah* offerings that were brought, it says concerning the *shelamim*, "*va-yizbachu zevachim shelamim*"—literally, "they slaughtered *zevachim* as a *korban shelamim*." More than the *korbanot olah* that were offered, the *korban shelamim* was a *zevach*—a feast of meat.[23] The notion that sharing and bonding are central to the essence of the *korban shelamim* is vividly expressed in a midrash cited by Rashi:[24] "[It is called] *shelamim* because it brings peace (*shalom*) to the *mizbe'ach* [i.e., on God's behalf], to the priests, and to the owner who offered it."

Salt as Symbol

One can witness today at a meal table a widespread custom, whose source lends further support to the conception of the *korbanot* as covenantal feasts. When a meal is commenced, many will sprinkle salt on the bread that initiates the meal. The gaonic source for this custom[25] cites the biblical injunction mandating that salt be added to every animal offering consumed on the *mizbe'ach* (Leviticus 2:13): "You shall season your every offering of a meal with salt; you shall not omit from your meal offering the salt of the covenant with God; with all your offerings you must offer salt." One phrase stands out here as peculiar. What is meant by the expression "you shall not omit from your meal offering the salt of your covenant with God"? As singular as the phrase sounds, the idiom "salt covenant" appears in two other places that are instructive for its meaning here. When God declares to the priests that they will always receive prescribed portions from the offerings of the Temple in place of a lot of ancestral territory in the land of Israel (Numbers 18:19), the covenant of salt reappears: "All the sacred gifts that the Israelites set aside for the Lord I give to you, to your sons, and to the daughters that are with you, as a due for all time. It shall be an *everlasting salt covenant* before the Lord for you and your offspring as well." The everlasting nature of an entity, in this case, God's pledge to the Priests, is characterized through the invocation of the preservative powers of salt. It is in this spirit that the midrash states: "*an everlasting salt covenant*—Just as something is preserved when it is salted, so too this *brit* shall be preserved before me forever."[26]

The final instance of a salt covenant returns us to the previous chapter, where we made mention of the civil war between Jeroboam, king of Israel, and his Judean counterpart Abijah, in the first generation following the split of Solomon's kingdom. One aspect of Abijah's rhetoric in attempting to ward off Jeroboam is germane to our present discussion (2 Chronicles 13:4–5): "Abijah stood on top of Mount Zemaraim in the hill country of Ephraim and said, 'Listen to me Jeroboam and all Israel. (5) Surely you know that the Lord God of Israel gave David kingship over Israel forever—to him and his sons—*by a covenant of salt.*'" Abijah characterizes the promise to David of eternal dynastic rule as a covenant of salt. The invocation of salt as a metaphor for something everlasting was Abijah's way of equating the preservative properties of salt, with the guarantee that the Davidic line would be preserved as well.

When the Torah mandates that salt be sprinkled on each and every *korban* because it is "the salt of the covenant with God," the implications here bear the same meanings as they do in Numbers, chapter 18, and 2 Chronicles, chapter 13. In those passages, salt symbolized the everlasting nature of God's pledges respectively to the priests and to the Davidic line. When the Torah mandates that salt be placed on the *korbanot* to mark the eternal nature of the covenant, it is, first and foremost, a statement about the lasting duration of the covenantal bond. It is also a statement about the very purpose of the *korbanot*.

The *korbanot* are singled out to serve as a vehicle for the symbolism of the salt because they themselves stand as a continuing testimony, as *zevachim*—celebratory feasts—to the ongoing rededication that Israel celebrates with its partner in the covenantal center that is the Temple.

Another source that vindicates the understanding of the *korbanot* as covenantal feasts is the section that outlines the communal *korban olah* offered twice daily in the Sanctuary. Earlier we examined some aspects of the personal *korban olah*, an *olah* brought by an individual out of his own volition. Numbers, chapter 28, mandates that a *korban olah* be offered on behalf of the entire congregation twice daily. Its symbolic function resembles that of the private *korban olah*; its meat is entirely consumed on the *mizbe'ach*, signifying the total dedication of its owner—in this case the entire Jewish people—to the service of God. Concerning this *korban olah*, the Torah says (Numbers 28:1–6):

> The Lord spoke to Moses saying: (2) Command the Israelite people and say to them: Be punctilious in presenting to Me at stated times the offering of food due Me, as offerings by fire of pleasing odor to Me (3). . . . As a perpetual *olah* every day, two yearly lambs without blemish. (4) You shall offer one lamb in the morning, and the other lamb you shall offer at twilight. . . . (6) [This] *perpetual olah* [*is like*] *that offered at Mount Sinai*—an offering by fire of pleasing odor to the Lord.

What is the import of the comparison in verse 6 between the perpetual *olah* and the *olah* of Sinai? The author of the thirteenth-century biblical commentary *Chizkuni* understood it as a desire on God's part to perpetuate the Sinai encounter: "Since you offered [the *olah*] at Sinai, as it is written, '[Moses] delegated young men among the Israelites, and they offered *olah* offerings' (Exodus 24:5), I do not want it to ever be discontinued." Once again, the motif of the *korbanot* as covenantal feasts is exhibited. The *olah* of Sinai, which symbolized Israel's total willingness to devote themselves to the terms of the covenant, emerges in the Temple as a perpetual token of that commitment. When the

Torah attributes to God sensual faculties, it is an anthropomorphism that underscores the fact that God participates in the covenantal feasts. The *korban olah* of Sinai, which is later perpetuated in the Sanctuary, constitutes His sustenance and is a pleasing odor to Him.

To summarize, the *korbanot* reflect two overarching themes: they are expiatory symbols, and they are symbols of covenantal feasting. One *korban* may highlight one of these leitmotifs while another of the categories will more prominently feature the other. The primary symbolism of the *korban chatat* and *korban asham* is in their role as agents of rehabilitation and catalysts of a penitential spirit. They are not referred to as God's sustenance, nor does the owner partake of the meat. Nonetheless, they bear characteristics of a covenantal feast. They are subsumed under the general term *zevach*, are offered together with loaves and wine, and are symbolically synchronized with salt imagery to provide an everlasting testimony to the renewal of the covenant.

The *korban olah* reflects the theme of a covenantal feast in even more pronounced fashion. On the one hand, man does not partake of the *korban olah* at all, for it symbolizes his selfless dedication to God. For precisely this reason, however, it constitutes a figurative feast for God; it is often termed "a pleasing odor before God," while the communal perpetual *korban olah* is termed by God, "My food" (Numbers 28:2). Of all the animal offerings, however, the shared meal par excellence is the *korban* whose very name is mentioned in conjunction with the word *zevach*—the *korban shelamim*.[27] When a *korban shelamim* is offered, the owner partakes of the meat and shares it with others, while God considers it "food" or "sustenance" (Leviticus 3:10) and a pleasing odor.

Breaking Bread with God

Another facet of the Temple service that is elucidated when considered as a gesture of covenantal partnership is the bread of display. Leviticus 24:8 refers to the bread of display as a "*brit* for all time on the part of the Israelites" (Leviticus 24:8). What is implied when the bread of display is termed a *brit*—or covenant—for all time?

In an earlier chapter we discussed some of the vessels of the *kodesh*—the outer chamber of the Sanctuary—and particularly the Altar of Incense. In that same chamber stood the table that held the bread of display. In Hebrew, the nomenclature for "bread of display" is somewhat ambiguous: *lechem ha-panim*, literally, "the bread of faces." R. Abraham Ibn Ezra writes that the meaning of the term can be garnered from the continuation of the verse that first mentions the bread of display: "And on the table you shall set them to be before Me always." He explains that *lechem ha-panim*—the bread of faces—is so called because it stands before, or "faces," God always.[28] Leviticus, chapter 24, delineates the laws of the *lechem ha-panim* and says that twelve loaves should be arranged on the table and replaced each Sabbath in a perpetual sequence. The number twelve immediately brings with it associations of the twelve tribes of Israel. That, coupled with the requirement of weekly replacement, suggests that the loaves are a new, and yet perpetual, repast presented to God by the entire nation of Israel. The motif of an ongoing series of meals in the Temple service is once again exhibited. This motif may also lend insight into the meaning of the designation of the *lechem ha-panim* as "a covenant for all time." It is not that the *lechem ha-panim* itself constitutes a covenant for all time, but that the *lechem ha-panim*, as Hoffman understands it, *symbolizes* the covenant that will last for all time.[29] Parallel to the imagery of the *korbanot* as *zevachim*, the laws of the *lechem ha-panim* allow it, too, to be cast as the ongoing presentation of a meal in recognition and celebration of constant covenantal renewal.

A final note about the meaning of feasting imagery in the Temple rites: the emphasis on the activity of eating as the most hallowed mode of worship is unexpected. We might presume that the highest form of worship would center around the capacities of man that are unique to him. In this vein, meditation or prayer, which utilizes the faculty of speech, would form the core of the most hallowed services. The feasting imagery of the sacrifices, however, highlights eating. Eating is a mundane, animate activity, seemingly removed from the sublime and majestic. How is it, then, that feasting becomes such an elevated activity in the Temple?

Rabbi Joseph B. Soloveitchik sees this emphasis as representative of Judaism's approach to the physicality of man. The entire halakhic system addresses man's corporeal nature and elevates it by calling upon man's drives and inclinations to become vessels of service of the Almighty. Confronting the seeming tension between the act of eating and the subliminal service of God in the Temple, Rabbi Soloveitchik writes,

> "And you shall *eat—before the Lord* your God" (Deuteronomy 14:23)— Could there be two greater opposites than these? Nevertheless! The Halakhah elevated the act of eating before God over that of prayer. The eating of the sacrifices, the eating of the paschal lamb, the eating of the second tithe . . . the eating of the matzah . . . —each one of these is enumerated amongst the 613 biblically mandated commandments. Prayer, however, is considered a biblical mandate only according to the opinion of Maimonides. The injunction to rejoice on the festivals [in our time] . . . is contingent on the eating of meat and the drinking of wine, and this rejoicing is the rejoicing of man before his Master.[30]

To stand before the Almighty in the Temple, says Rabbi Soloveitchik, is to experience the joy of God's nearness. When a man is joyous, he celebrates by feasting. The feasting symbolized by the sacrifices, therefore, is the expression of man's joy at experiencing God's closeness in the Temple.

The Blood Bond of Sinai

As we noted, a primary focus of animal offerings in the Sanctuary was the blood of the animal—its collection and its subsequent sprinkling on the altar. We have already examined the significance of these rites for the *korbanot* of atonement. We saw, variously, that the sprinkling of the blood represented the execution in effigy of the penitent or a rededication of the soul—but what of the *korban shelamim*? Like every other animal offering, the laws of the *korban shelamim* mandate that the blood of the animal be received at slaughter and sprinkled on the *mizbe'ach*. How can this rite be explained without expiatory overtones? Blood, we said, symbolizes a person's soul—his essence, his innermost identity and being. Blood rites, then, can be seen as uniquely evocative symbols of commitment and devotion. When a person commits his devotion to someone, he is not merely agreeing to a certain regimen or to execute certain actions. When someone commits his devotion to another, he commits his entire being—he defines his very essence in terms of the object of his devotion. To commit one's devotion, then, is to precipitate a transformation of the soul. No symbol could more vividly reflect this transformation of the soul than the blood, the substance that symbolizes the soul.

A covenant between two parties represents such a commitment, and in two significant biblical covenants, it is blood that signifies the depth of mutual commitment. In anticipation of the coming redemption, Zechariah calls in God's name to the Jews in exile and proclaims (Zechariah 9:11): "As for you, I shall release your prisoners from the dry pit, *on account of the blood of your covenant*." Both R. David Kimchi and R. Abraham Ibn Ezra suggest that the blood referred to here is the blood that stems from performing the rite of circumcision, the covenant of *milah*. Zechariah's words are, on the one hand, a comment on the reasons for redemption. Salvation will come, says Zechariah, because you maintained your identity and continued to perform the rite of circumcision. Zechariah's prophecy, however, is also a comment on the symbolism of circumcision. Zechariah emphasizes not just the rite of circumcision, but specifically, the blood that flows because of it. The covenant of *milah*, which commemorates God's promise to Abraham to be the God of his descendants and to grant them the land of Canaan, is a covenant, stresses Zechariah, that is consecrated in blood. The deep commitment engendered by this covenant is symbolically heightened by the demonstration that it is in our very blood, and it represents a transformation of our essence as members of the Jewish people.[31]

Once again, the rites of Temple service gain greater meaning when seen against the backdrop of events that transpired at the forging of the covenant at Mount Sinai. The importance of the sprinkling of blood as a symbol of deep devotion and commitment is central to the narrative of the establishment of Israel's covenant with God (Exodus 24:3–8):

> Moses went and repeated to the people all the commands of the Lord and all the norms; and all the people answered with one voice, saying, "All the things that the Lord has commanded we will do!" (4) Moses then wrote down all the commandments of the Lord. Early in the morning, he set up an altar at the foot of the mountain, with twelve pillars for the twelve tribes of Israel. (5) He delegated young men among the Israelites, and they offered *olah* offerings and sacrificed young bulls (*va-yizbachu zevachim*) as *shelamim* for the Lord. (6) Moses took one part of the blood and put in basins, and the other part of the blood he dashed against the altar. (7) Then he took the record of the covenant and read it aloud to the people. And they said, "All that the Lord has spoken we will faithfully do." (8) Moses took the blood and dashed it on the people and said, "This is the blood of the covenant which the Lord now makes with you concerning all these commands."

The mutual commitment engendered by entry into the covenant is consecrated and symbolized by the dashing of the blood. R. Obadiah Seforno in his commentary to Exodus 24:6 sees in the dashing of the blood a bilateral process. The blood is first sprinkled on the altar (verse 6), symbolizing God's commitment, and then on the people after their declaration of willingness to enter into the covenant (verse 8).[32]

The centrality of the dashing of the blood as an inherent part of the covenantal consecration is underscored in the Talmud as well. In *Kereitut* 9a, the Talmud discusses the rites of conversion, and compares the ritual steps taken by a convert to the steps taken by the Jewish people at Mount Sinai: "Rabi says, 'They shall be like your forefathers;

just as your forefathers entered into the covenant through circumcision, ritual immersion, and the presentation of blood, so too, [converts] shall enter into the covenant through circumcision, ritual immersion, and the presentation of blood.'" In his commentary to this passage, Rashi writes that the term "presentation of blood" with reference to the Forefathers alludes to the sprinkling of the blood on the altar. The implication, then, is that just as Israel entered the covenant by sprinkling blood on the altar, in subsequent generations converts are to do the same when they bring a *korban* at the conclusion of the conversion process, thereby entering into the covenantal bond.

We asked earlier what significance the sprinkling of the blood could have outside of an expiatory context. We now have an alternative explanation that accounts for the meaning of *zerikat ha-dam* for both the *korban shelamim* as well as the *korbanot* of expiation. The appearance of the term *zerikat ha-dam* in the Sinai narrative marks the only appearance of this term outside the context of the Temple service. There, both God and the Jewish people dedicated themselves to the covenantal bond. The *zerikat ha-dam* in the Temple, then, bears the same symbolism as the *zerikat ha-dam* of Sinai. When the blood of a *korban*—be it a *korban* of expiation, such as the *chatat* or *asham*, or a votive offering, such as the *shelamim*—is sprinkled on the altar, it represents the owner—whether an individual or the entire house of Israel—and the renewal of the covenantal partnership.

Expiation and Covenant

In this chapter we have offered two general interpretations of the Temple service: that the *korbanot* are founded on an iconography of expiation or, alternatively, that the rites of the Sanctuary are particular applications of gestures universally exhibited between parties entering into a pact. These two models, however, need not be viewed as mutually exclusive. Rather, the role of the Temple service as an expiatory agent can itself be construed as a function of the Temple as covenantal center.

Infractions not only diminish the spiritual stature of the transgressor, they strain the covenantal bond. At the end of Leviticus, God equates disobedience with the breaking of the covenant, "If you do not obey Me and do not observe all these commandments . . . and you break My covenant . . ." (Leviticus 26:14–15). If disobedience is damaging to the covenantal bond, it is only fitting that the rites of atonement—the korbanot—should be performed in the Temple. When the penitent seeks to repair the damage done to the covenantal bond, he goes to the covenantal center to formalize his feelings of contrition through the rites of expiation.

This relationship between expiation and covenant can help us understand a peculiar aspect of Temple theology—the notion of tum'at mikdash—that the Temple becomes defiled because of Israel's sins. This notion is evidenced in the laws concerning child immolation: "And I will set My face against that man and will cut him off from among his people, because he gave of his offspring to Molech and so defiled (tamei) My Sanctuary" (Leviticus 20:3). The same idea is borne out of the section that depicts the service of the High Priest on the Day of Atonement, this time in reference to the korban chatat: "He shall then slaughter the people's goat of korban chatat . . . thus he shall purge the Shrine of the uncleanliness (tum'ot) and transgression of the Israelites, whatever their sins" (Leviticus 16:15–16).[33] It is in this vein, as well, that Jeremiah refers to the abominations of Judah as bringing tum'ah to the Temple (Jeremiah 7:30).

The concept of tum'at mikdash seems peculiar because the Temple, ostensibly, is the seat of the divine presence. Why should Israel's misdeeds defile the abode and the vessels of a perfect God? This is because the Temple is not only God's house, but the focal point of the covenant between God and the Jewish people, and therefore, any breach in the covenant has ramifications for the Temple. When sin taints the covenant, its symbol in the realm of space, the Temple, becomes tainted as well.

The notion that sin taints the covenantal bond, and its symbol, the Temple, can shed light on an important aspect of the korban chatat. Through our investigation of the etymology of the word chatat, we defined the *korban chatat* as a vehicle of ablution. We discussed how sin taints a person's being and how, in the wake of sin, the transgressor is in need of purification. As a symbol of ablution and purification, the stage of *zerikat ha-dam* is more elaborate in the rites of the *korban chatat* than in any of the other *korbanot*. All other *korbanot* call for two acts of sprinkling the blood on the altar. A *korban chatat*, however, requires four such acts—but on who, or what, are these ablutions performed? The cleansing of the leprous domicile, we saw, was achieved by performing the *chitui*—ablution—on the dwelling. Likewise, we saw that the ablutions performed in the purification of someone who had been ritually defiled by contact with a corpse are executed on the body of the defiled person himself. The ablutions of the *korban chatat*, then, should be performed on the entity defiled—the sinner himself. Remarkably, however, the sprinkling of the blood is performed at different points on the altar—but never on the penitent himself!

When the laws of the *korban chatat* call for extra ablutions on the altar, or in the case of a communal *korban chatat* on the curtain of the *kodesh kodashim*, it is because the covenantal center itself has been tainted through the sin that engendered the bringing of the *korban chatat* in the first place. Through the ablutions of the *korban chatat*, not only is the individual restored to his former status, but the covenant between God and Israel emerges restored as well.

A Distinct Form of Commandments

This brings us to our final point concerning the symbolism of the *korbanot*. Why is there a chorus in the prophets about the evil of sacrificial worship when Israel fails to display proper devotion to God? Why are they not independent commandments—like the obligation to don phylacteries or to blow the shofar on Rosh Ha-Shanah—that are to be fulfilled under any circumstances?

If we construe the Temple service as an intricate web of covenantal gestures, the answer becomes quite clear. While the covenant between God and Israel is eternal, Israel's wayward behavior can leave the covenantal bond in severe strain. When Israel's general disposition is one of disobedience, *zevachim*—feasts in celebration of the covenantal bond—are not only inappropriate, they are a mockery. A husband who has been unfaithful to his wife and lives in estrangement from her cannot suddenly bring her a gift as a token of their relationship. To do so would be so out of line with the distance in their relationship that it would only add insult to injury. This is the spirit in which Jeremiah castigates the generation of the destruction of the First Temple (Jeremiah 7:21–23): "Add your *olot* to your other *zevachim* and eat the meat! (22) For when I freed your fathers from the land of Egypt, I did not speak with them or command them concerning the *olah* or *zevach*. (23) But this is what I commanded them: Do My bidding, that I may be your God and you may be My people; walk only in the way that I enjoin upon you, that it may go well with you." When Jeremiah invokes the phrase, "that I may be your God and you may be My people," it is a reworded reference to the terms of the Sinai covenant (Exodus 19:6–7). The point here is not, as some would have it, that Jeremiah was opposed to the institution of sacrificial worship. Sacrifices serve a crucial symbolic function, but only within the proper milieu. Jeremiah's message is that it is a mockery to bring an *olah* when Israel's actions belie the true meaning of this symbol of self-sacrifice to God. There is no point in celebrating the renewal of the covenantal bond through a *zevach*, he says, when the actions of an entire nation constitute a breach of the covenant.

The yearning we express, therefore, in our prayers for a return to sacrificial service is a yearning for the restoration and rejuvenation of the covenantal bond. It is a longing to live in covenantal union with the Almighty, and celebrate the renewal of the covenant on a continuing basis. It is a yearning that is at the center of our prayers each and every New Moon, in the additional service:

> In the service of Thy Holy Temple may we all rejoice and in the songs of Your servant David that are heard in Your City, when they are recited before Your Altar. May You bring them an eternal love *and the covenant of the forefathers may You recall upon the children.* May You bring us to Zion,

Your city, in glad song and to Jerusalem, Your Holy Temple in eternal gladness. *There we shall perform before You our obligated offerings*, the continual offerings according to their order, and the additional offerings according to their law.

THE MORALITY OF ANIMAL SACRIFICE

For all its evocative symbolism, the notion of sacrificial worship is still problematic to many individuals on moral grounds. It is troubling even to some who otherwise fully adopt the received tradition both in tenet and in practice. The moral opposition to animal sacrifice is usually expressed in one of two forms. The first, which represents the majority opinion in Western society, is that the killing and use of animals generally is acceptable. The use of animals for religious worship, however, seems excessive, even cruel. For a second group, comprising strict vegetarians and animal rights advocates, the notion of animal sacrifice constitutes a moral wrong of the highest order and violates their very sense of the relationship between man and the animal world. In this section, we will attempt to address both the more moderate and extreme forms of moral opposition to animal sacrifice.

We will begin by confronting the view that most strongly resists the legitimacy of animal sacrifice—that of the vegetarian and animal rights advocate. This is a minority opinion. Nonetheless, many of its underlying premises have been expressed in more moderate forms by those who are neither vegetarian, nor proponents of animal rights. By examining the most extreme positions, we will be in a position to better understand those that are more moderate and mainstream.

The issue at hand exhibits a classic confrontation between the world-view of traditional religious societies on the one hand, and that of the liberal Western tradition on the other. To understand, therefore, why animal sacrifice seems so morally odious to some, we need first to probe how Western society has evolved in its view of the human–animal relationship generally.

Man and Animal in the Modern World

Our society is in the midst of a moral convulsion as it attempts to resolve the weighty social issues confronting it. The underpinnings of how we face basic societal issues—the meaning of life and death, marriage and family norms—having come under heavy and critical review in recent decades. One area of thought that has undergone revolutionary reexamination in recent decades has been the way in which we view our relationship to the environment generally, and animals specifically.

It is only thirty years or so since the 1962 publication of Rachel Carson's *Silent Spring*, which discussed the effects of the pesticide DDT, spawned the environmental movement. Concerns over contamination from oil drilling, water and air pollution, and depletion of the ozone layer were early areas of concern. Attention to these problems stemmed primarily from utilitarian interests: the belief that it is in our own interest as users of this planet's resources to preserve the habitat as best we can. More recently, the term *biodiversity* has entered into our vocabulary on similar premises. Tropical rain forests should not be denuded, the reasoning goes, because they contain innumerable rare species which could prove invaluable for advances in medicine, material engineering, and the like. This argument is applied, of course, not only to flora, but to fauna as well. We must not tolerate the extinction of any species of animal, for we are the ones who may suffer as a result in the end.

Concomitant with the elevated environmental consciousness due to *utilitarian* concerns, has been an increased concern for nature and animals from *moral conviction* as well. We must preserve the environment in its pristine state, this argument maintains, not merely for our own material benefits, but because it is the ethical thing to do; nature is a force, or entity, that must be *respected*. When environmentalists fought the construction of the Tennessee Valley Authority dam in the 1960s in order to save the Darter snail from extinction, they were not thinking of the potential benefits man could one day harvest from

the little creature. To condone the extinction of a species, they argued—
no matter how insignificant—constituted a moral wrong. The environmental movement quickly spread. 1969 witnessed the creation of
the International Fund for Animal Welfare and the passage in the
United States Congress of the Endangered Species Act. Greenpeace
was founded in Vancouver in 1971.[34]

Arguments from moral conviction over this time have also been
expressed within the movement to prevent cruelty to animals. The
outcry that swelled from the indelible image of an eskimo bludgeon-
ing a fluffy little white-seal pup brought an end to worldwide trade of
that fur. More recently attention has been focused on the practices
of wildlife poachers in Africa and on the mistreatment of veal calves
as they are raised. The popular appeal of these causes has had the result
that in increasing measure we relate to animals in quasi-human, or
anthropic, terms. The pity, or sympathy, that we customarily feel for
a human being in distress is now experienced in greater intensity in
relation to animals as well. The casting of animal protection as animal *welfare*, according to James Jasper and Dorothy Nelkin, conjures
thoughts of *welfare recipients* and invests animals with emotions and
interests.[35]

The dynamic confluence of all these trends has engendered an
evolution in the way we view the human–animal relationship. It is
taken for granted today in Western society that we must view each
and every species as endowed with a quasi-sanctity that morally binds
us to safeguard it. From there, concern for the collective of certain
species has begot concern for the individual member of every species.
The cruel treatment of any animal is viewed as a moral offense, judged
in much the same way as cruelty toward a human being would. The
conceptual convergence of the sanctity of the life of an entire species
on the one hand, and the treatment of individual animals with
anthropic feelings on the other, has spawned in recent years the next
stage in the evolution of man's perception of the human–animal relationship: the notion that animals—no less than humans—are the
bearers of *rights*.

The Evolution of Animal Rights

The leap here is a quantum one. Animals rights activists claim that the use, let alone killing, nay *murder*, of any animal for any reason—medical research included—is immoral. At an international symposium held at an institution no less august than Cambridge University in 1977, 150 signatories endorsed a manifesto entitled, "A Declaration Against Speciesism": "We condemn totally the infliction of suffering upon our brother animals, and the curtailment of their enjoyment, unless it be necessary for their own individual benefit. . . . We believe in the evolutionary and moral kinship of all animals and we declare our belief that all sentient creatures have rights to life, liberty, and the quest for happiness."[36]

What are the ramifications of such a statement? The terms employed here are revealing. By *speciesism*, the animal rights movement means a discriminatory disposition accorded to members of another species (i.e., non–homo sapiens), in the same sense that prejudice toward members of another race is racism, or toward members of another sex is sexism. By *evolutionary kinship*, they mean that humans constitute merely another progression along the evolutionary continuum, and are thus intrinsically no different than animals. The term *moral kinship* implies that the same rights and privileges that we accord one another must be conferred upon the animal kingdom as well.

At the outset of this section we noted that such opinions do not represent the majority opinion in Western society today. However, two examples from the grass roots of popular culture will demonstrate the extent to which its influence is being increasingly felt. The children's tale of *Peter and the Wolf*, concludes with the killing of a wolf in a hunt. In a recent remake, however, the story concludes in a manner more politically correct for the times; the wolf is caught in a hunt—and taken to the zoo. The political correctness of the term *zoo*, however, has also been called into question. Zoo—short for zoological garden—implies a place where living beings are displayed. Animal rights advocates, however, view the term as exploitative because it implies that the animals are being penned for our pleasure. Under pressure, one of the largest zoos in the world, the Bronx Zoo in New York City, has changed its name to the New York Wildlife *Conservation* Society.

This analysis lends some insight into why the issue of animal sacrifice is a particularly troubling issue for many in our society: animals in recent years have attained a fair bit of status. This analysis alone, however, does not provide the full picture of why sacrificial worship is found to be so objectionable. As we stated at the outset of this section, the immorality that animal rights advocates perceive in sacrificial worship can only be understood against the backdrop of our society's perception of the human–animal relationship generally. Our perception of that relationship, then, is not only a function of how we regard the *animal world*. It is also a function of how we appraise *ourselves* as well. When some voices in our society declare that man and beast are equal, we need examine what has transpired in society's estimation of *man* that allows such a contention to be made in the first place.

The Low Estimation of Man in the Modern World

The belief in full kinship between man and beast has not been born in a vacuum, and it is no coincidence that such a theory is taking a foothold at this point in time. Society has historically affirmed the preeminence of man over animal on several grounds. Contentions today that man and beast are equal come in an age when the grounds for that preeminence are being called into question.

Challenges have been leveled against three arguments for man's ascendancy over the animals:

The superiority of his intellect—While man clearly has unsurpassed intellectual faculties, research reveals that some animals also possess a highly developed intellect, and that many are capable of an elaborate system of communication. Animal rights proponents assert that the disparity of intelligence between man and beast is a difference of degree, not of kind, and thus has no moral bearing.

Man is created in God's image—Western culture has become an increasingly secular one. With God relegated to the sidelines of public discourse, the notion that man is created in His image is no longer a fixed feature of our collective consciousness. Arguments, therefore, for man's supremacy on account of his relationship with God no longer provide a counterclaim to the assertions of equality between man and beast.

Data suggests, not surprisingly, that animal rights activists are far less inclined to bear a theistic orientation than is the rest of the populace. According to a 1984 Gallup poll, 90 percent of all Americans professed a belief in God, and 70 percent claimed to belong to a church. A year later, an animal rights periodical, *Animal Agenda*, released a poll of its subscribers in which 65 percent claimed to be atheist or agnostic.[37] This data is understandable. The belief that man *alone* is created in God's image is incommensurate with the conviction that man and beast exist in full ontic kinship.

Man's faculty for moral decisions—While man can uniquely distinguish between right and wrong, recent decades have displayed the moral malaise in which Western man finds himself mired. With many traditional values discarded while moral relativism takes the day, a consensus is emerging in our society that values are merely a matter of subjective, personal preference. When terms like *moral fortitude* are deemed anachronistic in the collective view and when morality is simply a pick-and-choose affair, arguments of man's preeminence on account of his moral faculties are found paltry.

To summarize, questions concerning the morality of sacrificial worship have stemmed in our generation from two concomitant social forces. On the one hand, our society has increasingly placed the animal world in higher esteem. Within this climate, if man wishes to take the life of an animal, he himself must demonstrate that he is of very worthy stature. Yet it is precisely in this day and age that the arguments for man's primacy are found lacking. When examined from the perspective of animal rights activists, the human–animal relationship appears quite changed from its status only three or four decades ago.

Man is not as great as he once was, nor are the animals quite so beastly. Instead, man and animal are full equals.

By identifying the social forces that have spawned the extreme assertions of the animal rights movement, we are now in a position to more clearly delineate and contrast the Torah's position on the human–animal relationship and examine how that bears on the morality of animal sacrifice.

Man and Animal—A Jewish View

It is difficult to make broad pronouncements on the Jewish view of the human–animal relationship, for Judaism's classical sources span a very broad frame of time.[38] Nonetheless, there are three themes that appear consistently across the tradition, and it is the interplay of these three that provides the key for our discussion—the morality of animal sacrifice from a Jewish perspective.

Man is created in the image of God—The Jewish view of the human–animal relationship begins with the postulate that man alone is created in God's image and that he is charged to dominate the natural order (Genesis 1:27–28): "And God created man in His image, in the image of God He created him; male and female He created them. (28) God blessed them and God said to them, 'Be fertile and increase, fill the earth and master it; and rule the fish of the sea, the birds of the sky, and all the living things that creep on earth.'" Medieval thinkers have variously understood man's primacy over the animals to be a function of his intellect. For R. Sa'adia Ga'on, this is manifest in man's capacity for speech, while according to Maimonides and Nachmanides, the significance of man's intellect is that it allows man to recognize and serve God.[39] Put in different terms, man's primacy, says R. Sa'adia Ga'on, is in his power of speech—what we may term the unique capacity to form relationships with his fellow man—while for Maimonides and Nachmanides, man's intellect uniquely allows him to enter into relationship with the Almighty.

Here, then, is the primary point of contention against assertions of equality between man and beast. Animal rights theorists claim that disparities of intellect between humans and animals are differences of degree but not of kind. From a religious perspective, this constitutes *kefirah ba-tov*—ingratitude and lack of appreciation. Man's capacity to express himself in a myriad number of ways and to relate to his fellow man in an according number of fashions does not place him simply a rung or two above the chimp on the evolutionary ladder. That capacity is a reflection of having been made in God's image, and hence, according to R. Sa'adia Ga'on, makes man qualitatively superior to the beast.

Within the thought of Maimonides and Nachmanides, the assertion that man and beast are equal represents nothing less than apostasy. It is an assertion that denigrates the significance of man's very calling—to serve God. Man alone can recognize His creator and serve Him, and he is thus qualitatively supreme over the beast.

Why May Man Use Animals?

Granted, one may claim that man is superior to the beast. Why, however, does that allow him to use animals for his own ends? This privilege may be viewed not merely as a license, but as a mandate. This idea is forcefully argued by Rabbi Joseph Soloveitchik in his landmark article, "The Lonely Man of Faith." The notion that man is created in the image of God, explains Rabbi Soloveitchik, means that man is to aspire to be a creator, even as God is. Just as God has glory because he rules over the universe, so, too, man reaches a state of dignity and majesty when he exercises dominion over the natural order. God's command to man, then, to "fill the earth and master it," is a calling to man to dominate the earth, to build, and to create.[40] Man's purposeful and proper use of animals, then, is not only legitimate, but critical for the attainment of his stature as a creative master of the world. This view stands in bold contrast to the belief that man and beast are in full kinship and that man has no right to use animals for his own ends. Rabbi Soloveitchik's view of man as a creative master may provide a clue as to why there are virtually no sources for vegetarianism in the entire corpus of biblical and talmudic writings. Because it is man's primal calling to have dominion over the natural order, the animal realm is available for his consumption.[41]

While man possesses dominion over the animal world he must act in a responsible fashion. The second and third themes that cut across the entire spectrum of Jewish sources concerning man's relationship to the animals serve to moderate and check the degree of control that man practices over the world of fauna.

Man must respect animals—While man possesses dominion over the animal world, he may not deal with animals in a cruel fashion. Many of the sentiments and opinions held in our society concerning animals can be traced back to biblical origins. The prohibition of tearing a limb from a living beast (Genesis 9:4), the mandate to chase away the mother bird before taking the eggs (Deuteronomy 22:6–7), and the prohibition of preventing an ox from eating by muzzling it while it works the threshing floor all demonstrate the Bible's sensitivity to the mistreatment of animals.

The respect that man must accord to the animals may stem from the notion that they, too, possess a soul. As we saw earlier in our study of the prohibition of eating the blood of an animal, Nachmanides' statement of the stature of the beasts was a statement that one would nearly expect of an animal rights proponent. Animals, he claimed, are possessed with a soul.[42] Like man, they have interests, can experience pain, and have the capacity of love and fealty. While Nachmanides' view is not consistently expressed throughout the tradition, it does represent a predominant medieval view of the stature of the animal world.[43]

While kindness toward animals is a constant theme in classical Jewish sources, the reasons why we are enjoined to behave as such are less clear. Throughout the tradition a tension exists concerning whether these statutes were meant to foster genuine concern for the animal as an end in itself, or whether their design is to foster within man a compassionate spirit so that he will in turn deal with his fellow man in kindness.[44]

Man must recognize that God is the ultimate master of the universe—
Here is a second theme that runs across the entirety of Jewish tradition that places man's dominion of the world in proper check. While
man is mandated to master the universe, he must always recognize
that true dominion is God's alone (Psalms 50:10–11): "For mine is
every animal of the forest, the beasts on a thousand mountains. I know
every bird of the mountains, the creatures of the field are subject to
Me." There are many commandments which require man to demonstrate that his mastery over the natural order is only partial. This idea
is the conceptual backdrop for the various tithes that the Israelite
farmer had to bring.[45] Other laws that pertain particularly to animals,
bear out this notion as well. One may not work his animal on the
Sabbath (Exodus 20:12), nor during the sabbatical year (Leviticus
25:6–7), in recognition that the world ultimately belongs not to man,
but to God.

To summarize, Judaism will agree that man must act with respect
toward animals and may not behave cruelly toward them. But to insist
that man and beast are equal is to deny the role that God bestowed
upon man to emerge as creative master of the world. It is to deny that
man was created in the image of God. We turn now to examine how
animal sacrifice may be viewed not only as morally acceptable, but
even a moral *necessity* for man to maintain a balanced approach in his
relationship to the animal world.

Minchah—Attributing Material Possessions

This brings us to a discussion of the fifth and final category of *korban*.
In the first section of this chapter, we saw three categories of
korbanot—the *chatat*, the *asham*, the *olah*—and cast them as penitential symbols and agents. In the second section, we examined the *korban
shelamim* and the notion of *korbanot* as covenantal gestures. The final
korban of our study is the *korban minchah*. It is the dialectic of man as
master of the world and man as servant of God that animates the
meaning of this *korban*.

Once again, insight into a phrase is garnered by examining its initial use. The first *korban minchah*—indeed, the first *korbanot* of any kind—are the *korbanot minchah* offered by Cain and Abel (Genesis 4:2–4): "Abel became a keeper of sheep, and Cain became a tiller of the soil. (3) In the course of time, Cain brought a *minchah* to the Lord from the fruit of the soil; (4) and Abel, for his part, brought the choicest of the firstlings of his flock. The Lord paid heed to Abel and his *minchah*." The passage is well-known because the ensuing epic of the murder of Abel is shrouded by the paucity of detail in the text. For our purposes, however, the text reveals much about the nature of a *korban minchah*. The term *minchah* commonly means a gift given in recognition of the stature of the recipient. In this spirit, Jacob commanded his emissaries to say to Esau, "[These animals are] Your servant Jacob's; they are a *minchah* sent to my lord Esau" (Genesis 32:18). The passage here bears the same connotation. It opens by informing us that Abel was a shepherd, and Cain, a farmer. From there, the Torah does not immediately tell of their offerings, but tells us that they did so only, *in the course of time* (verse 3). The offerings followed only after a period of time in which each had been working in his respective enterprise and had seen the fruits of his labor. Rather than keeping all of their handiwork, Cain and Abel saw fit to surrender a token part of their produce and credit God with what they had achieved. The *korban minchah*, then, is analogous to the *korban olah*. In an *olah*, one symbolically gives over his *life* to the service of God. In a *minchah*, he symbolizes the dedication to God of his *material possessions*.[46]

Vegetarians and animal rights advocates claim that in killing an animal man wrongly lords over his fellow beings. Through sacrifice, Judaism claims, man demonstrates precisely the opposite. Through sacrifice, man demonstrates that it is God who is the ultimate master of the universe and all that was created in it. It was this impulse that led Abel to take of the choicest of the firstlings of his flock and dedicate it to God.

Opponents of animal sacrifice will challenge: "Why need an animal die, to satisfy *man's* religious impulses?" Theirs is a voice that reverberates, however, only in a culture where man is at the center. The moral essence of their claim is that since man sets the rules of the game, even when worshipping his god, it is unnecessary and unfair to the animal to take its life for such a purpose. Sacrifice within this conception serves *man*.

The Torah, however, functions on the premise that God is at the center, and that He created man, "a little lower than the angels and has crowned him with glory and dignity" (Psalms 8:6). Man, as the creative master of the world, makes use of all that God has created, animals included. Because man has dominion over nature, however, he is required to relinquish control over part of his belongings and to acknowledge that God is ultimately the Master, and not he.

We have shown why the entire thrust of the Jewish tradition must reject the notion of full kinship between man and beast. However, we have yet to respond to other, more moderate forms of opposition to the notion of animal sacrifice. We have yet to respond to the concerns of those who assert that the use of animals for food, clothing, medicine, and so forth, is legitimate but for sacrificial purposes is not.

Here, the morality of animal sacrifice can be understood, nay, *mandated*, on two accounts. The first stems directly from the meaning of the *korban minchah*. It is precisely those who wear leather and eat meat—those who partake of the animal world for their own pleasure—who have the greatest obligation to demonstrate that their dominion over the animal realm is not absolute and that they recognize God's ultimate dominion over this realm as well. The Jew demonstrates this through *korbanot*. When man brings *korbanot* to God's presence in the Temple, all five categories bear an element of the conceptual import of the *korban minchah*. The *korbanot* taken together are comprised of inanimate, vegetative, and animate elements. The *korbanot* constitute a collective *minchah* of all the elements over which the Jew exercises dominion; they are a demonstrative declaration that all the possessions of man the creative master—inanimate, vegetative, and animate—are the true dominion of God Himself.

For those that countenance the general use of animals, sacrifices emerge as morally just on a second account as well. Throughout this chapter we have attempted to demonstrate how the sacrifices are singularly evocative symbols of religious impulses. Within the leitmotif of penitential symbols, the taking of an animal's life uniquely represents a dedication of one's total being to God, and a surrender of life in effigy in the wake of transgression. When seen as covenantal gestures, the sacrifice constitutes a shared feast with God in continual rededication of the covenantal bond initiated at Sinai. The symbolic significance of the sacrifices bears directly on their moral standing. The taking of an animal's life is deemed just for the satisfaction of man's mere physical desires. We can only approve then, of the taking of an animal's life for the loftier purpose of inspiring man's spirit in accordance with God's design.

7

The Lessons of Rebuilding

From the moment when the Jewish people left Mount Sinai until the destruction of the First Temple, one institution has stood at the center of Israel's national life: the Sanctuary. The spiritual crisis wrought by the Temple's destruction was addressed by the prophets Jeremiah and Ezekiel. They set themselves to the task of preparing the Jewish people for a Temple-less world and provided visions of how Israel might return to a state of affairs where the Temple would be rebuilt.

The process of Israel leaving exile and returning to her homeland is especially instructive for our generation. The sole analogy in the annals of our history to the present return of the Jewish people to their land is the return of the exiles from Babylon, two and a half millennia ago. Under what condition was Israel supposed to return to the land? What challenges did the returnees face upon their arrival? What mistakes were made, and how were they corrected?

TWO VISIONS OF THE RETURN

All the prophets who spoke of Israel's demise and the Temple's destruction also detailed Israel's redemption: the exiles would return,
Israel would regain her sovereignty, the Davidic king would return to
power, and the Jewish people would enjoy peace and prosperity. As
part of this vision of the return to Zion, the prophets had also envisioned the rebuilding of the Temple.[1]

Jeremiah and Ezekiel each proffered a different view of how this
redemption would unfold. According to Jeremiah, the redemption
would not come gratuitously. Exile had come because Israel had
sinned. Redemption would come when the Jewish people expressed
genuine desire to return to God. Jeremiah lays this out explicitly
(Jeremiah 29:10–14):

> For thus said the Lord: When seventy years of Babylon are over, I will
> take note of you, and I will fulfill to you My promise of favor—to bring
> you back to this place. . . . (12) When you call Me, and come and pray to
> Me, I will give heed to you. (13) You will search for Me and you will find
> Me, if only you seek Me wholeheartedly. (14) I will be at hand for you—
> declares the Lord—and I will restore your fortunes. And I will gather you
> from all the nations and from all the places to which I have banished you—
> declares the Lord—and I will bring you back to the place from which I
> have exiled you.

The exile would last a minimum of seventy years. After that, God
would redeem the Jewish people if they were worthy of it—"When
you call Me, and come and pray to Me, I will give heed to you" (verse
12). While Jeremiah urged repentance as the road to redemption,
Ezekiel saw redemption as occurring de facto, even if Israel did not
repent (Ezekiel 36:22–24): "Thus said the Lord God: Not for your sake
will I act, O House of Israel, but for My holy name, which you have
caused to be profaned among the nations to which you have come.
. . . (24) I will take you from among the nations and gather you from

all the countries, and I will bring you back to your own land." The scheme of repentance leading to redemption laid down by Jeremiah was the ideal path to be followed. However, even if Israel didn't repent, said Ezekiel, God would redeem the people for the sake of His own name. The redemption, however, would come through pain and tribulation (Ezekiel 20:34–38):

> With a strong hand and outstretched arm and with overflowing fury I will bring you out from the peoples and gather you from the lands where you are scattered. . . . I will enter into judgment with you face to face. . . . I will make you pass under the shepherd's staff and I will bring you into the bond of the covenant. I will remove from you those who rebel and transgress against Me; I will take them out of the countries where they sojourn, but they shall not enter the land of Israel. Then you shall know that I am the Lord.

For both Jeremiah and Ezekiel, the exile was to be rehabilitative and temporary. Either through their merits or otherwise, they would return to the land and the Temple would eventually be rebuilt.

SECOND TABERNACLE AND SECOND TEMPLE

What became of these visions? The redemption depicted in Ezra 1–4 reveals a process that moved forward only haltingly. A total of 42,000 exiles returned to Jerusalem and began work on the foundations of the Temple. After some twenty years, however, the restoration of which the prophets had spoken had barely been realized. Most of the Jews were still in exile, the Jews who had returned were still subjects of the Persian king and were harassed by neighboring tribes, and the Davidic king had not been reanointed. Economic fortunes were poor. The altar had been erected, but persistent attacks from nearby enemies precluded the building of the Temple itself. Why had these circumstances come to pass, and what were their ramifications? The period needs to be analyzed from two perspectives—that of the returnees, whose expectations had gone unfulfilled, and that of the prophets who explained why this had come to pass.

From the prophetic perspective, the degree to which the redemption would unfold was to be a function of Israel's behavior. The returnees, while desirous to return to the land, were derelict in their commitment to God's word. The prophet that declares this message to the returnees themselves is Zechariah (1:3–6):

> Turn back to me—says the Lord of Hosts—and I will turn back to you—said the Lord of Hosts. (4) Do not be like your fathers! For when the earlier prophets called to them, "Thus said the Lord of Hosts: Come, turn back from your evil ways and your evil deeds," they did not obey or give heed to Me—declares the Lord. . . . (6) But the warnings and the decrees with which I charged My servants the prophets overtook your fathers—did they not?—and in the end they had to admit, "The Lord has dealt with us according to our ways and our deeds, just as He purposed."

For the prophets, the full restoration of Israel's grandeur was available, but only on the condition that the people served God fully.[2] If the return had fallen short of expectations, said Zechariah, the blame was to be with those who returned.

The other perspective that is central to Ezra 1–4 is that of the returnees. For the people living through those early years of the return, the downturn of events had particular bearing on their view of the Temple and its reconstruction. All of the prophets, as we noted, had envisioned the rebuilding of the Temple as part of a greater process of restoration. Since none of the other elements of the prophetic vision of the return had unfolded, the Jews concluded that it was not the right time to rebuild the Temple either. Dispirited by the turn of events, and confused about the role the Temple was supposed to play in the new order, they desisted from the work altogether (Ezra 4:24). The opening words of the prophet Haggai recognize the sentiment of the people at this time (Haggai 1:2): "Thus said the Lord of Hosts: These people say, 'The time has not yet come for rebuilding the House of the Lord.'"

It is Haggai who recognizes the people's confusion about the role of the new Temple, and it is Haggai who defines for them its new identity (Haggai 2:3–5):

> Who is there left among you who saw this House in its former splendor? How does it look to you now? It must seem like nothing to you. (4) But be strong, O Zerubbabel—says the Lord—be strong, O high priest Joshua son of Jehozadak; be strong all you people of the land—says the Lord— and act! For I am with you—says the Lord of Hosts. (5) [*Fulfill*] *that over which I forged* [*a covenant*] *with you when you came out of Egypt and My Presence will dwell amongst you.*

The thrust of Haggai's message as the exiles rebuilt the Temple was that the conceptual paradigm for the new Temple was not to be their memory of Solomon's Temple. In verses 1 through 4 Haggai recognizes the returnees' expectation that the new Temple would resemble its predecessor in structure and in status. Haggai then reorients their thinking by hinting at the character of the new Temple in verse 5. What is the import of Haggai's message when he reminds the people of the forging of the covenant at Sinai and of the dwelling of the divine presence in the Tabernacle?

In chapter 3 we demonstrated how the Tabernacle perpetuated the Sinai experience. We noted that the Tabernacle is the Torah's primary focus immediately after the Revelation at Sinai, and that much of its physical structure is modeled after the revelatory elements that comprised the Revelation. In chapter 4 we noted that while the rites and services of the Tabernacle and Temple were essentially identical, each structure was of a fundamentally different character. The Tabernacle, we said, was particularist in scope—its function was to perpetuate the revelational experience of Sinai. The Temple, however, was to be universal in scope—it was to represent God's acclaim throughout the world, and its doors were to be open to gentile worshippers as well.

The initial function of the new Temple, said Haggai, was not to be the crown of a great society and a symbol of God's universally acclaimed glory. Rather, it was to serve as a symbol of a more basic, rudimentary stage. Haggai's exhortation, "[Fulfill] that over which I forged [a covenant] with you when you came out of Egypt and My Presence will dwell amongst you," is significant on two levels. On the most basic level, Haggai is emphasizing that the returnees are embarking on a fresh start, much like the Jews who left Egypt, and that the covenantal bond is being rekindled. On a more subtle level, however, the verse is reminiscent of the Torah's description of the role of the Tabernacle (Exodus 29:46): "And they shall know that I am the Lord their God who brought them out from the land of Egypt that I might abide among them." This allusion has significance for the identity of the new Temple. Haggai may be intonating that the order of the day is to establish the Sanctuary along the parameters of the Tabernacle. The return to the land would initiate the infancy of Israel's newly reestablished bond with God. The rebuilt Sanctuary, therefore, would conceptually reflect the Sanctuary erected in the infancy of Israel's relationship with God in the desert.

The parallel between the new Temple and the Tabernacle would be conceptual, not structural. Structurally, the new Temple would be a free-standing, solid structure, and not a tent, as the Tabernacle had been. The Tabernacle had been the portable, transient site at which the divine presence abode so long as a permanent location had not been established. Once Jerusalem became designated as the eternal site at which God's presence would dwell (Psalms 132:14), there was no longer any need of a portable structure. The revelation at Sinai initiated the covenantal bond. The return from exile to Zion reinitiated that bond. The Tabernacle had served as an exclusively Jewish monument to that bond. The returnees must build a Temple, said Haggai, that would also begin as a solely Jewish monument to the reinitiated covenant.

In this light, Haggai's urging for the Temple to be rebuilt is understandable. God had taken the initiative by revealing Himself at the covenantal encounter at Sinai. In the wake of the exile precipitated by their own misdeeds, the Jewish people would have to take the initiative to restore that bond by rebuilding the Temple. This initiative, said Haggai and Zechariah, would pave the way for Israel to return to her former glory. The rebuilding of the Temple, coupled with true devotion to God would bring Israel prosperity (Haggai 1:7–11, 2:15–19; Zechariah 8:9–12), rebuilt cities (Zechariah 1:16–17), and the reinstatement of the Davidic king (Zechariah 6:13), and would ultimately restore the Temple to its status under Solomon, as a symbol of God's acclaim in the world (Haggai 2:6–9):

> For thus said the Lord of Hosts: In just a little while longer I will shake the heavens and the earth, the sea and the dry land; (7) I will shake all the nations, and the precious things of all the nations shall come [here], and I will fill this House with glory, said the Lord of Hosts. (8) Silver is Mine and Gold is Mine—says the Lord of Hosts. (9) The glory of this latter House shall be greater than that of the former one, said the Lord of Hosts; and in this place I will grant prosperity—declares the Lord of Hosts.

THE BOOK OF ESTHER— ITS SECOND TEMPLE CONTEXT

The Book of Ezra reports that 42,000 Jews returned from exile. The vast majority of the Jewish community, it would seem, remained in Persia. In order to more fully grasp the Bible's perspective on the period of the return from exile, we need to examine the text that addresses the Jewish community of Persia at the time that Jews were already returning to Judea. This text is the Book of Esther.

Generally, the Book of Esther is read as a narrative independent from the rest of the Bible and interpreted as a story that is self-contained, yet Esther may also be understood on the premise that it must be seen integrally with the other books of the Bible that deal with its time period, the books that we have been studying in this chapter. The historical and theological currents described in Ezra, Haggai, and Zechariah create a backdrop for the Book of Esther from which the Second Temple emerges as an underlying theme.

The Book of Esther is a story of a Persian–Jewish encounter, and accordingly, it has two openings; one that introduces its Persian characters and one its Jewish ones. While most of the Book of Esther can be read without reference to other passages in the Bible, both of its "openings" compel the reader to step out of the pages of the Book of Esther and place its account within a broader historical and biblical context. It is the historical context that emerges from the twin openings of the Book of Esther that provides the key for understanding it within its broader biblical context.

The introduction to the Persian setting of the Book of Esther is in 1:1: "It happened in the days of Ahasuerus—that Ahasuerus who reigned over a hundred and twenty seven provinces from India to Nubia." The narrative assumes that we are familiar with this Ahasuerus, and in fact, Ahasuerus is known to us from one other passage, in Ezra 4. The context in which Ahasuerus is mentioned in the Book of Ezra provides background against which the entire drama of the Book of Esther unfolds. Recall that the early returnees were harassed by local tribes who felt threatened by the renewed Jewish presence. Concerning this harassment, we read (Ezra 4:4–7):

Thereupon the people of the land undermined the resolve of the people of Judah, and made them afraid to build. (5) They bribed ministers in order to thwart their plans all the years of King Cyrus of Persia and until the reign of King Darius of Persia. (6) *And in the reign of Ahasuerus, at the start of his reign, they drew up an accusation against the inhabitants of Judah and Jerusalem.* (7) And in the time of Artaxerxes, Bishlam, Mithredath, Tabeel and the rest of their colleagues wrote to King Artaxerxes of Persia a letter written in Aramaic and translated.[3]

Ahasuerus, then, was one of four consecutive Persian kings who heard regular reports about the Jews at Jerusalem and the disturbances they were causing as they built their Temple. While the narrative of Ezra does not specify the accusations leveled against the Jews, the letter to Artaxerxes referred to in verse 7 was perhaps indicative of the kinds of charges being leveled against the Jews throughout the first years after their return from Persia (Ezra 4:12–13): "Be it known to the king that the Jews who came up from you to us have reached Jerusalem and are rebuilding that rebellious and wicked city; they are completing the walls and repairing the foundation. (13) Now be it known to the king that if this city is rebuilt and the walls completed, they will not pay tribute, poll-tax, or land tax, and in the end it will harm the kingdom." Interestingly, the themes here are reminiscent of the charges of sedition that Haman levels against the Jews (Esther 3:8): "There is a certain people scattered and dispersed among the other peoples in all the provinces of your realm, whose laws are different from those of any other people and who do not obey the king's laws; it is not in Your Majesty's interest to tolerate them." Persian subjects in Judea had been warning for years that the Jews were plotting to rebel. Haman's indictments then, fell on royal ears already primed to hear unfavorable reports about the Jews.

The second opening of the Book of Esther introduces its Jewish context and likewise places the story within a broader historical context (Esther 2:5–6): "In the fortress of Shushan lived a Jew by the name of Mordekhai, son of Jair son of Shim'i son of Kish, a Benjaminite. (6) [Kish] had been *exiled* from Jerusalem in the group that was *exiled into exile* along with King Jeconiah of Judah, which had been driven into *exile* by King Nebuchadnezzar of Babylon." Verse 6, which mentions the word *exile* four times, leaves no question as to the nature of the Jews' presence in Persia. They were not there as dual-citizens, nor as a protected class. They were in *exile*.

Taking these two reference points together, Esther's overall biblical context emerges: the Jews of Shushan had remained in exile at a time when other Jews had already returned to Jerusalem and were struggling to rebuild the Temple.

The importance of this backdrop is intensified in light of the fact that one can detect in the narrative of Esther the pervasive interjection of Temple imagery. The setting in which the drama takes place is Shushan. The Book of Esther consistently refers to Shushan as *habirah*, which means "the fortress"(and not "the capital" as it is translated in modern Hebrew). This word is found in only one other context throughout the Bible, and that is with reference to the Temple or its precincts. When David transfers the reigns of power to Solomon he addresses the people in this vein concerning the building of the Temple, "As to my son Solomon, give him a whole heart to observe Your commandments, Your admonitions, and Your laws, and to fulfill them all, and to build this *birah* for which I have made provision" (1 Chronicles 29:19).[4]

The more specified setting of much of the tale of Esther is in the king's palace, and once again we see the broad presence of Temple imagery. The king's palace was decorated with *tekhelet* (blue wool) and *argaman* (purple wool), gold, and silver (Esther 1:6–7), materials that figured prominently in the construction of the Tabernacle (Exodus 25:3–4). The palace, we are told, had an inner court (Esther 4:11) and an outer court (Esther 6:4), as did the Temple (Ezekiel 42:1–3). Anyone who would enter the king's chamber without observing the proper protocol was subject to death (Esther 4:11), reminiscent of the law threatening the High Priest with death if he entered the Holy of Holies—the inner sanctum of the Temple—without the proper preparations (Leviticus 16:2).

What is the meaning of the Temple imagery laced throughout the Book of Esther? The biblical and historical contexts noted above may provide a clue. On a primary level, Esther is a story about heroism and about divine providence. However, all the evidence mentioned above points to a latent theme about the spiritual consequences of life in exile. In exile, God's sovereignty cannot be fully recognized because tribute must be paid to the mortal sovereign of the country.

All the characters in Esther must conduct their affairs while being mindful of how the king will respond. To be sure, Ahasuerus may be understood as a figure easily manipulated and as a buffoon, but this does not absolve his subjects—including Esther and Mordekhai—from paying lip service to his sovereignty and power.

Ideally, a Jew is called upon to serve the King of Kings, a service whose pinnacle is performed in the Temple at Jerusalem. When he lives in exile, however, he must perforce come to the palace—the would-be temple—of a king of flesh and blood, to offer homage and court his continued favor. It is no coincidence that God's name is absent from the entire Book of Esther, while the word *melekh*—king—appears nearly two hundred times. When God's name is entirely omitted, it is not merely because His guiding hand is hidden in the unfolding drama. It is because *God Himself* has been hidden by those who would serve Him. His subjects—even as they observe fasts to elicit His support (Esther 4:16)—perforce become preoccupied with serving the earthly king, with the result that the sovereignty of the King of Kings becomes overshadowed. Under these conditions, God's protective hand becomes concealed and the Jews of Shushan become subject to Haman's persecution. R. Judah Ha-Levi comments in a similar vein that the failure of the prophetic visions to materialize was in part because Jews remained in Persia when they could have returned to Judea:

> It is the sin which kept the divine promise with regard to the Second Temple, viz.: Sing and rejoice, O daughter of Zion (Zechariah 2:10) from being fulfilled. Divine providence was ready to restore everything as it had been at first, if they had willingly consented to return. But only a part was ready to do so, while the majority and the aristocracy remained in Babylon, preferring dependence and slavery, and unwilling to leave their houses and their affairs.[5]

This latent theme sheds light on the book's climax, in Esther, chapter 10. We often think of the conclusion of the Esther story as the steps taken to ensure its commemoration in the following generations, the steps recorded at the very close of chapter 9 (9:30–32): "Dispatches were sent to all the Jews. . . . 'These days of Purim shall be observed at their proper time as Mordekhai the Jew—and now Queen Esther—has obligated them to do.' . . . and Esther's ordinance validating these observances of Purim was recorded in a scroll." In fact, however, this is not the end of the tale. Chapter 10, a three-verse digression that seems to have little to do with the Purim story, constitutes the bottom line (Esther 10:1–3):

> King Ahasuerus imposed tribute on the mainland and the islands. (2) All his mighty and powerful acts, and a full account of the greatness to which the king advanced Mordekhai, are recorded in the annals of the Kings of Media and Persia. (3) For Mordekhai the Jew ranked next to King Ahasuerus and was highly regarded by the Jews and popular with the multitude of his brethren; he sought the good of his people and interceded for the welfare of all his kindred.

Ahasuerus's tax is seemingly irrelevant to the Purim story—if conceived, that is, solely as a story of heroism and hidden providence. If, however, the Book of Esther is also viewed as a comment on life in exile at a time when efforts should have been made to go to Jerusalem and build the Temple, the import of chapter 10 looms large. In several biblical passages, God's sovereignty over the world is depicted as stretching from the land to the islands of the sea (Isaiah 41:5, 42:4, Psalms 97:1). When the narrative of Esther invokes that image with regard to Ahasuerus's capacity to tax, it underscores the notion that in Esther, Ahasuerus's rule is supreme while the rule of God is eclipsed.

The closing note of the Book of Esther is one of irony. On the one hand, the final verse celebrates the triumph of Mordekhai and rewards him for his heroism. On the other, however, it underscores the fact that to provide for his brethren he must intercede to court the favor of a mortal king. Ideally, a Jew should feel dependence only on the King of Kings. When Israel sins and is cast into *exile*—the true status of the Jews of Shushan—it has no choice but to place its dependence on an earthly king of flesh and blood. In essence, the Book of Esther concludes on the same note upon which it began in its twin open- .ings; a king of flesh and blood rules from a false temple. Jews who should be building the new Temple to the King of Kings remain in exile where they must serve a false king in the court of his feigned temple.

The message that emerges from a close reading of the Book of Esther is stressed in the Talmud as well. The "vessels of various designs" used at Ahasuerus's great gala at the outset of the book (1:7), are taken by the Talmud to be the vessels of the Temple,[6] signifying the eclipse at this time of the Temple by the royal palace of Ahasuerus.

The notion that the Jewish presence in Persia at this time was in- appropriate and left them vulnerable to persecution is also echoed in the Talmud. The Jews of Shushan were subjected to Haman's decree of annihilation, says the Talmud, remarkably, for the crime of having absorbed themselves in Ahasuerus's banquet.[7] The punishment here seems unduly harsh relative to the offense. The severity of having partaken in the king's feast, however, is perhaps understood in light of remarks made about the *korbanot* in the previous chapter. Much of the Temple service, we saw, is based on the theme of a shared feast marking the intimate bond between two parties. The Talmud's state- ment here may be that when the Jews of Shushan not only partici- pated, but *absorbed themselves* in Ahasuerus's feast, it was a sign that they had cast their lot with him. In fully accepting him as their sover- eign, the sovereignty of the Almighty had been obscured. Their course of action constituted a shirking of the divine yoke, thus subjecting them to Haman's decree.

CHANUKAH—ITS BIBLICAL ROOTS

The themes outlined here about the meaning of the Second Temple are no less instructive for an understanding of the holiday of Chanu- kah. This may appear striking to some. Our reading of the Esther narrative is plausible only because the Book of Esther relates to the same period as do other books of the Bible. The events of Chanukah, however, took place some 270 years after the final accounts of the Book of Nehemiah. A careful study of the prophecies of Haggai suggests that the events of the Hasmonean period may have constituted the partial realization of earlier prophecies.[8]

As we saw earlier, both Haggai and Zechariah said during the early years of the return that Israel would be able to return to her former glory, and even surpass it. What became of these visions? When were they realized? Ezra, chapter 6, reports the completion of the Temple four years after the prophecies of Haggai and Zechariah, but what of the other elements of Israel's redemption of which the prophets had spoken? Some sixty years after Haggai and Zechariah, Ezra arrives in Jerusalem, and is witness to the rampant intermarriage that has plagued the community. Twenty-five years later, Nehemiah closes the biblical record on a dour note, noting the continued trend of intermarriage and overt desecration of the Sabbath (Nehemiah, chapter 13). The early prophets of the return to Zion foresaw a full restoration of Israel's glory—if it heeded God's word. The reality that Ezra and Nehemiah encountered fell far short of the mark. The earlier visions went unrealized, but perhaps even more significant is that the prophets of those later periods ceased to speak in the terms that the earlier prophets had used. Nowhere in Ezra and Nehemiah do we hear of aspirations toward Israel's renewed stature, peace with its neighbors, or reanointment of the Davidic king, and so forth. The pessimism of the times is summed up by Nehemiah (9:36–37): "Today we are slaves, and the land that You gave our fathers to enjoy its fruit and bounty—here we are slaves on it! On account of our sins it yields its abundant crops to kings whom You have set over us. They rule over our bodies and our beasts as they please, and we are in great distress."

The failure of that generation to fully heed God's word had ramifications for the Temple and its symbolism. Haggai had told the early returnees to commence work on the new Temple even if it wouldn't compare in stature to its predecessor. That stage, however, was only to be a temporary one. Haggai fully expected Israel to mature, and for the stature of the Temple to evolve consequently. Because Israel failed to heed God's word, the Temple never returned to its status as a symbol of God's acclaim in the world, as Haggai had envisioned (Haggai 1:6–9). It remained, instead, a sacrificial center in which the Jews worshiped their God.

The visions of the prophets of Israel's redemption went unfulfilled in their own day, and indeed, during the remainder of the period of the biblical record. Were these prophets mistaken, then?

The answer rests on an understanding of the very nature of prophecy. A distinction must be made between *prophecy* and *prediction*. A prediction can ultimately be shown to have been correct or incorrect, once the time frame of the prediction has passed. When a prophet presents a vision of what the future holds, however, there is no limited time frame in which that prophecy must take place. The prophet's vision represents an opportunity which his own generation can capitalize on by following the prophet's admonitions. Visions of the future that go unrealized in one generation can be fulfilled in a later one. It is for this reason that the words of the prophets are timely for our generation, indeed, for every generation. The prophets that spoke of Israel's redemption were speaking first and foremost of the opportunities that existed in their own times. But since their own generations did not warrant the fulfillment of these prophecies, Jews of subsequent generations can and should read them as potentially applying to themselves. Had Israel been worthy, the prophecies of Haggai and Zechariah would have become actuality in their own generation. The reality witnessed by Ezra and Nehemiah, however, did not warrant the fulfillment of these visions.

This takes us to the Maccabees. Looking forward from the time of Haggai, the next period of revival is that of the Hasmonean revolt in 164 B.C.E. Here we can see some evidence of the fulfillment of these prophecies. To be sure, the *full* restoration of which the prophets had spoken was not realized in that period either. But great armies had been defeated. Jewish sovereignty over Judah and Jerusalem had been achieved for the first time since the Babylonian exile.

Seen in this light, it is not surprising that Rashi writes that the prophecies of Haggai were ultimately fulfilled during this period. Haggai, as we saw earlier, had presaged an age when retribution would be measured on the nations of the earth, and glory returned to the Temple (Haggai 2:6–7): "For thus said the Lord of Hosts: In just a little while longer I will shake the heavens and the earth, the sea and the dry land; (7) I will shake all the nations and the precious things of all the nations shall come [here], and I will fill this House with glory, said the Lord of Hosts." In his commentary to the end of verse 6, Rashi writes "[this refers] to the miracles that were performed on behalf of the Hasmoneans." Rashi's comments throw light on an interesting correlation between the date and circumstances surrounding Haggai's final prophecies—the 24th of *Kislev*, and the date and circumstances commemorated by the holiday of Chanukah.

Recall the setting in which Haggai delivered his prophecy to the inhabitants of Jerusalem. The Jews had returned some twenty years earlier at the behest of Cyrus king of Persia. Due to harsh economic conditions and disputes with the neighboring peoples, they desisted from working on the Temple. Haggai's initial exhortations to move forward with the work on the Temple, the Bible records, were given on the first day of the sixth month (1 *Elul*) of the second year of Darius's reign (Haggai 1:1). The leaders of the Jewish community of Jerusalem responded affirmatively, and began preparations (Haggai 1:14). Three months later, on the twenty-fourth day of the ninth month, 24 *Kislev*, the construction began. On this day, Haggai offered two prophecies concerning Israel's future as the work on the Temple continued and the sacrificial rites commenced. The first spoke of the economic impact to be felt as Israel followed God's desire that the Temple be rebuilt (Haggai 1:15–19):

And now take thought, *from this day forward*: So long as no stone had been laid upon another in the House of the Lord, (16) if one came to a heap of twenty measures (of grain) it would yield only ten; and if one came to a wine vat to skim off fifty measures the press would yield only twenty. (17) I struck you—all the works of your hands—with blight and mildew and hail, but you did not return to Me—declares the Lord. (18) Take note *from this day forward—from the twenty fourth day of the ninth month, from the day when the foundation was laid for the Lord's Temple*—take note (19) while the seed is still in the granary, and the vine, fig tree, pomegranate, and olive tree have not yet borne fruit. *From this day on* I will send blessings.

The 24th of *Kislev* emerges as a pivotal date. Recall from our discussion earlier in this chapter that it was critical for Israel to endeavor in rebuilding the Temple; the return to Zion heralded a renewal of the covenantal bond, whose symbol was to be the new Temple. By toiling to rebuild the Temple, the people would be exhibiting their desire to return to God. The beginning of the Temple's construction, then, was a landmark event in that process, and was the occasion at which Haggai could spur the people onward with their work, with visions of things to come.

Haggai's first proclamation rings with a vision of a revitalized economy. Times were hard for you, says Haggai, "so long as no stone had been laid upon another in the House of the Lord." However, now that you have reached the milestone of completing the Temple's foundations and will now be able to perform the Temple service, your fortunes will change. From this day—the 24th of *Kislev*—onward, your produce will increase.

A second prophecy was offered by Haggai on that same day that saw in the resumption of the sacral rites a political revival as well (1:20–23):

And the word of the Lord came to Haggai a second time on *the twenty fourth day of the month*: (21) Speak to Zerubbabel the governor of Judah: I am going to shake heaven and earth. (22) And I will overturn the thrones of kingdoms and destroy the might of the kingdoms of the nations. I will overturn chariots and their drivers; horses and their riders shall fall, each by the sword of his fellow. (23) On that day—declares the Lord of Hosts—

I will take you, O My servant Zerubbabel son of Shealtiel—declares the
Lord—and make you as a signet; for I have chosen you—declares the Lord
of Hosts.

Haggai's second prophecy on the 24th of *Kislev* was a vision of Israel's
political maturation. Now you are still under foreign dominion, says
Haggai. However, should you continue in the path that you have
taken, of following in God's ways and continuing work on the Temple,
that will change. Great armies will fall, Israel will regain her independence, and Zerubbabel—a descendant of David—will be anointed as
king.

Haggai's final recorded prophecies occurred on the 24th of *Kislev*,
a date representing a turning point in the eyes of the prophet, because
on that date Israel had completed the foundations of the Temple. From
that day on, Haggai had said, Israel would know prosperity. From that
day on, the prophecy had been given that kings would be dethroned,
armies defeated, and the Davidic king reanointed.

It is perhaps not a mere coincidence that the commemoration of
the rededication of the Temple begins on the next day, the 25th of
Kislev. The Fourth Book of Maccabees tells us that the Hasmoneans
chose that date because it was the anniversary of the Temple's defilement three years earlier.[9] From their perspective the date was important because of what had transpired on that date in their own age.
However, looking at the prophecies of Haggai and looking at what
transpired in the time of the Hasmoneans, perhaps we can see a guiding hand in history.

In consonance with Rashi's comment linking those prophecies with
these events, we might add that the timing of the commemoration
backs his contention. From God's perspective the rededication of the
Temple occurs on the 25th of *Kislev* because the events of that time
represent the fulfillment of Haggai's prophecies. Just as the Temple
had been rededicated following the return to Zion on the 25th of *Kislev*
hundreds of year earlier, so too it would be now.[10] Haggai had said on
the 24th of *Kislev*, armies would fall and the Davidic king would be

restored. The victories in that generation and the newly won independence may have signaled the harbinger of Haggai's prophecies, which he had said would begin to be fulfilled "from this day—the twenty-fourth day of the ninth month on."

It may be that the commemoration date for the Maccabean victory is unrelated to the significance of that date within the prophecies. What is certain, however, is that Haggai's prophecies, which did not come to fruition in his time, began to be fulfilled in the time of the Hasmoneans, as Rashi noted. Their fulfillment, however, was not completed in the time of the Hasmoneans either. The vision of Haggai and Zechariah and the other prophets of Israel's restoration have lay entirely unfulfilled ever since the time of the Maccabees. After two thousand years of living as subjects to other rulers, it is only in our time that the prophecies of the ingathering of the exiles, and the return of Jewish sovereignty to the land, are again, partially, being concretized on the plane of reality.

Epilogue
The Temple Today

Thus far, we have traced the development of the Temple as a rich and central theme in biblical and rabbinic thought. Taking the lessons of Judaism's most ancient sources, we turn now to the present and the future. This chapter will probe two issues. The Temple was the central institution of Jewish life while it stood. The rabbis of the Talmud responded to its destruction in various ways—ways that have left a heavy imprint on our view of the Temple today. The first issue we will probe, then, is the rabbinic response to the Temple's destruction and its impact on our own perception of the Temple.

Beyond exploring how the present age relates to the Temple, we will also probe the ways in which the Temple sheds light on the present age. One of the primary themes of our study has been the relationship between the Temple and national sovereignty. In an age of national rebirth, the Temple has much to teach us about the currents of the times.

RELATING TO THE TEMPLE
IN A POST-TEMPLE AGE

The rabbinic prescription for an age when the Temple no longer stands reflects a dialectical tension—two strategies that seem mutually exclusive, and yet must be seen as complementary. Keenly aware of the Temple's centrality to the corpus of Jewish law and Jewish thought, and indeed to the essence of Judaism itself, the rabbis enacted a wide range of laws to perpetuate the memory of the Temple and its rites. Conversely, however, the sages who lived immediately after the destruction realized that the Temple's destruction had left the nation deprived of its central social and religious institution and that emphasis must be shifted to other existing institutions and precepts to fill the void left by the Temple's destruction. Otherwise, Judaism itself might wither as it fought to retain the centrality of an institution that would be only an ever-fading memory.[1]

What were the particulars of this dual agenda? We begin by examining the measures taken by the rabbis of the Talmud to perpetuate the memory of the Temple and its centrality. The sense of the Temple's centrality within Jewish life was to be preserved through two different approaches. The first was to institute the simulation of certain Temple rites, while the second was to legislate customs that would perpetuate a sense of loss for as long as the Temple lay in ruins.

Simulating the Temple Experience

One way to sustain the feeling of an earlier experience is not merely to recall it mentally or even orally, but to reenact or simulate it. The primary vehicle that simulated the Temple, already during the Babylonian exile, and to an even greater extent following the destruction of the Second Temple, has been the synagogue. In what manner does the synagogue assume the role in Jewish life formerly assumed by the Temple?

Following the destruction of the First Temple, God told Ezekiel that although the people would be scattered throughout the exile, far from Jerusalem and with their Temple destroyed, He would be for them in a figurative sense a *mikdash me'at*—literally, a small Temple (Ezekiel 11:16). Within the context of Ezekiel 11, God's words were a reassurance; even though the Temple no longer stood and the divine presence would no longer be as manifest, God had not abandoned His people. His presence would accompany them while in exile, though in a diminished capacity.

Following the Talmud's lead, many classical commentators understood the phrase "a small Temple" to mean the introduction of synagogues. If God's presence had been manifest in full measure in the Temple, then the focal point of His presence in diminished measure in exile would also be at an edifice of gathering. God's promise to remain with them in a *mikdash me'at*, then, was taken to mean that His presence would manifest itself through "small temples"—namely, synagogues and houses of study.[2]

The equation between synagogue and Temple is readily understood. The Temple, we noted, is the meeting place between God and the congregation of Israel. While no synagogue ever functions as the literal center for the entire Jewish people, the conceptual parallel exists. The *minyan*—the quorum of ten males needed to perform a collective prayer service—is taken by the Talmud to represent the entire congregation of Israel.[3] In the Temple, the entire people of Israel would come to encounter God. In the synagogue—the *mikdash me'at*—the *minyan* (representing the entire Jewish people) assembles to stand before God. In the Temple, God's presence was most immanent. In the synagogue—the *mikdash me'at*—God's presence is immanent, but in a diminished fashion.

The Temple, we said in chapter 5, was also a national center, an institution that served to unify the nation around a central institution. The very term for synagogue in Hebrew—*beit kenesset*, a house of gathering—suggests that this is a cardinal function of the synagogue as well.

The notion that the Temple is the paradigm for the synagogue is reflected in many of the laws of the synagogue. The Ark at the head of the synagogue bearing the Torah scrolls parallels the Ark in the Holy of Holies in the First Temple, which bore the tablets and a Torah scroll. The design of the synagogue entrance also parallels that of the Temple, according to the Tosefta: "The egress of a synagogue should only open toward the east, for we see that this was the practice in the Temple, that its egress opened toward the east, as it says [concerning the Tabernacle] (Numbers 3:38), 'Those who were to camp before the Tabernacle, in front—before the Tent of Meeting, *on the east.*'"[4] In customs later adopted, appurtenances of the synagogue were also patterned after those of the Temple, such as the seven branched candelabra and the eternal light. Most significantly, the three daily prayer services, says the Talmud,[5] were instituted to correspond to different aspects of the sacral service in the Temple. The relationship between prayer and sacrifice will be addressed later at greater length.

From a conceptual standpoint, the paradigm of synagogue as Temple is borne out in striking fashion in a talmudic statement, which echoes one of the cardinal points raised in chapter 4. The Book of Deuteronomy referred to the Sanctuary as the place where God would establish His name, meaning His reputation in the world. Comparing the synagogue to the Temple, the Talmud states: "When Israel enters the synagogues and houses of study and answers [the *kaddish*], 'May His great name [be blessed forever and ever],' The Holy One Blessed Be He shakes His head and says, 'Fortunate is the king, whose [subjects] praise him so in his palace [i.e., the Temple]; what is to be of the father who banishes his sons? And woe unto the sons that have been banished from the table of their father!'"[6] In the wake of the Temple's destruction, God ruefully wishes that the Jewish people could exclaim, "May His great name be blessed forever and ever," in the Temple rather than in the synagogue. Their exclamations leave God lamenting that He has banished them from His table—the Temple.

What is it about Israel's declaration, "May His great name, and so forth," that elicits this response?

We posited that a cardinal function of the Temple was to serve as the place where God would establish His name—meaning His *reputation* as sovereign in the universe. The notion of proclaiming God's name, or reputation, is the essence of the declaration "May His great name be blessed forever and ever." It is an echo of Abraham's gesture when he first arrived in the land and proclaimed the name of God. When the Jewish people—through their actions and achievements— serve as a vehicle for the glorification of God's reputation, the Temple stands as a symbol and focal point for that process. When the Jewish people enter the synagogue—the "small Temple"—and proclaim the greatness of God's name, they express their desire to fulfill that role once more. Upon hearing this, God desires only to restore them to "the table of their father"—the Temple—so that the message can be heard the world over.

Simulation of the Temple experience can be seen as an underlying theme uniting the new rituals inducted by the rabbis, which are performed *zekher la-mikdash*—as a commemoration of the Temple and its rites. While there were perhaps hundreds or even thousands of different activities performed in the Temple service, the Talmud only perpetuated three Temple rites through the agency of *zekher la-mikdash*. An examination of the three reveals that the communal and national role of the Temple was paramount in their thinking.

In the time of Temple, the four species taken on the festival of Tabernacles were waved for seven days in the Temple courtyard, but elsewhere, on the first day of the holiday alone. R. Yochanan ben Zakkai, the rabbinic leader of the generation of the destruction, decreed that the four species should be waved outside the Temple for all seven days of the holiday, *zekher la-mikdash*—to commemorate that which was done in the Temple itself.[7] It is popularly assumed that it is a commandment to wave the four species the entire holiday of Sukkot. In fact, however, this is done to commemorate that which was done in the Temple.

The other two practices which we perform *zekher la-mikdash* according to the Talmud, are central to the seder service of the first night of Passover. The "Hillel Sandwich"—matzah taken together with bitter herbs and *charoset*—commemorates the eating of the paschal lamb in a similar fashion during the time of the Temple on account of *zekher la-mikdash*.[8] Similarly, the shank bone and egg respectively commemorate the paschal lamb and the festival sacrifice that are offered when the Temple stands.[9]

These three rites were enacted during different periods by different sages. Nonetheless, we may be able to discern a common thread linking the three rites designated as *zekher la-mikdash*. The waving of the four species in the Temple, and the partaking of the paschal and festival sacrifices share a common attribute—they represented the most palpable experience of the Temple rites for the vast majority of the Jewish people while the Temple stood. Nearly all the rites of the Temple were performed exclusively by the Priests and Levites. The only participatory role in the Temple played by the common Israelite on a regular basis was during the festival pilgrimages. The waving of the four species in the Temple Mount courtyard was performed by the entire male population that had made the pilgrimage to Jerusalem for the festival of Sukkot. The paschal sacrifice and festival sacrifice were likewise consumed within the precincts of Jerusalem by the entire congregation that had made the pilgrimage to Jerusalem for Passover. The Talmud's rationale, then, for perpetuating these acts as *zekher la-mikdash* can be understood. The rabbis wished to perpetuate, not so much the Temple itself, but rather the popular encounter and sense of the Temple as experienced by the entire nation during the festival pilgrimages.

The rituals that are *zekher la-mikdash* and the propagation of Temple imagery within the synagogue underscore a common theme. Common to all of these is the sense of *communal worship*. The rites that are performed *zekher la-mikdash* all recall the experience of pilgrimage and mass worship at the Temple, even as they are carried out today in the more localized domains of the synagogue and the home. The synagogue, whose services pivot around the representative presence of the entire people of Israel—the *minyan*—also highlights the perpetuation of the experience of the entire Jewish nation gathering together and coming before God at the Temple. When the rabbis sought to simulate the Temple experience, they were seeking to perpetuate the sense of communal encounter with God which had become jeopardized with the loss of Judaism's central institution.

Perpetuating a Sense of Loss

A second strategy to preserve and heighten the memory of something lost, is to demonstrate how life is changed because of its absence. The sense of loss permeates the fast days on the Jewish calendar. All, with the exception of Yom Kippur and the Fast of Esther, commemorate some aspect of the Temple's destruction and, more important, what the Temple's destruction represents—a severely strained relationship between God and the Jewish people.

The perpetuation of a sense of loss after the Temple's destruction is the underlying premise of a series of customs that fall under the heading of *zekher la-churban*—commemoration of the destruction. The Talmud[10] bases this notion on Psalms 137:5–6: "If I forget you, O Jerusalem, let my right hand wither; let my tongue stick to my palate if I cease to think of you, if I do not keep Jerusalem in memory even at my happiest hour." Even at moments of great joy, a sense of void and lacking must be felt on account of the fact that the Temple lies in ruins. The Talmud enumerates four venues in which the notion of *zekher la-churban* applies. One who builds a home must leave a portion of a wall unfinished; one who makes a great feast must omit a small dish from the offerings; a woman who dresses to her finest must omit a small accessory. Finally, and perhaps best known, is the mandate that a bride and groom commemorate the destruction of the Temple during the marriage ceremony, which is observed today through the breaking of a glass.[11] The verse in Psalms that is the backdrop for these laws emphasizes the memory of Jerusalem over the chiefest of joys. The joys that are to be overshadowed by Jerusalem's destruction are the joys of *completion*—a complete house, a complete meal or wardrobe, a completed bond between man and wife. The message of the customs of *zekher la-churban* is that in the absence of the Temple, the joy of full completeness in any realm is unattainable.

The Talmud prefaces the enumeration of the customs of *zekher la-churban* with an anecdote that takes on an added dimension in light of the theme developed earlier of *korbanot* as covenantal feasts:

> When the Temple was destroyed for a second time, many in Israel desired to abstain from the consumption of meat and wine. R. Joshua replied taunt-ingly, "My sons, why do you refrain from eating meat and drinking wine?" They replied, "Shall we eat meat that was once offered on the altar but is no longer? Shall we drink wine that used to be poured in libations upon the altar, but is no longer?" [R. Joshua] replied to them, "If so, let us desist from eating bread, for we no longer offer *minchah* offerings [whose pri-mary component was loaves of bread]. And should you suggest that we eat only fruit, why, fruit we should desist from as well, for we can no longer bring the first fruits. And should you suggest that we eat other types of fruit [that are exempt from the laws of the first fruits], then [consider that] we should desist from drinking water as well, for the libations of water upon the altar have desisted! . . . My sons, come and let me tell you. To abstain from mourning is impossible, for this evil decree [that is, the de-struction of the Temple] has indeed befallen us. Yet we cannot mourn excessively either, for we do not enact a decree that the people cannot tolerate. . . . Rather, the sages have said, let a man build a house and leave a portion unfinished, and so forth."

The ascetics of the generation of the destruction of the Temple chose their symbols with great care. Of all the ramifications of the Temple's destruction, the one that preoccupied them the most was the cessa-tion of sacrificial worship, and the area of life that they wished to limit in response was the feast. Inherent in their declaration of abstention is the underlying explanation of the sacrifices offered in chapter 6.

The sacrifices, we demonstrated, may be viewed as a covenantal feast shared by God and the Jewish people. When sacrifices are no longer offered, it is as if the Jewish people are no longer welcome to feast with God. If we cannot feast with God, asserted the ascetics, then it is improper to feast at all.

What are to we make of Rabbi Joshua's derision of their position? To mourn is critical and proper. To mourn in a fashion that is self-destructive is prohibited. It is interesting that R. Joshua's prescriptions speak of building as much as they speak of mourning. "Let a man build his house," he begins. Houses are to continue to be built, but even as life continues, the Jew must be ever mindful of the state of incompletion that he lives in—"yet let him leave a portion unfinished."

Commandments "Equal" to the Temple

As we noted, the rabbis of the postdestruction period realized that emphasis would need to be shifted to other existing institutions and precepts to fill the void left by the Temple's destruction. In many passages, the Talmud claims that certain commandments are in some way equal to the Temple and its rites. Some view such statements as a *rejection* of the Temple. This view envisions a "progressive" Judaism: once upon a time, Jews stressed Temple worship. The rabbis of the postdestruction period, however, brought Judaism to other, more "enlightened," and less ritualistic forms of worship, abandoning the Temple as a relic of the past.

It is true that rabbinic Judaism emphasized certain rites and values to fill the void created by the Temple's destruction. These emphases, however, do not reflect a renunciation of the Temple. Rather, the opposite can be demonstrated: rabbinic Judaism sought to *highlight* the practices and values that represent the essence of what the Temple stood for. They set to this agenda by stressing the importance of four activities in the wake of the Temple's destruction:[12]

Charitable Acts—The urgency of the question of how to cope with the Temple's destruction is poignantly depicted in the following anecdotes of two prominent sages from the period of the Temple's destruction:

> Once as Raban Yochanan ben Zakkai was coming out of Jerusalem, Rabbi Joshua followed him and beheld the Temple in ruins. Said Rabbi Joshua, "Woe unto us that this place, the place where the iniquities of Israel were atoned for, is in ruins." Said [Rabban Yochanan] to him, "My son, be not grieved. We have another atonement that is like it, and what is it? It is acts of lovingkindness, as it is said (Hosea 6:6), 'For I desire mercy, not sacrifice.'"[13]

This passage and the others like it that we will examine are easily misunderstood. What we have before us, it could be claimed, is shining evidence of the enlightenment of Judaism in process. Once upon a time, when Judaism was in its primitive infancy, atonement was achieved through the mechanistic act of slaughtering an animal. However, with the Temple destroyed the rabbis realized that true spiritual development could only come through a refinement of one's traits. The passage is evidence to the inferiority of the sacrifices, it could be said, and constitutes a rejection of them as a mode of worship.

The key to understanding the passage lies with R. Yochanan ben Zakkai's prooftext—Hosea 6:6—"For I desire mercy not sacrifice." Read in context, Hosea's words were not a rejection of the institution of sacrifice as such. Hosea spoke in a manner consistent with the entire biblical tradition. Sacrifices have value—within the proper setting. When sacrifices are seen as symbols—symbols of the process of expiation or of the covenantal bond between God and the Jewish people—they have value as a physical embodiment of a process of true spiritual striving. As stated in the introduction, such acts achieve something that feelings or thoughts alone cannot. They represent a concretization on the plane of action of the abstract thoughts and feelings that the penitent harbors in his heart. What Hosea and other supposed prophetic "opponents" of sacrifice rejected was sacrifice as a symbol with no substance behind it.[14] Hosea 6 speaks of Jews who

violate the covenant and of Jews who exploit their fellow man. Under
these circumstances, sacrifices become an abomination. Under these
circumstances, the prophet can only admonish the people: "For I desire
mercy" (i.e., true substance of spiritual striving), "not sacrifice" (that
is, a representative act incommensurate with the behavior and atti-
tude of the person offering it).

With this understanding of the prooftext cited, let us return to the
anecdote as a whole and reexamine its implications. Rabbi Joshua's
lament was focused on the organizational and structural devastation
that the Temple's fall had engendered. Without sacrifices—the symbolic representation of the inner spiritual process of repentance—
R. Joshua questioned whether Israel would be able to achieve expiation in the wake of sin.

What, then, was the meaning of R. Yochanan's response—that
loving-kindness is of equal efficacy as are the sacrifices? Like Hosea
in his generation, R. Yochanan ben Zakkai was responding to the ills
that plagued the generation that witnessed the fall of the Second
Temple. The Temple had been the cornerstone of Jewish social and
religious life. The sacrificial rites were being performed with regular-
ity, if by a corrupt priesthood. The rabbinic tradition states firmly that
the Second Temple fell because of sin'at chinam—wanton discord
between man and his fellow man. An imbalance had crept into the
social and religious fabric of the Jewish community of that generation.
Ritual symbol had been elevated over the essential acts and feelings
of true spiritual striving. If sacrifices were being dutifully offered, while
men had no regard for another, then the Temple's destruction would
have to herald a redress to this imbalance. By stressing the value of
charitable acts over and above that of the sacrifices, the rabbis may
have been saying that heretofore, too much emphasis was being placed
on the role of ritual and cult. Their statements equating the efficacy
of charity with that of sacrifice are essentially a return to basic prophetic values. Hosea had said that sacrifice was meaningless when men
dealt corruptly. The rabbinic statements of the postdestruction period
are a retrumpeting of that same message. In the post-Temple period

expiation would come through precisely the kind of behavior that had been lacking beforehand. *Sin'at chinam* can only be countered with acts of loving-kindness towards one's neighbor. "It is within this spirit that we find another talmudic statement: R. Yochanan and R. Eleazar both said, 'When the Temple existed, the altar atoned for a person; and now when the Temple no longer exists, a person's table atones for him.'"[15] The context in which the equation is made is with reference to hosting the poor at one's table. When the Temple stands and Israel is faithful to her calling, sacrifice embodies the spirit of the process of atonement. Symbol reflects inner strivings. When the Temple no longer exists because Israel has failed in her calling, symbol can no longer be allowed to culminate the process of repentance. Instead, a redoubled emphasis must be returned to the essence of repentance— the deeds themselves, in which case a person's table atones for him as he opens it before others.

Whereas these two sources *equate* the expiatory potency of acts of kindness and sacrificial worship, a third source goes even further and ranks loving-kindness as *superior* to the sacrifices in the eyes of God:[16] "Said R. Eleazar, 'The one who does charity is greater than all the sacrifices, as it is said (Prov. 21:3), "To do charity is more pleasing to God than sacrifices."'"[17] The meaning of the verse from Proverbs is not to reject sacrifice, but to qualify it; as a symbol, sacrifice is subordinate to the attitudes and actions that it symbolizes.

Repentance—A second equality that is drawn in this vein is between Temple and repentance: "Whoever repents is considered as if he had gone up to Jerusalem, built the Temple, built the altar, and offered upon it all the sacrifices of the Torah."[18] Once again, the equality is not meant as a replacement. Repentance did not suddenly emerge on the rabbinic plane in place of sacrifice. Repentance had always been the substantial core of sacrifice. Without true penitence, we saw, sacrifice was meaningless.

Once again, we see how the institutions that are equated with sacrifices are not entirely distinct from them, but rather reflect the values that stood behind them. The Temple, as a perpetuation of the

Sinai encounter, is the site at which Israel symbolically renews and reexperiences anew the covenantal bond. However, the essence of that process is repentance—for in repentance the penitent strives to renew the bond with God that had been strained by his misdeeds.

Torah Study—In a well-known dictum, the Talmud says, "Since the fall of the Temple God has no place in His world except the four cubits of the *Halakhah*."[19] So long as the Temple stood, God's presence was manifest in the entirety of the Temple. In the aftermath of its destruction, however, God's manifestation in the world is figuratively diminished to the smallest dimensions of a personal domain as defined in *Halakhah*—four cubits.[20] When the Talmud claims that God has but four cubits in His world—those of the *Halakhah*—the implication is that the most manifest exposure to God's presence in a post-Temple age is through the study of Torah. While this comparison heightens the significance of Torah study, the implication here is that on some level the Temple is still superior. On the most minimal level, God's presence is manifest in the four cubits of His laws. When the Temple stands, however, His presence is manifest in far greater measure in the entirety of the Temple.

Other sources see in Torah study a value equivalent to that of the Temple rites: "'In every place offerings are presented unto My name even pure oblations' (Malachi 1:11)—refers to the scholars who study in purity. . . . He who occupies himself with Torah is like a man tending 'a burnt offering, a meal offering, a sin offering and a guilt offering' (Leviticus 7:37)."[21] By utilizing references to the sacrificial service as a metaphor for the endeavor of Torah study, the Talmud creates an equality between the two activities. Other statements, however, posit Torah study as superior to the sacrificial rites: "Greater is a single day of your Torah study," says God to David, "than all of the sacrifices offered by Solomon."[22] Another source even asserts that the enterprise of Torah study is greater than that of building the Temple.[23]

Once again, the themes developed earlier shed light on the comparison. The Temple is a symbol of the covenantal bond, we said, and the sacrifices represent a covenantal feast. When the Temple lies in

ruins it is a sign that the covenantal bond is strained, and the partners, distanced. Within this context, the emphasis of the importance
of Torah study as equal or even superior to Temple worship is understood. The Temple is a perpetuation of the Sinai experience, of entering into covenantal bond. If the Temple lies destroyed, then Israel
must respond by strengthening her awareness of those responsibilities.
The road to repairing the breach between God and Israel is through
the study of the Torah—the very content of the covenant.

Torah study may be equated with the Temple experience in a second fashion. To come to the Temple was to come before God—to
reexperience a feeling of revelation. When the Temple no longer
stands, that sense of revelation can only be partially retained through
the encounter with His words and laws. This is the principle that
underlies Judaism's stress on Torah study.

Prayer—Temple worship, we noted, constituted a unique realm of
commandments. Most commandments, we said, are divine mandates
to be obeyed. Temple worship, however, was not merely a call to perform and fulfill a requirement, but represented an act of coming before
God in direct address. It is not surprising then, that in an age when a
direct address could no longer be accomplished in the Temple, the
Sages saw prayer as the natural vehicle to fill this void. Again, we will
see that an emphasis after the fall of the Temple has its roots in values
and practices already extant while the Temple still stood.

Perhaps the single rabbinic response to the fall of the Temple that
has had the greatest bearing on our practice today is with regard to
prayer. The Talmud claims that the practice of institutionalized daily
prayer is patterned after the offerings of the *korban tamid*—the daily
communal sacrifices—in the Temple.[24] Many of the sacrificial services
included the recital of prayers that we still say today, including the
shema and parts of the *amidah*.[25] The succession of prayer over sacrifice, then, should not be described as a process of substitution and
replacement. Rather, it represents the preservation and embellishment
of a single element from the service of the offering of the communal
sacrifice.

Much like the laws that were enacted *zekher la-mikdash*, the patterning of three daily prayers in the model of the daily sacrifices underscores the rabbis' desire to perpetuate the centrality of communal worship. The sacrifices that serve as the paradigms for the prayer services are specifically those brought on behalf of the entire people of Israel. It is, perhaps, for this reason that the central prayer of the three daily services is phrased entirely in the first person *plural*.

While *Berakhot* 26b claims that the prayer services were patterned after the daily sacrifices, other sources go even further: "If you cannot go to a synagogue to pray, pray within your house, [if necessary,] pray within your bed. And if you are unable to speak, meditate within your heart. And if you follow this prescription, [it is concerning this that] it is written (Psalms 4:6) 'Offer sacrifices in righteousness'—I consider it as if you had built the altar and offered upon it many sacrifices."[26]

Another source goes further still: And said R. Eleazar, "Prayer is *greater* than all the sacrifices, as it is said (Isaiah 1:11), 'What need have I of all your sacrifices,' and it is written [afterward] (Isaiah 1:15), 'And when you lift up your hand [I will turn My eyes from you; though you pray at length, I will not listen, your hands are stained with blood].'"[27] After first rejecting sacrifices, it was still necessary for Isaiah to reject the prayers of his generation, indicating the superior status of prayer.[28]

In discussing how charitable acts, repentance, and Torah study were cast as equal in efficacy and importance to the sacrifices, a common theme emerged: each of these is not merely a *symbol*, but a *substantive* act or disposition. It is difficult for any of these to degenerate to the point that they are purely mechanical, and no longer a substantive spiritual act. What of prayer, however? Cannot prayer become just as mechanized as had the sacrifices?

Prayer poses a challenge. On the one hand it is like sacrificial worship in that it is a symbolic, representative act—having only as much value as the thoughts that stand behind it. However, the relationship between the symbolic act and the substantive feelings behind it is a closer one in prayer than in sacrifice. The formal act of prayer involves a text, whose words can readily inform the mind and heart of the worshipper if his attention is focused upon them. It is a challenge to us to make the institution of prayer a reflection of a true, inner spiritual process.

We have examined four realms of practice that the rabbis stressed as equal to the Temple and its rites. We close with an observation that cuts across each and every one of the sources we have examined. One cannot discern in them any hint of the permanent abolishment of the sacrificial rites. The rabbinic agenda is clear. With the Temple in ruins, values and practices that reflect its substance are to be emphasized. However, with the rebuilding of the Temple, sacrifices are to be reinstituted and function as they had always been intended—as powerful symbolic acts that concretize and manifest the inner stirrings of the Jew desiring to come closer to his Maker.

Where does this leave us today in our thinking about the Temple? The sages set out on a dual agenda: on the one hand, to commemorate the Temple and its centrality to Jewish life, and on the other, to give Judaism renewed vitality in the wake of the Temple's fall. The success of the shift to new emphases, however, has had the result that the image of the Temple has become diminished. If we do not feel an intuitive grasp for the Temple's importance in our time, it is not merely because its memory has faded in the two millennia since its destruction. The process spawned by the rabbis—out of necessity—to highlight extrasacral modes of worship has eroded our comprehension of the Temple's significance. In our day, most identifying Jews would certainly place at Judaism's core the institutions of synagogue, charity and kindness, prayer, Torah study, and repentance more readily than they would the Temple and its rites.

While the various customs encompassed under the headings of *zekher la-mikdash* and *zekher la-churban* continue to animate Jewish practice, and do serve to remind Jews of the Temple and its importance, the most direct reminder the contemporary Jew encounters of the Temple is in the liturgy. It is fitting to conclude these remarks on how our generation looks at the Temple, therefore, with an insight into the structure of the daily *amidah*.

The central portion of the *amidah* contains requests or petitions for individual and collective concerns. It includes, therefore, a petition for the rebuilding of Jerusalem and the return of God's presence to it. The petitional blessings conclude, appropriately, with a collective request that our prayers be heard. Following this conclusion, we proceed with yet another request: "Be favorable, O God, toward Your people Israel and their prayer and restore the service to the Holy of Holies of Your Temple. The fire-offerings of Israel and their prayer accept with love and favor, and may the service of Your people Israel always be favorable to You."

Even after asking of God that our prayers be heard, one more request is submitted that touches on the nature of prayer itself and its ideal form. At the dedication of the First Temple, Solomon had depicted the Temple in primary terms as a place of prayer. With God's presence near at hand, the Temple was to be the focal point for prayer, for those in the land of Israel and outside it, Jew and non-Jew alike. Therefore, our final supplication in the daily *amidah* is that we return to the state of covenantal closeness, symbolized by the presence of the Temple. Prayer is efficacious in all generations. Only when Israel returns to its covenantal partner, however, is the true ideal of prayer—of addressing God directly in close proximity—possible. It is this thought which ends our supplications in the *amidah*, and it is with this thought that we step out of God's presence at the close of the *amidah* as well:

> May it be Your will O Lord our God and the God of our forefathers, that the Holy Temple be rebuilt, speedily in our days *and may You grant us our share in Your Torah, and may we serve You there with reverence*, as in days of old and in former years. Then the offering of Judah and Jerusalem will be pleasing to God as in days of old and in former years.

When we conclude the *amidah*, we do so with a request for the re-building of the Temple. However, we do so in recognition of the fact that the rebuilding of the Temple is not a unilateral action to be taken on the part of God. Accompanying our final petition for the rebuild-ing of the Temple, we ask that we be granted our share in the Torah. Moreover, we ask that we be given assistance in understanding our covenantal responsibilities, for only if we fulfill our part may we be able to serve God in the covenantal center as in days of old and in former years.

THE MODERN AGE IN LIGHT OF THE TEMPLE

What relevance does the Temple have for our generation? How can its meaning and symbolism help us make sense of the contemporary Jewish landscape?

Many are prepared to dismiss the Temple as irrelevant for our times. Two millennia have elapsed since it last stood, nor do we see the pros-pect of its rebuilding in the near future. However, the question takes on more relevance if we consider the ideal progression of stages that led to the building of the Temple in the time of Solomon. The con-struction of the actual structure took thirteen years, but the social and religious foundation that was laid prior to that construction was a generation in the making. The physical construction of the Temple began in the fourth year of Solomon's reign; the grooming of a stable, prosperous, and just society that would be worthy of a Temple, how-ever, began in the early years of the reign of David. When assessing how the Temple can shed light on our times, we need to remember a cardinal point: the construction of the Temple represents the pinnacle of a *process*.

When we ponder, therefore, the ramifications of the Temple for our generation, we should not be so myopic as to shrug off the Temple as meaningless for us merely because it is not part of our reality. The Temple—in our day no less than in David's—needs to be seen ideally, as the culmination of a social, political, economic, and religious development on a national scale. To assess, therefore, the Temple's implications for our times, we need to take stock of where we are in the process whose pinnacle is the rebuilding of the Temple. We are midstream in this process; this means that achievements have been attained that must be recognized as such. Being midstream in the process, however, we must also identify long-term goals that will bring us closer to the ideal conditions necessary to rebuild the Temple.

In taking account of what has been achieved, we will focus on that which has already been rebuilt, at least partially—the city of Jerusalem. Here we will probe the import and identity of Jerusalem in an age when the Temple is not standing. Looking forward in time, at what remains to be achieved, we will explore the theological and halakhic issue of when the Temple will be rebuilt.

Jerusalem—Its Meaning without the Temple

Throughout this book, we have touched upon the topic of Jerusalem in tangential fashion; our discussion of it has generally related to it as the host site of the Temple. When perceived solely as the host site for the Temple, one could posit a view of Jerusalem in our day via the analogy of a tree stump. One who happens across a large tree stump may be impressed by its girth and by the years of longevity and productivity it enjoyed, as evidenced by the rings of its cross section. The impression that such a stump makes, however, is not on account of its own identity as a stump, but as the remnant of a larger, flourishing entity—the great tree, which has since been felled.

In similar fashion, one may be tempted to regard Jerusalem in theological terms as a large tree stump. Jerusalem, it may be argued, is significant in our day—but only on account of the vicarious importance that it draws from its association with the Temple in days of yore. With the Temple in ruins, according to this view, we can only look upon Jerusalem and yearn for the day when it will be fully rebuilt with the Temple as its crown.

To be sure, Jerusalem is not complete without the Temple. However, both biblical and rabbinic sources emphasize that Jerusalem has a value and identity of its own—an identity that is related to its function as the site of the Temple, and yet extant even when the Temple is not standing. A cognizance of Jerusalem's identity is the key to understanding what we have achieved in the process of laying the social and religious foundations for the Temple's renewal.

What significance is there to Jerusalem when the Temple no longer stands? Maimonides rules, as do most halakhic decisors, that with the dedication of the First Temple by Solomon, Jerusalem became immutably endowed with *kedushah*, and that this endowment remains an inherent part of the city's character even when the Temple lies in ruins and Israel is exiled from her land.[29] Maimonides claims that the *kedushah* of Jerusalem is enduring and permanent because the seat of the *shekhinah*—the divine presence—is located there.[30]

The notion that the *kedushah* of Jerusalem is eternal on account of the divine presence that resides there echoes themes that we have seen in biblical sources. Recall the discussion in chapter 4 concerning the structural differences between the Tabernacle and the Temple. The structure of the Sanctuary in its different forms, we said, was a reflection of the degree of association between God and the Jewish people. In several pre-Temple references, we saw, the Bible refers to God as "He who dwells on the cherubim."[31] The appellation referred to the fact that Moses had received the divine word from between the cherubim (Exodus 25:22, Numbers 7:88–89), indicating that within the Tabernacle, God's presence was most immanent atop the cherubim. In the Temple, however, no explicit mention was made of the cherubim atop the Ark. Rather, Solomon erected two enormous cherubim on the floor of the Holy of Holies, whose wings spread open from wall to wall (1 Kings 6:23–28).

The contrast between the location of the cherubim in the Tabernacle and the Temple, it was noted, was symbolically significant. As long as Israel's bond with God was not fully realized, God's presence remained, figuratively, a passenger atop the cherubim of the Ark. However, when that bond was maximized, the only cherubim highlighted were the ones planted on the floor of the Holy of Holies, symbolizing the rootedness of God's presence.[32] It is in this sense that the psalmist describes God's choice of Jerusalem (Psalms 132:13–14):

> For the Lord has chosen Zion;
> He has desired it for His seat.
> (14) "This is My resting-place for all time;
> here I will dwell for I desire it."

The ramifications of this notion for our generation are great. The divine presence is most manifestly immanent when the Temple stands. However, even when it does not, it is special privilege for the Jewish people to have sovereignty over Jerusalem and access to the Temple Mount, for at all times Jerusalem is the *mekom ha-shekhinah*—the seat of the divine presence.

If we see the contemporary situation as a stage along the process toward the full renewal of the covenantal bond and the rebuilding of the Temple, then there are also other dimensions to Jerusalem's current status that emerge as salient. To appreciate these dimensions, we need only examine one of the psalms that illustrates how Jews of the First Temple period related to Jerusalem. For the Jewish pilgrim ascending toward Jerusalem, the focal point of his trip was to be his experience together with the entire nation outside the Temple. Psalm 122, which is a record of one pilgrim's thoughts on his way to Jerusalem, reveals several other associations with the city, which today we could make as well:

> A song of ascents. Of David.
> I rejoiced when they said to me,
> "We are going to the house of the Lord."
> (2) Our feet stood inside your gates, O Jerusalem.
> (3) Jerusalem built up, a city knit together,
> (4) to which tribes would make pilgrimage,
> the tribes of the Lord,

—as was enjoined upon Israel—
to praise the name of the Lord.
(5) there the thrones of judgment stood,
thrones of the house of David.
(6) Pray for the well-being of Jerusalem:
"May those who love you be at peace.
(7) May there be well-being within your ramparts, peace in your citadels."
(8) For the sake of my kin and friends,
I pray for your well being;
(9) for the sake of the house of the Lord our God
I seek your good.

What does Jerusalem mean to the author of this psalm, and how does he view Jerusalem's relationship to the Temple? The devotee both opens and closes his psalm with mention of the Temple. His attention, however, throughout most of the psalm, is not on the Temple, but on Jerusalem as an extension of the Temple.

Within this context, the first point that emerges is that he sees in Jerusalem a potent force for Jewish unity; he stands at its gates not in solitude but with his fellow pilgrims: "*Our* feet stood inside your gates, O Jerusalem" (verse 2). He lauds the fact that all the tribes of Israel gather there (verse 4), and concludes by praying for the well-being of his kin and friends, bound together by the common endeavor of pilgrimage to Jerusalem (verse 8). Here, Jerusalem has an identity that is a by-product of its status as the host site of the Temple. The common goal of the pilgrims is to reach the Temple for the festival; but it is in greater Jerusalem that the gathering and unity occur. Jerusalem, then, develops its own dynamic as a unifying force for the Jewish people.

The devotee also sees Jerusalem as the center of justice: "there the thrones of judgment stood" (verse 5). As was pointed out in chapter 4, the Temple, as a perpetuation of Sinai, was the geographic point from which the law emanated. There sat the highest court of the land, and from there the Priests and Levites went out across the land to administer justice in the district courts. Once again, an idea that is central to the Temple is given application to Jerusalem as a whole. In the eyes of the pilgrim, Jerusalem constitutes the judicial center of the country.

Though the devotee of Psalm 122 does not mention Jerusalem as the center of Jewish education, we may recall that within the Temple the realms of education and justice went hand in hand. The Priests and Levites—the same agents who went out across the land to adjudicate disputes—also taught the laws and precepts of the Torah. The notion that not only the Temple, but indeed the city of Jerusalem was considered the source of authoritative values is underscored in Isaiah's statement (Isaiah 2:4): "For instruction shall come forth from *Zion*, the word of the Lord from *Jerusalem*."

The final association that the pilgrim makes with Jerusalem is one that is only residually a function of the city's association with the Temple. He recognizes Jerusalem as the seat of government and offers tribute to it when he says: "[there stood] thrones of the house of David" (verse 5).

What does Jerusalem mean for us today? All of the dimensions that animated and invigorated the spiritual meaning of Jerusalem for the psalmist centuries ago, have returned to animate her—if on a diminished scale—again today, two thousand years later. We await the reinstatement of the Davidic king, but we can already see in Jerusalem today the seat of a sovereign Jewish government. The Sanhedrin has not yet returned to its residence in the Chamber of Hewn Stone in the Temple, but the Supreme Court of the State of Israel adjudicates from Jerusalem. We have no formal guild of Priests or Levites who bring the word of God out from Zion, but Jerusalem is today the world capital of Jewish learning of all forms. We do not fulfill the halakhic requirement of gathering as a nation on the pilgrimage festivals in the Temple courtyard, yet Jews from all over Israel and all over the world flock to Jerusalem and to the Western Wall on each of these occasions. Jerusalem today stands as a symbol of the unity of the Jewish people as the largest Jewish city in the world, and the point toward which all Jews look as the center of the Jewish world. While the divine presence is not yet fully immanent in the Holy of Holies, in Jerusalem today Jews can worship at a place eternally endowed with *kedushah*—the site that is the eternal seat of the divine presence. In chapter 5, we attempted to demonstrate how the Temple, and Jerusalem as its extension, comprised a multifaceted facility. The variety of activities and commandments that could only be fulfilled there made Jerusalem a national center. Even without the Temple, Jerusalem today has once again emerged as our national center.

For some, these comparisons will be invidious; to compare modern-day Jerusalem with the Jerusalem of Solomon, they will argue, is to mock Solomon and his achievements. No Jerusalem will compare to the Jerusalem of old, they will assert, until all of the redemptive elements are in place, including the rebuilt Temple, and the reinstatement of the Davidic king.

The rebuilding of the Temple, in the author's opinion, needs to be seen as the pinnacle of a process that is measured in *collective* and *national* terms. Stated in religious terms, we must realize that we serve God not only as individuals observing the commandments, but as a nation that must identify its calling and strive to achieve its collective goal. The very first stage of this process, then, is the self-perception that we have a national identity and will. This has only begun to emerge with the return of the people to their land, and the founding of the State of Israel. To be sure, Jerusalem today is not what it once was under Solomon, nor what we yearn for it to become in the age of redemption. Yet in light of all the misery of the last two thousand years of Jewish history, it seems that we have come to a turning point with the rebirth of the State of Israel. In looking at Jerusalem today, even bereft of a Temple, we can begin to see the reclamation of the ideals and institutions that gave rise to the Temple's construction under David and Solomon.

A biblical synonym for Jerusalem is Zion. Zionism, from a religious perspective ought to be perceived as a movement dedicated to building a nation around the highest ideals of the Zion of old—around a city that stands as a symbol of Jewish sovereignty in the land, justice,

the wisdom of the Torah, Jewish unity, and the opportunity for a collective encounter between the Almighty and His people, Israel. The
ultimate achievement of this goal remains a distant prospect. However, the *process* is well under way.

Looking toward the Third Temple

What are the next steps of this process? How do we get from where
we are to that which we pray for several times a day—the rebuilding
of the Temple? Phrased in perhaps more tantalizing terms, when will
the Third Temple be built?

While the question is of enormous importance, and is the natural
topic with which to close this study, we need first to limit the parameters of the question. There is no one who can predict the Temple's
rebuilding with certainty, or even the precise causal chain that will
precede it. When the question is posed head on, "when will the
Temple be rebuilt?" in expectation of a precise chronological answer,
Maimonides' words at the close of the *Mishneh Torah* should be
heeded:

> These are matters that no man can know until they have actually tran-
> spired. For these concerns are cryptically depicted in the words of the
> prophets. Neither do the sages have a received tradition concerning these
> matters. . . . Neither these matters nor their details are of cardinal reli-
> gious significance. A person should not indulge himself in speculation
> based on the rabbinic sayings pertaining to these concerns nor place great
> importance in them. For such activity leads neither to the fear [of God]
> nor the love [of Him].[33]

Taking Maimonides' advice, we will probe the issue not as an exer-
cise in apocalyptic forecasting, but with an eye toward those aspects
of the Temple's rebuilding that may contribute to "the fear of God
and the love of Him."

There are many positions in the corpus of rabbinic writings concerning the question of who will rebuild the Temple and under what

circumstances.[34] The disparity between them only underscores how futile it is to predict definitively when the Temple will be built. Each position, however, represents a commentary on the nature of the Temple to be rebuilt. We will mention here three of the primary opinions that represent the parameters of the debate. Rashi maintains that the Temple will be rebuilt by God Himself, and that it will literally descend from the heavens onto the Temple Mount in completed and finished form.[35] While a clear depiction of what Rashi means is difficult to attain, one element of Rashi's opinion is clear: the physical rebuilding of the Temple is an endeavor that will be executed by God alone.

A less supernal projection is provided by Maimonides.[36] The Davidic king will reascend the throne through conventional sociopolitical forces. He will rule over a sovereign Israel whose laws are those of the Torah. Through strong leadership, he will bring about the ingathering of the exiles and bring the people to observe the stringencies of the sabbatical and jubilee years. This is the person, says Maimonides, who will rebuild the Temple. Maimonides' vision is a challenge to the Jewish people; when the Jewish people perfect their state, culminating in the ascent of an effective and popular leader of Davidic descent, the time will be ripe for the Jewish people themselves to rebuild the Temple:

> Should a king arise from the House of David who is learned in the ways of the Torah, and engages in the commandments like his forefather David, according to the mandates of the written and oral laws, and he leads all of Israel to obey them and be exacting in their observance, and who wages God's wars—this man may be considered the Messiah. And should he flourish and go on to build the Temple in its place, and return the exiled of Israel—he may be considered the Messiah with certainty. He will restore the world to the service of God, as it says (Zephaniah 3:9), "For then I will make the peoples pure of speech, *so that they all invoke the name of the Lord*, and serve Him with one accord."[37]

The quote from Zephaniah is a telling one. Maimonides' conception of the Third Temple resembles the portrayal of the First Temple pre-

sented in chapter 4. In the time of Solomon, Israel had achieved greatness in the eyes of her neighbors. The Temple was erected as a symbol of God's *name*—His reputation and acclaim in the world. The
Third Temple, claims Maimonides, will be built in an age when the
nations will be brought to "invoke the *name of God* and serve Him
with one accord."

Perhaps the most mundane opinion found amongst the major
decisors within the rabbinic tradition is that of the nineteenth-century Polish talmudist, R. Joseph b. Moses Babad, in his commentary
to the medieval *Sefer HaChinukh, Minchat Chinukh*. In his essay on
the commandment to build a Sanctuary he cites a midrash that tells
of an attempt to rebuild the Temple shortly after its destruction, under
the aegis of the Emperor Hadrian, prior to the Bar-Kokhba rebellion.[38]
The effort was led by R. Joshua ben Hananiah, a disciple of R. Yochanan ben Zakkai, the rabbinic leader at the time of the Temple's destruction. The fact that a prominent Tanaitic leader spearheaded the
efforts to rebuild the Temple, without the presence of a Davidic king,
writes R. Babad, is evidence that we have an obligation to rebuild the
Temple at the moment that the opportunity affords itself.[39] The notion
that the Temple may be built even as Israel is subject to foreign dominion recalls the conditions prevalent at the onset of the Second
Temple period. Recall that during that period, conditions were far from
ideal; Israel was subject to a foreign power, most of the Jewish people
had not returned to Israel, and religious observance was weak. The
Second Temple, we said, was not built as a symbol of God's sovereignty in the world, but was rather constructed with the particularist
aims of the Tabernacle: to serve narrowly as the focal point of the
covenant between God and the Jewish people. By drawing evidence
from the movement led by R. Joshua ben Hananiah, the author of the
Minchat Chinukh is essentially staking the claim that the Third Temple
may be constructed with this particularistic function at the fore.

We cannot know whether the Third Temple will be built under
conditions more closely approximating those of the age of Solomon
or the age of the return to Zion. However, we might take a cue as to

what our responsibilities are at this time from the historical and political landscape that God has laid before us. As stated before, we live in an age that more closely approximates the Israel of Solomon than has any other period in Jewish history. Conversely, we have the peculiar distinction of being the only Jews in history who have lived under their own government in their own land *without* a Temple standing atop Mount Moriah. These are the conflicting symptoms of being at mid-process.

What is it then, that prevents us from rebuilding the Temple? Some ruefully point a finger at the Dome of the Rock and bemoan the fact that prevailing geopolitical considerations make the Temple's reconstruction an impossibility at this time. Would that we could somehow rid ourselves of that obstacle, some feel, and the road to the rebuilding of the Temple would be clear. Such a view, however, is simplistic. As covenantal partners with the Almighty, we must surely believe that it is His will that the Temple eventually stand atop Mount Moriah. If we see in our time that He does not allow the Temple to be rebuilt, then we ought not point a finger at others, but at ourselves. The very presence of the Dome of the Rock atop Mount Moriah is not the obstacle toward the rebuilding of the Temple. Its presence atop Mount Moriah is rather a *sign* to us that we are not yet deserving of the covenantal symbol that is the Temple. It is a *symptom* of the fact that we need arrange our own house, before the House of God is to be rebuilt. In our generation, God challenges us—indeed, almost allures us—by creating conditions that harken to Israel's most glorious age, and at the same time deny us the capacity to erect a symbol to His covenant with us. However, it is a challenge, or even an enticement, designed to spur us further in the development of our collective covenantal behavior.

What, then, is beckoned of us at this juncture? The dominant theme of this work has been that the Temple stands as a symbol of the covenant between God and the Jewish people. We need, then, to focus on those objectives that define us as ideal covenantal partners. To be sure, this means that we must work toward a spiritual revival throughout the whole of the Jewish people—but it means more. To be God's covenantal partner in the fullest sense means creating a great society that will be a model for others to emulate. Thus it was in the time of David and Solomon, and thus we must set our sights today. Within this context, all areas of public life—economics, diplomacy, social welfare, and education—become religiously significant. By excelling in all these areas, we create a society that will serve the glory of God. In his inaugural address as the seventh president of the State of Israel, Ezer Weizman claimed that Israel had a calling to excel in all areas of higher education. He cited Isaiah 2:3, "For out of Zion shall go Torah and the word of the Lord from Jerusalem." On one level his statement represented a corruption of the prophet's intention, applying the term "Torah" and "word of the Lord" to biochemistry and economic forecasting. However, on another level, his message was strangely appropriate within religious terms as well. It is the religious calling of the State of Israel to excel in all areas of public life. Nonetheless, even as Israel embraces many endeavors and opens its doors to visitors from the world over, it must be careful not to fall into the snare of Solomon's generation. Without proper emphasis on Jewish ideals, foreign cultural influence will rot the core of this society, and distract it from its covenantal task.

Perhaps more than anything else, the aim of developing our covenantal behavior mandates us to reorient the way we view one another as members of the Jewish people. Writing at the time of the inception of the Jewish State, R. Joseph Soloveitchik incisively remarked that the covenant does not only create a vertical bond between God and the Jewish people. It creates a horizontal bond between Jews as well. He termed this *brit goral*—the covenant of fate. In the wake of the covenant, he wrote, every Jew must know that an attack on any Jew anywhere, is an attack on all Jews everywhere. The meaning of covenant is that at all times the suffering of any Jew is the suffering of every Jew, and mandates mutual sympathy and action from us on behalf of all other Jews.[40] The value of Jewish unity is very much undermined in our time, as ideology is often trumpeted in justification of needlessly inflammatory remarks and defensive positions that drive ever deeper wedges between us. Greatly diminished in our time is the communal spirit engendered by the covenant of *kol Yisrael arevim zeh la-zeh*—that all Israel are sureties for one another.[41]

To rebuild the physical components of the Temple in this age is hardly a difficult task, yet without developing our covenantal behavior, the Temple will never be able to stand as a meaningful symbol of our covenantal bond. In yearning for the rebuilding of the Temple, we ought to be ever mindful of the words of the nineteenth-century chasidic master, R. Judah Aryeh Leib Alter of Gur (1847–1905), in his collected homilies, *Sefat Emet*: "We must know that even when the Temple stood, it took great effort and refinement to perceive its inner power. We must therefore diligently refine ourselves in preparation for the ultimate rebuilding of the Temple, and not merely pray for the rebuilding of the Temple alone."[42] May we set ourselves to the task ahead of us, so that the Temple be rebuilt speedily in our days.

Notes

INTRODUCTION

1. *Shulchan Arukh, Orach Chaim* 94:1, based on *Berakhot* 30a.

2. A term exists to denote a time when a majority of the Jewish people resides in the land of Israel—*rov Yisra'el sheruyim be-admatam*. A term also exists to denote an age in which Israel is sovereign on its land—*yedei Yisra'el tekeifah*. The use of these terms, however, is far less ubiquitous in rabbinic writings than the terms used to denote the ages when the Temple stands and those when it does not.

3. This is the foundational assumption of the writings of R. Samson Raphael Hirsch. See Yitzchak Heinemann, *Ta'amei Ha-Mitzvot Be-Sifrut Yisra'el* 2 (1956):91–161. Maimonides also ascribed symbolic importance to the *mitzvot* (see Maimonides, *The Guide of the Perplexed*, trans. Shlomo Pines and Leo Strauss [Chicago: University of Chicago Press, 1963], 3:26) as did the author of the thirteenth-century work, *Sefer Ha-Chinukh*.

4. Clifford Geertz, *The Interpretation of Cultures* (New York: Basic Books, 1973), p. 99.

CHAPTER 1

1. *The Encyclopedia of Religion* (Macmillan: New York, 1987), 12:516.

2. *The Encyclopedia of Religion,* 12:511.

3. To date, no comprehensive work has been written that traces the development of the concept of *kedushah* from its biblical roots through its evolution as an aggadic, halakhic, kabbalistic, and philosophical term. For a discussion of the biblical meaning of *kedushah,* see Yissakhar Ya'akovson, *Chazon La-Mikra,* 2 vols. (Tel Aviv, Sinai, 1957), 1:183–191. Nechamah Leibowitz surveys the understandings of the medieval biblical exegetes in *her Iyunim Chadashim Be-Sefer Va-yikra* (World Zionist Organization, 1983), pp. 212–220. Essays on *kedushah* that draw from the broad spectrum of the rabbinic tradition can be found in Warren Zev Harvey, "Holiness: A Command to Imitatio Dei," *Tradition* 16 (1977): 7–28; and in Alan Grossman, "Holiness," in *Contemporary Jewish Religious Thought* (New York: Free Press, 1987), 389–397. Writing in the wake of Rudolph Otto, R. Joseph Soloveitchik discusses the concept of *kedushah* in "Sacred and Profane: *Kodesh* and *Chol* in World Perspectives," *Gesher—A Publication of the Student Organization of Yeshiva University* 3:1 (*Sivan* 5726, June 1966): 5–29. The concept of *kedushah* in the thought of R. Abraham Isaac Kook is explored in Zvi Yaron, *The Philosophy of Rabbi Kook* (Heb.) (Jerusalem: World Zionist Organization, 1974), pp. 107–130.

4. In a similar vein, see Psalms 60:8, 89:36, 108:8. For a fuller treatment of *kedushah* as a reference to God's essence see *Encyclopedia Mikra'it* (Jerusalem: Bialik Institute, 1982), 7:55.

5. This point is mentioned in Ya'akovson, *Chazon La-Mikra,* p. 188, and in *Encyclopedia Mikra'it,* 7:52.

6. See Nachmanides, commentary to Leviticus 19:2.

7. Cf. Exodus 22:30, 29:34, 30:32, 30:37; Leviticus 11:43–45, 19:2, 20: 25–26, 21:7–8; Numbers 15:39–40; Deuteronomy 7:3–6, 14:1–2, 14:21, 23:15.

8. Ya'akovson, *Chazon La-Mikra,* p. 186.

9. See also Deuteronomy 14:2 concerning the prohibition against ritual self-mutilation.

10. Biblical quotations generally follow the translation of the Jewish Publication Society of America (JPS). In many instances, however, the JPS version has sacrificed literal precision for ease of reading and contextual flow for the English reader. Because the methodology employed herein relies heavily on nuanced readings of the biblical text, I depart from the JPS translation on many occasions in favor of a more literal rendering.

11. The revelation of the Sabbath—which was consecrated at the close of creation but related to man only after the crossing of the sea—is well explained by this thesis. Following the six days of creation, God made the Sabbath *kadosh*—distinct and set apart. However, the Sabbath is only revealed as a day of special norms, as a day whose *kedushah* gains expression through the limitation of activity, once the nation of Israel emerges (Exodus 16:29) and approaches the covenantal rendezvous at Sinai.

12. *Pirke De-Rabi Eliezer*, chap. 40. There are many instances where the root *kdsh* does not pertain to the commandments per se, but to ad hoc impositions of limitation and restriction. Thus, in Exodus 19:10, when God wants Moses to prepare the people of Israel for the giving of the Torah by having them wash their clothes and abstain from marital intercourse, He tells Moses to make them *kadosh*. This *kedushah* is not a call to perform one of the 613 commandments, but a call to proscriptions that prepared the nation for entry into the covenant. See also Joshua 7:11–13 and the commentary of *Da'at Mikra* (Jerusalem: Mossad Harav Kook).

13. The term *ish-Kadosh* may not refer to Elisha's spiritual stature. See 2 Kings 4:9–10. Elisha's visits mandate a *separate* loft for he is *Kadosh*—socially *distinct* and *separate*.

14. The meaning of *kedushah* as "separate" is alluded to in *Midrash Torat Kohanim* on Leviticus 19:2; "'You shall be *kedoshim*'—you shall be separated." Nachmanides understood this as a general call to abstinence, above the requirements of the *Halakhah*. See his commentary to Leviticus 19:2. Other aspects of this characteristic are explored in Grossman, "Holiness," p. 390, and Ya'akovson, *Chazon La-Mikra*, p. 187.

15. The relationship between Sabbath and Sanctuary in the Bible has been well documented. See Nechamah Leibowitz, *Iyunim Chadashim Be-Sefer Shemot* (World Zionist Organization [1983]), pp. 348–352; Mordekhai Breuer, *Pirkei Mo'adot*, 2 vols. (Jerusalem: Chorev, 1986), 1:23–47; M. Weinfeld, "Sabbath, Temple Building and the Enthronement of the Lord" (Heb.) *Beit Mikra* 5737 (1976–77): 188–193; Jon D. Levenson, "The Temple and the World," *Journal of Religion* 64:3 (1984):275–298; Arthur Green, "Sabbath as Temple: Some Thoughts on Space and Time in Judaism," in *Go and Study: Essays and Studies in Honor of Alfred Jospe*, ed. Raphael Jospe and Samuel Z. Fishman (Washington, DC: B'nai B'rith–Hillel Foundations, 1980), pp. 287–305. In his article, Green beautifully traces the connection between Sabbath and Temple through biblical, aggadic, halakhic, kabbalistic, and chasidic literature.

16. *Pesikta Rabbati* 6. See in a similar vein, *Pesikta De-Rav Kahana* (Buber ed.), 5b–6a.

17. This parallel is noted in Breuer, *Pirkei Mo'adot*, p. 33.

18. *Berakhot* 55a. Other *midrashim* take the Sanctuary-creation link a step further. Beyond positing that the Sanctuary completes the process of creation, they maintain that the very process of creation began at the spot on Mount Moriah that lay under the Holy of Holies and spread outward from there. See in this vein, *Midrash, Tanchuma, Kedoshim* 10, *Yoma* 54b, and *Midrash Bereishit Rabbah* 3:4.

19. The concept of *menuchah* figures prominently in the discussion of the transition from Tabernacle to Temple. See chapter 4.

20. On the precise meaning of the term *melakhah*, skilled craftsmanship, as opposed to *avodah*, physical labor, see Jacob Milgrom, *Studies in Levitical Terminology I: The Encroacher and the Levite* (Berkeley: University of California Press, 1970), p. 78.

21. See Exodus 31:3; 35:31, 33, 35; 36:1, 5, 6, 7, 8.

22. The juxtaposition of the *melakhah* of the Sabbath and of the Sanctuary appears a second time. The prohibition from engaging in *melakhah* on the Sabbath is later the opening note of Moses' address to the nation concerning the *melakhah* of the Tabernacle (Exodus 35:1–3).

23. This call to desist from work on the Sabbath is distinguished from earlier calls of the same nature and is not a repetition. Exodus 20:9 begins, "Six days you shall labor and do all *your* work." Likewise, Exodus 23:12 opens, "Six days you shall do *your* work." The commands to refrain from work on the Sabbath here and in Exodus 35:2 both begin, "Six days work may be done," omitting the qualifying *your*. In the earlier references to the Sabbath, the Torah prohibited mundane work—*your* work—to be carried out on the Sabbath. However, this verse reveals that work done for God's Tabernacle is prohibited as well.

24. *Shabbat* 49b.

CHAPTER 2

1. See Nachmanides, commentary to Genesis 3:22.

2. Nachmanides points out this connection in his commentary to Genesis 3:8.

3. The midrash to Leviticus 26:12 portrays God as figuratively strolling with the righteous in the garden of Eden. See *Midrash Torat Kohanim, Bechukotai* 3:3. The midrash is brought by Rashi to Leviticus 26:12. Similarly, see Nachmanides on Leviticus 26:12.

4. The theme of exile across the Bible is explored by Nachmanides in his commentary to Genesis 1:1.

5. In Numbers 8:26, Joshua 22:27, and Isaiah 19:21, the sacrificial tasks of the Priests are referred to as *avodah*, which is the common phrase used by the rabbis to refer to the Temple services. The auxiliary duties of the Levites are referred to as *avodah* in the Book of Numbers, chapters 4 and 8. For an extensive treatment of the different forms of *avodah* enumerated in these passages, see Jacob Milgrom, *Studies in Levitical Terminology I: The Encroacher and the Levite* (Berkeley: University of California Press, 1970), pp. 60–88. The role of the Priests as sentries is delineated in Numbers 3:38, and of the Levites, in Numbers 1:53. These responsibilities are restated in Numbers 18:2–7. See also Milgrom, *Studies in Levitical Terminology I*, pp. 8–15.

6. These and other parallels are addressed in Jon D. Levenson, *Sinai and Zion* (Winston Press, 1985), pp. 128–131.

7. Nachmanides 2:17. For an analysis of the concept of death by the hands of heaven in the Bible, see Milgrom, *Studies in Levitical Terminology I*, 16–22.

8. *Bereishit Rabbah* 21:8.

9. *Midrash Ha-Gadol, Bereishit* 3:23. A similar idea appears in *Pirkei De-Rabi Eliezer* 20: "'He drove the man out' (Genesis 3:24)—He was driven from the garden of Eden, and settled on Mount Moriah, for the entrance to the garden of Eden opens onto Mount Moriah. From there [man] was taken and unto there he was returned, to the place from which he had been taken, for it says (Genesis 2:15) 'The Lord God took the man.' Where did he take him from? From the site of the Temple, for it says (Genesis 3:23) 'to till the soil from which he was taken.'"

10. This view, which is contrary to that of R. Saadiah Gaon and Nachmanides mentioned above, is consistent with the simple meaning of the text and is mentioned by *Midrash Bereishit Rabbah* 6:17.

11. *Midrash Ha-Gadol, Bereishit* 3:24.

12. The parallel between the cherubim as guards in Eden and as guards within the *Kodesh Kodashim* is made in a midrash (original source unknown) cited by the fourteenth-century Italian kabbalist, Menachem b. Benjamin Recanati, in his commentary to Genesis 3:24. The midrash depicts the jour-

ney and travails the souls of the righteous endure on their way to their final destination. The relevant segment says as follows: "The soul then approaches the second gate, the gate of the garden of Eden. There, it encounters the cherubim and the fiery ever-turning sword. If the soul is found meritorious, it enters unscathed. If it is judged unfavorably, it is punished there with the fiery ever-turning sword. Parallel to these [cherubim], were the cherubim in the Temple. If the High Priest was judged meritoriously when he would enter the *Kodesh Kodashim* on the Day of Atonement, he would enter unscathed. But if he was found to be lacking in merit, a flame of fire would leap out from between the two cherubim [atop the Ark] and would consume him internally and he would perish."

13. A similar parallel can be observed concerning the clothing of Eden and the clothing of the priests in the Temple. Genesis 3:21 reads, "And the Lord God made tunics of skin for the man and his wife, and He dressed them." Employing almost identical sentence structure, God commands Moses concerning the investiture of the priests, "And for the sons of Aaron, you shall make tunics . . . and you shall dress your brother Aaron with these" (Exodus 28:40–41). In the wake of the sin, man's base nature, as embodied in his nakedness, could no longer stand unmasked in the presence of God. Similarly, the priests cannot appear before God unless they are properly attired. A link between the tunics of skin that Adam received and the priestly garments is made in *Midrash Avkir*, brought in M. M. Kasher, *Torah Shelemah*, 41 vols. (New York: American Biblical Encyclopedia Society, 1951), 2:287; and in *Bamidbar Rabbah* 4:8.

14. *Baba Batra* 25a.

15. Maimonides, *The Guide of the Perplexed*, trans. Shlomo Pines and Leo Strauss (Chicago, University of Chicago Press, 1963), 3:45.

CHAPTER 3

1. Deuteronomy 26:1–9.
2. Exodus 13:9.
3. Deuteronomy 5:15.
4. Mishnah, *Berakhot* 12b.
5. *Yad, Hilkhot Keri'at Shema* 1:3.

6. Many commentators have attempted to explain why the Torah omitted this information. For an overview, see Menachem Kasher, *Torah Shelemah*
(Heb.) (New York: American Biblical Encyclopedia Society, 1955),16:282.

7. *Shabbat* 86b.

8. The earliest explicit source that describes Shavu'ot as a commemoration of the giving of the Torah is in the Talmud, *Pesachim* 68b. Refuting
Abarbanel's contention that the Torah did not intend Shavu'ot to be a celebration of the revelation, R. David Zvi Hoffmann maintains that the connection between the two was implicit from biblical times. See his commentary to Leviticus 23 in D. Z. Hoffmann, *Sefer Vayikra* (Heb.), trans. Zvi Har
Shefer and Aharon Leiberman (Jerusalem: Mosad Harav Kook, 5732), 2:158–
168. See also Hayyim Leshem, *Ha-Shabbat U-Mo'adei Yisra'el* (Tel Aviv: Niv,
5725), 2:504–506.

9. This approach reflects Maimonides' listing of the 613 biblically mandated commandments. Nachmanides however, in his commentary to Maimonides' *Sefer Ha-Mitzvot* (end of the listing of prohibitions, commandment
2), cites Deuteronomy 4:9 as the source for the commandment that we must
perpetually remember the giving of the Torah at Sinai.

10. It should not trouble the reader that the Rabbis highlighted the connection between the holiday of Shavu'ot and the Revelation at Sinai, even
as the Bible obscured it. The Rabbis wanted to ensure that the Jewish people
would identify with the Sinai experience. Since the tradition holds that the
Revelation occurred on the sixth of *Sivan*, they featured Shavu'ot as *zeman
matan Torateinu*. This would seem to put the rabbinic approach to the nature
of the Revelation at direct odds with that of the Bible. The Bible makes every
attempt to remove the Revelation from the bounds of time so that it not be
associated with a particular generation of Jews. Conversely, however, the
Rabbis enacted a commemoration of the event on its anniversary, which
seems to stress its nature as an event rooted in a particular historical period,
like any other event. The rabbinic agenda on this issue should be seen as a
compliment to the message that stems from the simple meaning of the biblical text, and not as a negation of that meaning. Taken together, the biblical and rabbinic emphases allow a balanced approach to the Revelation to
emerge. A sensitive reading of the Torah that is faithful to its simple meaning,
teaches that the Revelation bears a timeless dimension, as we have discussed
in the body of the text. In full awareness and acceptance of this important

lesson, the Rabbis then chose to stress the identity of Shavu'ot as *zeman matan Torateinu* in order to allow later generations a greater sense of identification with the Sinai event.

There are many instances where the simple meaning of the biblical text is at variance with the rabbinic interpretation. To some, this is especially disturbing when the rulings of the Oral Law contrast sharply with what the Bible itself has to say on that topic. The approach that we have utilized here recognizes the differences that exist between the simple meaning of the biblical text and the interpretation of the Oral Tradition. One classical approach to such differences is to attempt to explain them away, in an effort to show how the Written and Oral Traditions speak with the same voice at every turn. Such an approach, however, often seems stretched and challenges the Orthodox Jew with a choice between his common sense and his loyalty to the rabbinic tradition. Further, such an approach often results in a complete departure from the simple meaning of the text, thereby insulting the text itself, which is divine in origin. In recognizing that issues often have more than one side, we can examine the differences between the Written and Oral Traditions as complementing views, while allowing each source to retain its own integrity and speak with its own voice. For a fuller discussion of this approach see M. Breuer, *"Limud Peshuto Shel Mikra: Sakanot ve-Sikuyim," Ha-Ma'ayan, Nisan* 5738 (1978), 1–13. For an overview of the relationship between the Written and Oral Traditions within classical rabbinic sources, see M. M. Kasher, *Torah Shelemah* (New York: American Biblical Encyclopedia Society, 1956) 17:286–312.

11. *Tanchuma Yashan, Yitro,* 8.

12. This is in keeping with the position of the thirteenth-century commentator, Nachmanides. Nachmanides held that events happened in the order that the Torah reports them and rejected the principle of *ein mukdam u-me'uchar ba-Torah.* Nachmanides generally displayed a propensity to render explanations that were faithful to the simple meaning of the text and without invoking midrashic embellishments, unlike Rashi. See his commentaries to Leviticus 8:1 s.v. *kach et Aharon,* and to Numbers 16:1 s.v. *va-yikach Korach.*

13. Nachmanides, Exodus 35:1.

14. *Seder Eliyahu Rabbah,* 17, s.v. *d.a. ba-atarah.*

15. The close of the Revelation narrative is further linked to the Tabernacle chapters in its use of a significant phrase that heralds the command to build the Tabernacle. Throughout the narrative of Exodus, chapter 19, the

Bible consistently employs the word *va-yered* ("descended") to refer to God's arrival upon the Mount. Here, in chapter 24, a new term appears: *va-yishkon kevod Hashem*—"God's glory dwelled" upon Mount Sinai. This phrase is significant as it is the key phrase in both the opening and closing statements of the Tabernacle sections: "Make for me a Tabernacle, and I shall dwell in their midst (*ve-shakhanti betokham*)" (Exodus 25:8); and "And I shall dwell amongst (*ve-shakhanti betokh*) the children of Israel, and shall be for them a God. And they shall know that I am the Lord their God who took them out of the land of Egypt to dwell amongst them (*le-shokheni be-tokham*), I am the Lord their God." (Exodus 29:45–46). Thus, the passage at the close of Exodus, chapter 24, not only concludes the Revelation at Sinai but, by dividing the narrative of the tablets and utilizing the key word "to dwell" (*sh.kh.n.*) it also prefaces the chapters of the Tabernacle.

16. There are two exceptions to this. The first is the list of commandments in Exodus, chapter 34, following the sin of the Golden Calf. These are all commandments originally issued in Exodus, chapter 23, during the Revelation at Mount Sinai. Their reemergence here is part of a larger theme of the reconsecration of the covenant following the sin of the Golden Calf. See Nachmanides, Exodus 34:11. The second exception is the mention of the Sabbath in Exodus 31:12–17 and 35:1–3. Though quantitatively they are an insignificant presence, their meaning amid the chapters of the Tabernacle is great. See chapter 1, "What Is *Kedushah*?" See also Jon D. Levenson, *Sinai and Zion* (Winston Press, 1985), pp. 142–145.

17. This is said concerning the Ark, the Table, and the Candelabra in Exodus 25:40, concerning the surrounding tent in Exodus 26:30, and concerning the Altar of Burnt Offering in Exodus 27:8.

18. See U. Cassuto, *A Commentary on the Book of Exodus*, trans. Israel Abrahams (Jerusalem: Magnes Press, 1967), p. 319.

Another established voice in the tradition understands that the command to erect the Tabernacle did not immediately follow the Revelation, but was issued only after the people sinned in the building of the Golden Calf. See Rashi, Exodus 33:11, for the chronology of the 120 days that Moses spent on Mount Sinai. According to this view, the Jewish people should have been prepared to worship God without physical representations of his presence. The building of the Golden Calf, however, demonstrated that the people needed physical forms to embody their service to God, and so God sanctioned the building of the Tabernacle. This line of thinking represents a long tradition in the midrashic and exegetical literature. See *Midrash Aggadah Terumah,* 27:1, *Shemot Rabbah* 33:3, *Tanchuma Terumah* 8, Seforno to Exodus 24:18, and Rabbeinu Bahya to Exodus 25:5, s.v. *ba-shamayim.*

This view is sometimes misconstrued as a statement that if the people had not sinned, there would have been no need of a Tabernacle. In our age, critics of the concept of a Temple point to this voice in the tradition as evidence that when there is no idol worship, the Temple no longer serves a function. In Exodus, chapter 23, however, at the close of the juridical section that follows the giving of the Ten Commandments, Moses receives several commandments concerning the "house of the Lord." All voices in the tradition concur that this revelation took place before the details of the Tabernacle were transmitted in chapter 25, and before the people committed the sin of the Golden Calf. The basic notion, therefore, of a Sanctuary—of a place where God dwells among the people—does not represent a concession, but a hallowed ideal. When Rashi and the *midrashim* speak of the Tabernacle as a concession to the idolatrous tendencies of that age, this is only in regard to the details of the Tabernacle and its rites, but not the basic concept of a Sanctuary itself. See Rashi, Leviticus 9:3, concerning the calf that was offered in the consecration of the Tabernacle in Leviticus, chapter 10.

Although this position divorces the chronological link between Sinai and Sanctuary, it can still cast the Sinai motif as a significant symbol in Tabernacle theology. According to this understanding, God spoke to Moses concerning the Tabernacle for the first time at the beginning of Exodus, chapter 35. Exodus 34 is the chapter in which the children of Israel are forgiven for their transgression and their covenant with God, reestablished. This narrative borrows many elements from the first Sinai theophany narrative, ranging from the account of Moses' ascent to receive the tablets, to the enumeration of holidays after the covenant is restored. In essence, then, the Golden Calf narrative concludes with a re-creation of the Revelation at Mount Sinai. The Tabernacle section in chapter 35 follows the account of the re-creation of the Sinai revelation to show that the Tabernacle will be the vehicle that perpetuates the restored relationship between God and Israel, the most potent symbol of which is the Revelation at Sinai.

19. According to Rashbam, Leviticus 9:24, the fire that consumed upon the altar was itself the Glory of God, thus creating a parallel to the narrative in Exodus, chapter 24. For a discussion of the term "the Glory of God" and its different meanings, see Nechamah Leibowitz, *Iyunim Chadashim Be-Sefer Va-Yikra* (World Zionist Organization, 1983), pp. 94–98.

20. See Nachmanides, introduction to Exodus, chapter 25.

21. In chapter 25, the vessels are ordered as follows: The Ark, the Table, the Candelabra, and the tent itself. In chapter 35, however, the order reads first the tent, and then the Ark, the table, and the candelabra. In chapter 25, the Torah lists the vessels according to their hierarchy as vessels of *kedushah*, and hence, the Ark is given first billing. In chapter 35 the Torah recounts the actual construction and assembly of the Tabernacle and its constituent parts. The Bible lists the tent first because once it is built, it can house the other vessels, which are then mentioned in the same order as in chapter 25.

22. This tenet is assumed throughout the Bible, as many figures express shock that they survived encounters with angels. See Genesis 16:13; Deuteronomy 5:22; and Judges 6:23, 13:22.

23. The identity of a group known as priests prior to the election of the house of Aaron is discussed in the commentary of the Mossad Harav Kook publishing house, *Da'at Mikra*, to Exodus 19:22.

24. *Midrash Sifrei Zuta, Korach* 18:4, as quoted by Nachmanides in his introduction to the Book of Numbers.

25. *Zohar, Pekudei* 229a.

26. This perspective on the *anan ha-ketoret* is discussed, in conjunction with the sins of Korach in Numbers, chapter 17, the sins of Nadab and Abihu in Leviticus, chapter 10, and other episodes in Baruch Katz, "Ve-Chisah Anan Ha-Ketoret," *Alon Shevut* (Heb.) 106 (*Adar II, 5744*): 53–62.

27. *Mekhilta de-Rav Shimon ben Yochai* to Exodus 19:18, as quoted in *Torah Shelemah* 19:105.

28. "Pilgrimages," *The Encyclopedia of Religion* (New York: Macmillan, 1987), 11:338.

29. *Yoma* 53a.

30. *Yad, Hilkhot Chagigah* 3:6.

CHAPTER 4

1. A tower is seen to be a fortified structure in nearly all biblical references. See Judges 9:50–52; Psalms 61:4; and Song of Songs 4:4. For further treatment of the term *migdal* (tower), see *Encyclopedia Mikra'it* (Heb.) (Jerusalem: Bialik Institute, 1970), 4:633–636.

2. The anthropomorphism, "God came down" is common and gener-

ally refers to divine intervention in the affairs of man, as in Exodus 3:8, or to an act of divine revelation, as in Exodus 19:20. Here, however, God's omnipotence is contrasted with the tower, which would reach the sky, thus licensing the understanding of God's descent here as almost mocking condescension.

3. Nachmanides, commentary to Genesis 12:4.

4. The etymology of the word *name* is from the Latin *nomen*. In its connotation as reputation or renown, this root is the source of the word *ignominy*.

5. Examples of this are seen in Proverbs 22:1, "Repute (*shem*) is preferable to great wealth," and Ecclesiastes 7:1, "A good name (*shem*) is better than fragrant oil."

6. Interestingly, it is the practice of religious Jews to refer to God in casual speech as *Hashem*—literally, the Name—in a reference to the unutterable tetragrammaton. However, since the word *shem* also implies reputation, to mention God's name—*Hashem*—is to immediately bring to mind His reputation.

7. *Midrash Tanchuma* (Buber ed.) 50b (to Genesis 20:1); *Yalkut Shim'oni* 2:703.

8. See the parallel section in 2 Chronicles 6:9–10. The establishment of dynastic rule as a precondition for the erection of the Temple is also seen in 1 Kings 5:19.

9. 1 Samuel 4:4, 2 Samuel 6:2, 1 Chronicles 13:6.

10. This is the understanding of the medieval exegete R. David Kimchi. Other commentators contend that the poles remained in center position but protruded into the curtain between the Holy and the Holy of Holies because of their length.

CHAPTER 5

1. Maimonides, *The Guide of the Perplexed* 3:39, trans. Shlomo Pines and Leo Strauss (Chicago: University of Chicago Press, 1963), 2:551. See also 3:46 at end.

2. *Megillah* 26b, *Yoma* 12a.

3. Other biblical sources also portray the Priests and Levites as educators. See Nehemiah 8:5–8, Malachi 2:6–7, and 2 Chronicles 30:22, 35:3.

4. Maimonides, *Yad, Hilkhot Shemitah Ve-Yovel* 13:12.

5. This understanding is also reflected in *Midrash Tehillim* (Buber ed.), Psalm 18 s.v. (21) *yatsileini*.

6. S.v. *mai Har Ha-Mori'ah*.

7. *Sefer Ha-Hinnuch—The Book of [Mitzvah] Education*, trans. Charles Wengrov (Jerusalem: Feldheim, 1984), 3:509.

8. *Kuzari* 3:39.

9. *Yad, Hilkhot Sanhedrin* 14:11. This law is an application of the halakhic principle of *ha-makom gorem*—literally, "a function of location." Its meaning is that the courts only possess certain powers by virtue of God's inspiration, which is extant only when the Temple is standing and the seat of the Sanhedrin is in the Chamber of Hewn Stone. See *Avodah Zarah* 8a, *Shabbat* 15a, and *Sanhedrin* 14b. For the distinction between the four forms of capital punishment that are biblically enumerated, and the broader powers given to the king to enact the death penalty, see *Derashot Ha-Ran* of Rabbeinu Nissim of Gerona, essay no. 11.

10. *Megillah* 1:12. For a halakhic discussion of private sacrifice outside of the Sanctuary see "*Bamah*," *Encyclopedia Talmudit* 3:339–346.

11. *Yad, Hilkhot Beit Ha-Bechirah* 6:15–16.

12. Psalms 2:1–2 equates war against the king with war against God: "Why do nations assemble/and peoples plot vain things;/kings of the earth take their stand,/and regents intrigue together/*against the Lord and against His anointed*."

13. See Jon Levenson, "The Jerusalem Temple in Devotional and Visionary Space," in *Jewish Spirituality*, vol. 1, *From the Bible through the Middle Ages*, ed. Arthur Green (New York: Crossroad, 1986), p. 49. Levenson sees this idea expressed in Psalms 2:6: "But I have installed My king/on Zion My holy mountain."

Psalms 78:68–69 also attests to the connection between the Temple and the monarchy: "He did choose the tribe of Judah/Mount Zion, which He loved/ (69) He built His Sanctuary like the heavens/like the earth that He established forever." The choice of the tribe of Judah may be a geographic reference to Jerusalem and the site of the Temple, or it may refer to the choice of the Davidic line to rule over Israel. According to this second interpretation, verse 69 pairs the choice of the Davidic line with the choice of Mount Zion as the site of the Temple.

14. *Vayikra Rabbah* 17:3.

15. *Sifrei Bamidbar* 99.

16. See in this vein, Nachmanides, commentary to Genesis 49:10.

CHAPTER 6

1. See, e.g., 1 Samuel 15:22 and Jeremiah 7:22–23.

2. In medieval Jewish thought, this remains the dominant view. Some opinions, however, interpreted anthropomorphic statements in the Bible and Midrash as indications of God's corporeal nature. See *Yad, Hilkhot Teshuvah* 3:7, and the commentary to that ruling of R. Abraham b. David.

3. *Encyclopedia of Religion* (New York: Macmillan, 1987), 12:555.

4. *Encyclopedia of Religion* 12:556.

5. *Yad, Hilkhot Ma'asei Ha-Korbanot* 3:13.

6. Nachmanides, *Commentary on the Torah*, Leviticus 1:9, trans. Charles B. Chavel (New York: Shilo Publishing House, 1974).

7. *Sefer Ha-Chinukh*, commandment 95.

8. See commentary of R. Abraham Ibn Ezra to Exodus 29:14.

9. R. David Zvi Hoffman (1843–1921) was the supreme halakhic authority of Orthodox Jewry in Germany in the early part of the twentieth century. On top of a classical yeshiva background, Hoffman also studied at the universities of Vienna and Berlin. His commentaries on the Books of Leviticus and Deuteronomy utilize classical rabbinic exegesis in an attempt to refute interpretations offered by schools of higher biblical criticism.

10. The passages of Leviticus do not explicitly implicate the leper as guilty of a sin. The midrash, however, concludes that the mandate to bring a *chatat* is indicative that an offense was committed. See *Midrash Vayikra Rabbah* 17:3. In a similar vein, the Talmud feels compelled to identify the sin that mandates a new mother to bring a *korban chatat*. See *Niddah* 31b.

11. David Zvi Hoffman, *Sefer Vayikra*, vol. 1, trans. Zvi Har Shefer and Aharon Leiberman (Jerusalem: Mosad Harav Kook, 5732 [1971–72]), p. 150.

12. Pinchas H. Peli, *On Repentance: In the Thought and Oral Discourse of Rabbi Joseph B. Soloveitchik* (Jerusalem: Oroth Publishing House, 1980), pp. 59–60.

13. Nachmanides, *Commentary on the Torah*, Leviticus 4:2, trans. Charles B. Chavel (New York: Shilo Publishing House, 1974).

14. Hoffman, *Sefer Vayikra*, p. 151.

15. See also the case of the man obligated to bring a *korban asham* in the wake of sexual relations with a servant designated for another man (Leviticus 19:20–22).

16. Leviticus 1:4 refers to the *korban olah* as performing an expiatory function without delineating the infractions that would mandate its offering. The Talmud lists several categories of transgressions for which no other *korban* is brought and for which the *korban olah* could atone. See *Yoma* 8:6, *Yad, Ma'asei Ha-Korbanot* 1:8 and 3:14; and Nachmanides in his commentary to Leviticus 1:4 s.v. *ve-nirtzah lo.*

17. See *Yad, Hilkhot Ma'asei Ha-Korbanot* 5:6–17.

18. *Midrash Ha-Chafetz* Leviticus 1:2, as quoted by *Torah Shelemah* 25:17.

19. Hoffman, *Sefer Vayikra*, p. 115.

20. Nachmanides makes this point explicitly in his commentary to Genesis 31:46. Some commentators have seen a similar phenomenon in Joshua 9:14–15, at the establishment of the *brit* between the Israelites and Gibeonites. The consumption of the Gibeonite victuals by the elders of Israel, however, was more likely a test of the veracity of their story.

21. R. David Kimchi, commentary to Genesis 31:54, s.v. *va-yizbach.*

22. *Chizkuni* to Exodus 24:11.

23. The offering of *korbanot olah* and *zevachim* at Mount Sinai sheds light on a point raised earlier. We noted in line 2, chapter 3, that the thrice-annual pilgrimage can be construed as a collective re-creation of the Sinai experience. It is worthy of note, in this context, that the Oral Law mandates that every pilgrim must offer a *korban olah* and *korban shelamim* when he comes to Jerusalem for the three festivals. See *Yad, Hilkhot Chagigah* 1:1.

The laws of the *korban shelamim* can be seen as a covenantal gesture in a second venue. Generally speaking, the *korban shelamim* is brought by an individual. The only occasion on which the entire congregation of Israel offers a collective *shelamim* is on the festival of Shavu'ot (Leviticus 23:19). This is one of the strongest supports from within the Bible itself for the identity of Shavu'ot as a holiday commemorative of the establishment of the covenantal bond between God and Israel.

24. Rashi, Leviticus 3:1.

25. Brought in the commentary *Beit Yoseph* of R. Joseph Karo to *Tur, Orach Chaim* 167.

26. *Midrash Ha-Gadol* Numbers 18:19, also cited in *Torah Shelemah* 25, 109, n. 110.

27. Some modern scholars have referred to the *korban shelamim* as a *korban*

se'udah—a feast offering. See Hoffman in his quote of Zunz, in Hoffman, *Sefer Vayikra*, p. 116.

28. R. Abraham Ibn Ezra, commentary to Exodus 25:30.

29. Hoffman, *Sefer Vayikra* 2:212. Hoffman derives this reading of the verse from Exodus 31:16, where the Sabbath is described as an everlasting covenant (*brit olam*). The Sabbath, according to this opinion, is not an independent covenant, but rather a sign of the covenant entered into at Sinai.

30. Joseph B. Soloveitchik, *"U-Vikashtem Mi-Sham," Ish Ha-Halakhah— Galui Ve-Nistar* (Jerusalem: World Zionist Organization, 5739 [1978–79]), p. 208.

31. The centrality of blood imagery to the rite of circumcision gains greater amplification in rabbinic writings. It is the custom today to recite verses that pertain to the commandment of circumcision immediately following the ceremony. One of these is Ezekiel 16:6, "I said to you, 'Live in spite of your blood.' Yea, I said to you, 'Live in spite of your blood.'" See *Shulchan Arukh, Yoreh De'ah* 265:1. When a convert undergoes circumcision, the blessing recited refers to the "blood of the covenant." See *Yad, Hilkhot Milah* 3:4.

32. *Midrash Ha-Gadol* to Exodus 24:8 also sees the significance of the blood as a symbol for the soul: *"This is the blood of the covenant*—Through this blood you have entered into the covenant; if you sustain the covenant, your souls will be sustained. And from where do we learn that the soul is called blood? For it says, 'for the soul of all flesh is its blood' (Leviticus 17:14), and it says, 'for the blood is the soul' (Deuteronomy 12:23)."

33. Hoffman, *Sefer Vayikra*, p. 150.

34. Alan Herscovici, *Second Nature: The Animal Rights Controversy* (Toronto: CBC Enterprises, 1985), p. 46.

35. James M. Jasper and Dorothy Nelkin, *The Animal Rights Crusade: The Growth of a Moral Movement* (New York: Free Press, 1992), p. 69.

36. David Paterson and Richard D. Ryder, eds., *Animal Rights—A Symposium* (London: Centaur Press, 1979), p. viii.

37. Jasper and Nelkin, *The Animal Rights Crusade*, p. 38.

38. A very good study of this issue can be found in Elijah Judah Shochet, *Animal Life in Jewish Tradition: Attitudes and Relationships* (New York: KTAV, 1984). Shochet is particularly sensitive to how the Jewish view of the animal world has evolved from biblical, through rabbinic, to modern sources. See also Roberta Kalechofsky, ed., *Judaism and Animal Rights: Classical and Contemporary Responses* (Micah Publications, 1992).

39. Shochet, *Animal Life in Jewish Tradition*, pp. 210–212. Other sources that address the primacy of man are, A. Tkhrusch, *Tif'eret Ha-Adam* (Jerusalem: Mossad HaRav Kook, 1951); and E. Urbach, *The Sages: Their Concepts and Their Beliefs* (Jerusalem: Magnes Press, 1971), pp. 189–226.

40. Joseph B. Soloveitchik, "The Lonely Man of Faith," *Tradition* 7:2 (Summer 1965):11–16.

41. For an overview of the Jewish sources for vegetarianism, see Shochet, *Animal Life in Jewish Tradition*, pp. 288–298.

42. Nachmanides, Leviticus 17:11.

43. See Maimonides, *Guide of the Perplexed* 3:48; and Shochet, *Animal Life in Jewish Tradition*, p. 211.

44. See Shochet, *Animal Life in Jewish Tradition*, chaps. 4, 5, 9.

45. With regard to animals, see Leviticus 27:32 concerning the tithe of livestock, and Exodus 13:11–15 and Deuteronomy 12:17, concerning the dedication of the firstborn.

46. Hoffman, *Sefer Vayikra*, p. 65.

CHAPTER 7

1. See Ezekiel 37:15–28; Isaiah 2:1–4, 56:7. Other passages that address the final redemption are Jeremiah 30:1–33; Hosea 2:16–25; Amos 9:8–15; Zechariah 8:1–23; Malachi 3:19–24.

2. See Haggai 1:3–11, 2:10–19.

3. The identity of the biblical Ahasuerus is a subject of dispute. Rabbinic sources place his rule between those of Cyrus and Darius. Historical records indicate that he reigned between Darius and Ataxerxes. The evidence and dates for each position are discussed in the introduction of the *Da'at Mikra* commentary to the Book of Esther by Amos Chakham (Jerusalem: Mossad Harav Kook, 1973), pp. 4–6. This dispute, however, has little bearing on the present discussion. All opinions concur that Ahasuerus's reign was during the first years of the Second Commonwealth.

4. See also 1 Chronicles 29:1; Nehemiah 2:8, 7:2.

5. Judah Halevi, *The Kuzari: An Argument for the Faith of Israel*, trans. Hartwig Hirschfeld (New York: Shocken, 1964), 2:24, p. 100.

6. *Megillah* 12a.

7. *Megillah* 12a.

8. See, in a related vein, R. Yoel Bin-Nun, *"Yom Yusad Heikhal Hashem,"* *Megadim* 12 (*Tishrei* 5751): 49–97.

9. 4 Maccabees 4:52–57.

10. The correlation between the 24th of *Kislev* in Haggai and the holiday of Chanukah is drawn in similar fashion by the German halakhist R. Jacob Emden (1697–1776) in his commentary to the *Shulchan Arukh, Mor U-Ketzi'ah,* chap. 670.

EPILOGUE

1. On this topic, see Baruch M. Bokser, "Rabbinic Responses to Catastrophe: From Continuity to Discontinuity," *Proceedings of the American Academy for Jewish Research* 50 (1983):37–61; Gedaliah Alon, *The Jews in Their Land in the Talmudic Age,* vol. 1 (Jerusalem: Magnes Press, 1980) pp. 46–52, 107–118, 253–287; E. E. Urbach, "Political and Social Tendencies in Talmudic Concepts of Charity" (Heb.), *Zion* 16 (1951):1–27; Robert Goldberg, "The Broken Axis: Rabbinic Judaism and the Fall of Jerusalem," *JAAR Supplement* 45 (1977):869–882.

2. *Megillah* 29a. See, in this vein, the commentaries of Rashi and R. David Kimchi to Ezekiel 11:16.

3. *Megillah* 23b.

4. *Tosefta Megillah* 3:14. In actual practice, today, the egress need not face eastward if the structure of the synagogue does not allow for it. The *Halakhah* does, however, call for the portal to be opposite the direction of the Ark, which is the direction toward which the congregants face. See *Shulchan Arukh, Orach Chayim* 150:5.

5. *Berakhot* 26b.

6. *Berakhot* 3a.

7. *Sukkah* 41a.

8. *Pesachim* 115a.

9. *Pesachim* 114b.

10. *Baba Batra* 60b.

11. For a full enumeration of these customs, see *Shulchan Arukh, Orach Chayim* 560.

12. For a lengthier treatment of the modes equated with sacrificial worship, see Nahum Glatzer, "The Concept of Sacrifice in Post-Biblical Juda-

ism," in *Essays in Jewish Thought* (University, AL: University of Alabama Press, 1978), pp. 48–57.

13. *Avot De-Rabi Natan* 4.

14. Cf. Isaiah 1:11–14; Jeremiah 7:22–23, Amos 5:22–24.

15. *Berakhot* 55a.

16. In his essay, Baruch Bokser maintains that in mishnaic and early amoraic sources, other modes of worship and service to God are equated with the sacral rites, and that it is only in later amoraic material that the rabbis began to see extrasacrificial acts as superior in value to the rites of the Temple. See Bokser, "Rabbinic Responses to Catastrophe."

17. *Sukkah* 49b.

18. *Midrash Vayikra Rabbah* 7:12.

19. *Berakhot* 8a.

20. For a halakhic overview of this concept, see *"arba amot," Encyclopedia Talmudit* (Heb.) (Jerusalem: Talmudic Encyclopedia Publishing, 1959) 2:153–159.

21. *Menachot* 110a.

22. *Shabbat* 30a.

23. *Megillah* 16b.

24. *Berakhot* 26b.

25. *Yad, Hilkhot Temidin U'Musafin* 6:4, *Hilkhot Kelei Ha-Mikdash* 6:4.

26. *Midrash Shochar Tov* 4:6.

27. *Berakhot* 32b.

28. See also *Berakhot* 2:1, which indicates that prayer is equivalent to offering a *korban minchah* and that charity and justice are superior to sacrificial worship.

29. *Yad, Hilkhot Beit Ha-Bechirah* 6:14–16.

30. *Yad, Hilkhot Beit Ha-Bechirah* 6:16.

31. 1 Samuel 4:4, 2 Samuel 6:2, 1 Chronicles 13:6.

32. One of the foremost contemporary Orthodox biblical scholars, R. Mordekhai Breuer, has seen enormous theological and historical significance in this concept. As long as God's presence rested amid the cherubim atop the Ark, His presence was tenuous; moreover, during periods when the Ark was in captivity or when the Tabernacle fell into disuse altogether, the divine presence withdrew. The progression from Tabernacle to Temple, claims Rabbi Breuer, was a process of anchoring the divine presence in the world. Moreover, once the divine presence became affiliated with a parcel

of land—Jerusalem, something with permanence—it meant that the divine presence would never leave that spot. Subsequent Temples, argues Rabbi Breuer, do not require the conditions extant in the ages of David and Solomon. To bring the divine presence to a state of rootedness in the world required the ideal conditions of the age of Solomon. Once the divine presence is rooted in the world, however, it is the obligation of the Jewish people to erect a Temple to acknowledge that fact. Hence, the returnees from the Babylonian exile could—indeed, were obligated to—build the Temple as soon as they returned, even though conditions at the time were hardly what they had been under Solomon. See Rabbi Breuer's essay "*Kedushat Yerushalayim Ve-Ha-Mikdash,*" in *She'alu Shelom Yerushalayim: Ir Ha-Kodesh Ba-Halakhah Ba-Aggadah U-Va-Machshavah*, ed. Yo'el Baris and Ya'akov Bir, pp. 15–31 (Jerusalem: *Tenu'at Ha-No'ar Ha-Chareidi Be-Eretz Yisra'el "Ezra,"* 5745 (1984–1985); Pirkei Mo'adot (Heb.) (Jerusalem: Chorev, 1986), 2:476–491, particularly pp. 483, 487.

33. *Yad, Hilkhot Melakhim* 12:2.

34. The former Chief Rabbi of the State of Israel, R. Shelomo Goren, explores these positions in greater halakhic depth in *Har Ha-Bayit* (Heb.) (Jerusalem, 1992), pp. 161–171.

35. Rashi to *Sukkah* 41a, s.v. *'i nami*, based on *Mekhilta* to Exodus 15:17.

36. *Yad, Hilkhot Melakhim* 11:1.

37. *Yad, Hilkhot Melakhim* 11:4.

38. *Bereishit Rabbah* 64:10.

39. *Minchat Chinukh* to *Sefer Ha-Chinukh*, commandment 95.

40. Joseph B. Soloveitchik, "*Kol Dodi Dofek,*" in *Ish Ha-Emunah* (Jerusalem: Mossad Harav Kook, 1988), pp. 88–90.

41. *Sifra*, Leviticus 26:37.

42. *Sefat Emet, Chanukah* 5642–43.

Glossary

Amidah The central prayer of the traditional liturgy, recited three times daily.

Anan Ha-Ketoret The incense that was offered in the Sanctuary.

Asham One of the five categories of sacrificial worship. See pp. 122–123.

beit Midrash The study hall of a *yeshivah*.

brit The Hebrew word for *covenant*, it often refers more particularly to the covenant established at Sinai between God and the Jewish people.

charoset A mixture of wine and nuts served at the Passover Seder to commemorate the mortar used by the Israelite slaves in Egypt to make bricks.

Chatat One of the five categories of sacrificial worship. See pp. 120–122.

cherubim Two human figures that were molded atop the Ark of the Covenant.

churban Literally, "destruction," usually in reference to the destruction of the Temple.

Hakhel A biblically mandated convocation of the entire nation in Jerusalem, held every seven years during the festival of Sukkot following the sabbatical year.

kaddish A prayer of public declaration of God's greatness and sanctity, recited only in the presence of a quorum of ten men.

karet Literally, "to be cut off," it refers to a divine punishment tantamount to capital punishment. According to some opinions, this took the form of early death, while others maintain that it meant childlessness.

Kodesh Kodashim The inner sanctum of the Sanctuary, and its holiest site.

ma'aser sheni Literally, "the second tithe," so called because it was the second tithe taken by the Israelite farmer, following the first tithe, which was given to a member of the tribe of Levi.

mechitzah Literally, "a divider," it generally refers to the partition separating the men's and women's sections in a synagogue.

Minchah One of the five categories of sacrificial worship. See pp. 154–156.

minyan A quorum of ten men needed for a public prayer service.

Olah One of the five categories of sacrificial worship. See pp. 123–124.

Semikhah The ritual in which the owner of an animal places his hands upon it prior to its slaughter for sacrificial purposes. See pp. 117–120.

Shelamim One of the five categories of sacrificial worship. See pp. 128–133.

Shema A prayer recited during the morning and evening services comprising Deuteronomy 6:4–9, 11:13–21, and Numbers 15:37–41.

shlita A Hebrew acrostic meaning "he should live long and good years," used after the mention of someone's name.

tefillin Phylacteries of leather boxes containing parchment scrolls with biblical passages, donned by men during the morning prayer service.

Zerikah　The sacrificial ritual in which the blood of the sacrificial animal was sprinkled at various points on the altar. See pp. 124–126.

z"l　A Hebrew acrostic meaning "may he rest in peace," or, literally, "may his memory be blessed."

Bibliography

WORKS IN ENGLISH

Anderson, Gary. *Sacrifices and Offerings in Ancient Israel: Studies in Their Social and Political Importance.* Harvard Semitic Monographs 41. Atlanta, GA: Scholars Press, 1987.

——. "Approaching Sacred Space—The Problem of Divine Omnipresence and Sacred Places in Biblical, Post-Biblical and Rabbinic Judaism." *Harvard Theological Review* 78:3–4 (1985): 279–299.

Bokser, Baruch M. "Rabbinic Responses to Catastrophe: From Continuity to Discontinuity." *Proceedings of the American Academy for Jewish Research* 50 (1983): 37–61.

Brown, J. R. *Temple and Sacrifice in Rabbinic Judaism.* Seabury-Western Theological Seminary, 1963.

Cassuto, Umberto. *A Commentary on the Book of Exodus.* Trans. Israel Abrahams. Jerusalem: Magnes Press, 1967.

Eliade, Mircea. *The Sacred and the Profane.* Trans. William R. Trask. San Diego, CA: Harcourt Brace and Jovanovitch, 1959.

Fishbane, Michael. "The Sacred Center in the Bible." In *Texts and Responses:*

Studies Presented to Nahum N. Glatzer, ed. Michael A. Fishbane and Paul R. Flohr, pp. 6–27. Leiden, Holland: E. J. Brill, 1975.

Goldberg, Nahum. "The Rabbinic Concept of *Shekhinah* and Its Development in the Thought of Sa'adia Ga'on and Judah Levi." *Nitzanim* 2 (1983): 101–117.

Green, Arthur. "Sabbath as Temple: Some Thoughts on Space and Time in Judaism." In *Go and Study: Essays and Studies in Honor of Alfred Jospe*, ed. Raphael Jospe and Samuel Z. Fishman, pp. 287–305. Washington, DC: B'nai Brith–Hillel Foundations, 1980.

Greenberg, M. "The Design and Themes of Ezekiel's Program of Restoration." *Interpretation* 38 (1984): 181–208.

Grossman, Alan. "Holiness." In *Contemporary Jewish Religious Thought*, pp. 389–397. New York: Free Press, 1987.

Halpern, Baruch. "The Centralization Formula in Deuteronomy." *Vetus Testamentum* 31:1 (1981): 20–38.

Haran, Menachem. "The Ark and the Cherubim—Their Significance in Biblical Ritual." *Israel Expeditionary Journal* 9 (1959): 30–38, 89–94.

———. "Shilo and Jerusalem." *Journal of Biblical Literature* 81 (1962): 14–24.

———. "Temple and Community in Ancient Israel." In *Temple in Society*, ed. Michael V. Fox, pp. 17–25. Winona Lake, MN: Eisenbrauns, 1988.

———. *Temples and Temple Service in Ancient Israel*. Oxford: Clarendon Press, 1978.

Harvey, Warren Zev. "Holiness: A Command to Imitatio Dei." *Tradition* 16 (1977): 7–28.

Herscovici, Alan. *Second Nature: The Animal Rights Controversy*. Toronto, Canada: CBC Enterprises, 1985.

"Holy." *The Encyclopedia of Religion*. New York: Macmillan, 1987 ed.

Jasper, James M., and Nelkin, Dorothy. *The Animal Rights Crusade: The Growth of a Moral Movement*. New York: Free Press, 1992.

Kalechofsky, Roberta, ed. *Judaism and Animal Rights: Classical and Contemporary Responses*. Micah Publications, 1992.

Kumaki, F. Kenro. "The Deuteronomistic Theology of the Temple as Crystallized in 2 Samuel 7 and 1 Kings 8." *Annual of the Japanese Biblical Institute* 7 (1981): 16–52.

Levenson, Jon D. *Sinai and Zion*. Winston Press, 1985.

———. "The Jerusalem Temple in Devotional and Visionary Space." In *Jewish Spirituality*, Vol. 1, *From the Bible through the Middle Ages*, ed. Arthur Green, pp. 32–61. New York: Crossroad, 1986.

————. *Theology of the Program of Restoration of Ezekiel 40–48*. Missoula, MT: Scholars Press, 1976.

————. "The Temple and the World." *Journal of Religion* 64:3 (1984): 275–298.

Levine, Baruch A. "The Language of Holiness; Perceptions of the Sacred in the Hebrew Bible." In *Backgrounds for the Bible*, ed. Michael Patrick O'Connor and David Noel Freedman, pp. 241–255. Winona Lake, MN: Eisenbrauns, 1987.

Lundquist, John M. "The Legitimizing Role of the Temple in the Origin of the State." *Society of Biblical Literature Seminar Papers* 21 (1982): 271–297.

Milgrom, Jacob. *Studies in Levitical Terminology I: The Encroacher and the Levite*. Berkeley: University of California Press, 1970.

Patai, Raphael. *Man and Temple*. New York: KTAV, 1967.

Paterson, David, and Ryder, Richard D., eds. *Animal Rights—A Symposium*. London: Centaur Press, 1979.

Peli, Pinchas H. *On Repentance: In the Thought and Oral Discourse of Rabbi Joseph B. Soloveitchik*. Jerusalem: Oroth Publishing House, 1980.

"Pilgrimages." *The Encyclopedia of Religion*, vol. 11, p. 338. Macmillan, 1987 ed.

Rabe, V. W. "The Temple as Tabernacle." Dissertation, Harvard University, 1963.

"Sacrifice." *The Encyclopedia of Religion*. Macmillan, 1987 ed.

Shochet, Elijah Judah. *Animal Life in Jewish Tradition: Attitudes and Relationships*. New York: KTAV, 1984.

Soloveitchik, Joseph B. "Sacred and Profane: *Kodesh* and *Chol* in World Perspectives." In *Gesher—A Publication of the Student Organization of Yeshiva University* 3:1 (*Sivan* 5726/June 1966): 5–29.

————. "The Lonely Man of Faith." *Tradition* 7:2 (Summer 1965): 11–16.

Valentine, James. "Theological Aspects of the Temple Motif in the Old Testament and Revelation." Unpublished dissertation, Boston University, 1985.

Wenham, Gordon. "Deuteronomy and the Central Sanctuary." *Tyndale Bulletin* 22 (1971): 103–118.

WORKS IN HEBREW

Aptowitzer, Victor. "*Beit Ha-Mikdash Shel Ma'alah*." *Tarbiz* 2 (1931): 137–153, 257–287.

Breuer, Mordekhai. "*Kedushat Yerushalayim Ve-Ha-Mikdash*." In *She'alu Shelom Yerushalayim: Ir Ha-Kodesh Ba-Halakhah Ba-Aggadah U-Va-*

Machshavah, ed. Yo'el Baris and Ya'akov Bir, pp. 15–31. Jerusalem: Tenu'at Ha-No'ar Ha-Charedi Be-Eretz Yisra'el "Ezra," 5745 (1984–85).

———. *"Limud Peshuto Shel Mikra: Sakanot ve-Sikuyim." Ha-Ma'ayan (Nisan 5738 [1978])*: 1–13.

———. *Pirkei Mo'adot.* 2 vols. Jerusalem: Chorev, 1986.

Frank, Pesach Tsevi. *Sefer Mikdash Melekh: Berurim Be-Hilkhot Kedushat Yerushalayim U-Mekom Ha-Mikdash.* Ed. Shabtai David Chazantal. Jerusalem, 5728 (1967–68).

Gevaryahu, Ch. M. *"Beit Ha-Mikdash Birushalayim Le-Elokim She-Ein Lo Demut U-Temunah: 'Hashem Amar Lishkon Ba-Arafel'."* Beit Mikra 100 (5755): 142–155.

Goren, Shelomo. *Sefer Har Ha-Bayit—Meshiv Milchamah.* Jerusalem, 5752 (1991–92).

Hoffmann, David Zvi. *Sefer Vayikra.* 2 vols. Trans. Zvi Har Shefer and Aharon Leiberman. Jerusalem: Mosad Harav Kook, 5732 (1971–72).

Isserles, Moshe. *Torat Ha-Olah* [1570]. Tel Aviv: Yeshivat Chidushei Rim, 5752 (1991–92).

"Kedushah." *Encyclopedia Mikra'it.* Jerusalem: Bialik Institute, 1982.

Kliras, Shelomo. *Ha-Mikdash Ve-Kadoshav: Berurim Ve-Iyunim Be-Avodat Beit Ha-Bechirah Bi-Zeman Ha-Zeh.*

Leibowitz, Nechamah. *Iyunim Chadashim Be-Sefer Shemot.* World Zionist Organization, 1983.

———. *Iyunim Chadashim Be-Sefer Va-Yikra.* World Zionist Organization, 1983.

Luria, Moshe Refa'el. *Or Ha-Mikdash.* Jerusalem: Machon Sha'arei Ziv, 5753 (1992–93).

Soloveitchik, Joseph B. *"U-Vikashtem Mi-Sham."* In *Ish Ha-Halakhah—Galui Ve-Nistar.* Jerusalem: World Zionist Organization, 5739 (1978–79).

Weinfeld, M. "Sabbath, Temple Building and the Enthronement of the Lord." *Beit Mikra* 5737 (1976–77): 188–193.

Ya'akovson, Yissakhar. *Chazon La-Mikra.* 2 vols. Tel Aviv: Sinai, 1957.

Index of Biblical Verses

1:45, 27
2:2, 15
3:1, 70
3:2, 99
5:1, 69
5:2–14, 69
5–10, 95
5:15–26, 70–71
5:27–28, 96
6, 78
6:1, 58
6–7, 113
6–9, 108
6:23–28, 79, 198
6:35, 14
7:51, 15
8, 15
8:2, 14
8:8, 80
8:12–53, 14
8:17–19, 68–69
8:20–21, 12
8:41–43, 71
9:10, 95
9:15–19, 95
9:22, 96
9:24, 95
9:26, 95
10:4–9, 71
10:26, 95
11:1–4, 97
11:28, 96
11:31–39, 96
11:33, 97
12:4, 96
12:26–27, 100
12:28, 100

12:31, 100
15:14, 99
19:21, 129
22:44, 99

2 Kings

4:9, 4
12:4, 99
14:4, 99
15:4, 99
15:35, 99

1 Chronicles

22, 66
22:7–9, 80
22:7–10, 73–74
23:4, 92
23–24, 87
29:19, 168

2 Chronicles

1:3, 99
3:1, 5
6:41, 17
13, 134
13:4–5, 134
13:9–12, 100
13:15–20, 101
17:7–9, 88
23:5–8, 87
26:4–10, 103
26:11–21, 103

General Index

245

About the Author

Joshua Berman is director of admissions and a lecturer in Bible at Nishmat—
The Jerusalem Center for Advanced Jewish Study for Women. He holds a
bachelor's degree in religion from Princeton University and received his
ordination from the Israeli Chief Rabbinate following extended study at
Yeshivat Har Etzion in Alon Shevut, Israel. His articles on biblical theology
and on contemporary issues in Jewish life have appeared in the pages of *Amit
Woman*, *The Jerusalem Post*, *Judaism*, *L'Eylah*, *Megadim*, *Midstream*, and *Tradition*. He has lectured widely on these topics in Israel, the United States,
and Great Britain. Rabbi Berman, his wife, Michal, and their son now reside
in Beit Shemesh, Israel.